Hammering on the mind's door

Frontispiece, full of history, is my teddy bear from when I was a small child. His name was, prosaically, not Rupert or Aloysius, but simply Teddy. He is sitting in a chair made for my grandfather, when he was a small child in the early 1890s, as a copy of his father's big chair. My grandfather was a coal miner in County Durham, and the poverty, and his ill health, resulted in my grandmother organising for them to leave the country, on a £10 migrant scheme, and head for the fresh air of Australia. The chair was one of the few things my grandparents were able to bring from England in 1929, on the migrant ship *Vedic*, on its way to Fremantle, and the economic furies of the Wall Street Crash while they were at sea, and faced with a farming exam in Margaret River that was impossible to pass, no matter how hard you worked. Teddy is wearing red overalls, with a rabbit (Sandy perhaps), which I had worn when he first came to me, so he is the same size as I was, aged two, when I proudly sat on my granddad's chair. Teddy had come, from America, in 1946, as one of the first toys imported from America after the war (transport by ship of toys being too frivolous during the war). A war in which my father had fought (Middle East, New Guinea) before returning home on leave in 1944, just in time to marry my mother and get her pregnant. With me.

David Horton

Hammering on the mind's door

Hammering on the mind's door
ISBN 978 1 76109 628 0
Copyright © text David Horton 2023
Front cover photo: the author, aged eleven, on steps outside the front door of his home, in uniform, on the morning of his first day at high school, 7.30 a.m., 11 February 1957. Colours used are the school colours.

First published 2023 by
GINNINDERRA PRESS
PO Box 3461 Port Adelaide 5015
www.ginninderrapress.com.au

Contents

What's past is prologue		9
1	Perfectly still, remembering things	16
2	'Pawn to King 4'	32
3	Working to capacity	47
4	Thrown out of the nest	63
5	'He's (not) a physiologist	80
6	Farewell to New England forever	88
7	A room with a view	105
8	Picking up the pieces	123
9	'I come from a land down under'	133
10	Forms known by pure reason	147
11	Year without a Summer	163
12	Arthur and me	178
13	Penguins can't fly	193
14	Following your career with interest	214
15	In the blood	226
16	The roads more taken	245
17	Consequences	260
What's future is epilogue		267

For Vicki
who gave me emotional reserves
and who saved my life
many times

I think we are well-advised to keep on nodding terms with the people we used to be, whether we find them attractive company or not. Otherwise they turn up unannounced and surprise us, come hammering on the mind's door at 4 a.m. of a bad night and demand to know who deserted them, who betrayed them, who is going to make amends. We forget all too soon the things we thought we could never forget. We forget the loves and the betrayals alike, forget what we whispered and what we screamed, forget who we were.

Joan Didion

What's past is prologue

'For the rhythm of life is a powerful beat.' – Dorothy Field

Normally in an autobiography there should be a comparison between the primitive days of one's own youth and the conditions enjoyed by today's youth. Can't be resisted, really, though I will try to approach it a little differently.

I often say, in that boring and infuriating way in which old fellows make pronouncements, that mine was the last generation in tune with the past. That is the past which was so rudely interrupted by World War II. When I read Dickens or any other Victorian writer, I am reading of a world instantly recognisable as contiguous with the one I grew up in. For my children's generation, this connection no longer exists. Dickens and Balzac and Chekhov are as remote to the baby boomer's baby boomers as Shakespeare, or the Beowulf poet, or Homer.

But perhaps that's just my perception, and this is not an academic analysis of the evolution of society and technology from 1822 to 2022. More important to me is my lived experience, and I'll try to explore that here, not very systematically.

First, we lacked technology, almost entirely. No car, no phone, no TV, no computer, no power tools, no fridge, no electric stove (no electric kitchen appliance of any kind except a toaster), no washing machine, no hot water heater, no flush toilet. Our most advanced technology, most of the time I was growing up, from birth to fifteen, was a radio and a record player, although a fridge arrived some time during that period.

That all sounds like an introduction to another common theme, the 'how poor was I?' approach to autobiography, but that should have been killed forever by the Monty Python skit on people trying to outdo each other in poverty and finishing with someone living in a shoebox sleeping on broken glass and eating coal, or something similar.

So no, I'm not doing that, but in any case I didn't think of us as being poor, nor did I make comparisons with richer people. We were poor, very poor, but we weren't dirt poor, thanks to my grandparents, Charles and Emma Young (especially my grandmother, who took in laundry and ironing and did babysitting to help pay the mortgage my grandfather's gardening wage couldn't have managed), we had a house to live in, and we never lacked food on the table or clothes on my back. Presents came at Christmas and birthdays, and, if the scale of them was low key (a second-hand bike, not a new one), then so what?

If we are now in the digital age, then my childhood was spent in the analog age. Home entertainment in the evening was the radio, especially the seemingly endless serials (like *Appointment in Samarra*), sometimes the record player (*Reader's Digest Great Classical Music*), always books. The radio also had the new 'hit parades' – 'Hi-lilli hi-lo', 'How much is that doggie in the window', 'Que sera sera', 'Green door' some of the songs still hammering in my mind seventy years later.

Outside entertainment was the movies. Occasional big films – *Anchors Away* is the first I can remember, *Ma and Pa Kettle* doing anything. But the regular was Saturday-morning matinee, again with the serials and the cliffhangers. We knew the projectionist, Ken Schneider, and he gave me, from time to time, some of the glass slides which were used at interval to advertise coming attractions. Nothing special, I think, but they have become lost along the way, like so much else.

Ken was married to Glenys, who was the daughter of Phyllis, friend of my grandmother. She was enormous – I don't know, twenty stone, twenty-five stone? So big she was almost unable to move, or at least unwilling to when people could see her. She was married to a tiny man with the look of a retired jockey. He bred budgies and canaries in a large aviary which he dismantled and gave to me when he was building an even bigger one.

Phyllis was the first person we knew to have a television. She welcomed us into her lounge room, along with her own family, children on the floor, adults on chairs, Phyllis in her bed, which was set up in there permanently. Every Saturday night, *Perry Mason*.

Phyllis had a sister, Roma, who was married to Bob Humphreys, a leading figure in the Rechabites. They lived, ironically, immediately behind the pub, sharing a back fence. Bob was a keen breeder of Modern Game bantams, and I once was allowed to visit and inspect, dripping with envy at a backyard full of pens and cages and birds. He owned a very large black car with huge leather bench seats, which we sat on as he drove us to Rechabite functions/sports in exotic and far-flung locations like Victoria Park and Fremantle.

Another aspect of the movie world I shared with my grandmother, I guess in school holidays: we would catch bus or train for a rare trip into Perth. There we would go to the Mayfair Theatrette. Small, as the name suggests, the Mayfair didn't show Hollywood blockbusters, nor did it have sessions. Instead, it just ran all its content on a continuous loop an hour long. The hour was made up of a news bulletin, *Passing Parade*, some cartoons and a Three Stooges short film. It didn't matter where you came in, you sat there until you reached that spot again (as a result there was constant movement), though there was nothing to stop you watching it all twice or more if you wanted.

The news bulletin was important because in those pre-TV days it was the only way to see world events, though, given the need to send reels of film all over the world and then copy and combine them, they were always a week or so after the events they portrayed. *Passing Parade*, with its unforgettable theme, was human interest stories from around the world.

After we had spent the hour or so watching the offering, my grandmother would take me upstairs (the theatrette was in a basement) to a café for tea (for her) and scones. It wasn't a normal café, but one run by a church group, or possibly even the Rechabites, so it wasn't the frivolous outing that a normal café would have been seen as by my grandmother. Besides, the scones were good, and cheap, and that mattered too.

Having no car meant that holidays that didn't involve staying home and reading books had to be formally arranged. My mother Elsie went on one to South Australia when I was very young, and she went by train, I think on some kind of package tour. When I was a bit older, she took me on a bus tour of the south-west of Western Australia, as far as Albany. It was a coach full of people, most, I guess, as unused as we were to being tourists (though I doubt that word was used much then). Anyway, we stopped at all the notable spots along the way, and I stood dutifully in front of each one to be photographed by my mother. I rarely remember jokes, but here is a tourist bus driver joke from about 1955: 'What is a bulldozer?' 'A cow's husband sleeping in the sun.' Did we laugh? Probably. And so the jokes continued all the way there and back.

In everyday life, not having a car meant that our lives were lived geographically in a two-dimensional world like an ant walking on a string. Essentially, our world consisted of the line from Perth to Fremantle. We could travel along that line by rail and by bus. But getting away from that line, as for the ant, was almost impossible – so we spent almost no time at the beach, and none in the Darling Ranges.

The other effect of being carless was that everything took so long. My mother and I went to the public library in Claremont every Saturday morning. It was a walk, carrying bags of books, that took us about an hour. So, to spend an hour at the library took three hours of our time. The number of things you could do, and the time between them, stretched out like the approach to a black hole. Friends offering rides would make a difference, and later bikes made a difference (although limited to journeys not involving carrying great loads). But when I was young, shanks's pony was as relevant to me as it was to the people of Dickens's time and earlier.

One aspect of life, though, made a car less essential. There were no supermarkets (nor could I have imagined such a thing). Just as they had for hundreds of years, individual people ran individual shops specialising in particular things. And, even more oddly from the perspective of 2022, all essential goods were delivered to the door or better. And, as they had been for hundreds of years, they were delivered by horse-drawn vehicles, although that was changing even when I was still quite young.

Groceries were delivered from the grocery store by the owner, carrying a big basket, and delivered right on to the kitchen table! He did have a motor van, though. But not far from us, just a block or two, was a stables which I passed on the way to music lessons, pausing to say hello to the horses. They were used to pull the baker's cart.

In the holidays, there was a relay of kids waiting to have a turn on the baker's cart. You sat up front, maybe held the reins briefly, helped deliver bread (like groceries – in a basket, to the kitchen table), got to eat a bit of broken crust, then handed over to the next child a few houses down.

Milk was delivered to the front gate. I think they had changed from horses by the time I was aware. The milk bottling plant was several blocks away. In fact, it was over the road from my music teacher's house. My music theory teacher, the nice Mrs Birkbeck, had married into the milk Birkbecks. You could go over the road, after the lesson, watch bottles being whirled overhead hanging from a conveyer belt in the cavernous, cold and wet space. If you were lucky, someone might give you one of the small bottles of milk to drink on the spot, ice cold. They were the size bottle we had at school too, but by the time you got to drink them, they were warm from the sun.

Finally, the ice man also cameth. Again, I think he had switched from horse to truck. The ice man, a giant it seemed, wet leather apron, and wet leather shoulder pads, would grab the ice picks, swing them hard into the big ice block, swing it in one movement up onto his shoulder and hurry into the house, where he would put it into the ice chest for you. The previous ice had melted away, the water running out the bottom, into a funnel stuck into a hole in the floor. The new block in place, the ice man ran on to the next house. Even then, I guess he must have known the writing was on the wall as fridges gradually took over the street, leaving holes in the floor as the only reminder of a lost business.

The only staple goods that weren't delivered were fruit and veg. So once a week my grandmother, aged in her sixties, would set off up the extremely steep hill trailing a small shopping cart behind her and return, an hour or two later, with potatoes and carrots, apples and pears – whatever was in season. It was fresh produce, not frozen, grown locally and not shipped from California. If she saw someone in their front garden or on their veranda, she would stop for a quick chat. They all knew her.

Some years earlier, while I was still in primary school, she had worked in that greengrocers (Bassett's – Syd and sons) on Fridays. Sometimes, I would go there after school if she was going to be late, sit in the back office doing homework, or help out on the counter, learning to estimate the weight of a bag of onions or potatoes. She didn't earn much, I'm sure, but what she did earn, plus free or discounted vegetables, was a vital addition to our family economy based otherwise only on her old age pension and my mother's low salary as an office worker. Then they sacked her, abruptly. One of the young Bassetts told me, viciously beforehand, 'Getting rid of your grandmother. She's too old.' Her self-esteem took a battering and so did our economy. But hey, just business, right?

She kept on walking up the hill to the shops until she was in her eighties. Kept her fit, I guess. But walking to church was easier, downhill all the way, every Sunday. Like clockwork. Methodist of course, what else? (The snooty C of E were up the hill.) I think now she wasn't religious in any deep sense except one. She was convinced, or needed to be convinced, that she would one day be reunited with Charles.

Apart from that, I think church was a social occasion at a time and in a place which needed all the social occasions it could get. Same for children. I was forced to go to Sunday school, every Sunday, but so were all my peers, and Sunday was a chance to catch up, perhaps arrange a game of cricket for later, pretend to chat up girls. Later, there was a badminton club established for Friday nights, but with a ceiling so low that it affected my style as I learned to play.

There was a church fete every year. Every church had one, as did every school, and they were not only also social events but a chance to get a nice cake, a jar of jam, a potted geranium, some second-hand books.

And so it went, rhythms which were daily, weekly, monthly, yearly. Rhythms as fixed, and familiar, as the phases of the moon, the alternation of seasons.

Until they weren't.

1

Perfectly still, remembering things

'Capture your reader, let him not depart, from dull beginnings that refuse to start.' – Horace

I have a brain aneurysm, a tiny thing, two millimetres or so in length, a small thing but mine own. It may have been there since birth, the result of genetics or some environmental factor, nature or nurture, or may have developed recently as a result of the medical traumas of recent years. It may stay harmless forever, or may rupture unexpectedly, like so many invisible but damaging events in my life, only later discovered. I knew nothing of this one until December 2020, when that *annus horribilis* ended with me having a stroke. Out of nowhere, I couldn't speak or write. After seventy-five years of communicating, I was struck dumb, unable to inform, guide, lead people, as they clustered around my bed, asking how many fingers they were holding up, or the name of the prime minister of Australia, or what caused the extinction of the megafauna, or why prescribed burning is bad for ecology. Thrombolycin cleared the clot, as two brain scans eventually revealed, and I slowly began to speak again, but the scans, hammering on the mind, had also revealed that small kink in another blood vessel, and who knew where that would lead.

Earlier in the year, on one of my three-monthly oncology reviews, I expressed concern that I had gained a lot of weight during the years of chemotherapy from 2011 to 2016 and had not been able to lose it again. Emma the oncologist told me not to worry. Put on plenty of weight, she said, so you will have more to lose, a buffer for when the cancer comes back. Seemed to me another metaphor for my life – build up reserves of emotional well-being (something like having vaccinations for Covid) so that you have a buffer when the bad times come. So I did, but there were times when the buffer was tested almost to breaking point.

When the catastrophic Australian bushfire season 2019–2020 had begun, I felt it was my duty to become involved in the debate that soon raged. I asked my publisher about a new edition of my book, and I began trying to re-establish contact with my peers, and develop on on-line intellectual presence again. As propositions about prescribed burning and a newly invented term – 'cultural burning' – were pushed strongly in the media, with no dissenting voices, I felt more and more determined that I should try to make myself heard. All to no avail. I also felt an obligation to contribute to climate change debates with my knowledge of animal extinctions in Pleistocene Australia. Not wanted on voyage. Impotent.

Years of cancer treatment had left me, since 2016, with sensory isolation from the world – no smell, no taste, sense of touch almost gone, sight and hearing problems partially solved by operations. Then coronavirus struck and with it came social isolation, trying to avoid clouds of invisible, but deadly, virus in the air. Which was added to my academic isolation – the publisher totally rejected the idea of a new edition, and no one was interested in having any interaction with me. The media had no idea who I was, nor any idea that I represented a countervailing view to the cultural burning mythology, nor, as a result, any idea that there was a countervailing view. I was reduced to anonymous comments in response to articles in online newspapers, uploading my publications to a research site, and writing poetry on an anonymous blog.

One day twenty-five years earlier, I was shaking hands with the prime minister as he prepared to launch my *Encyclopaedia of Aboriginal Australia* in Parliament House in front of a large crowd; another day (Grandfather's pocket watch in my pocket), I was receiving the award for best book of the year from the NSW premier at a grand evening dinner; on yet another, I was being awarded a Doctor of Letters degree by the chancellor of UNE. So how did I get from there to here? I am reminded of the old joke about the Scotsman who is asked by a tourist how to get to some tourist destination. 'Well, I wouldna start from here' is the reply.

We could start with a young lad being taught to read and write by his mother (a schoolteacher manqué) before he started school, a grandfather reading to the child in the brief few years before he died, and a grandmother providing a loving and supporting home. No, no father, he would not be met until the lad was thirty years old and on his way to his life's work in Canberra, but plenty of emotional well-being.

So what was Charles Young reading to his grandson while lying on a couch with him? The earliest book was *Curly Kitten*, who was 'never still; here and there he skips and plays'. Curly has many adventures, including climbing a monkey puzzle tree and having to be rescued. The monkey puzzle tree has fascinated me ever since, in my mind I think a tree like a vertical maze, where you could get lost or stuck, rather than one you could climb easily. Some people have lives like pine trees, I seemed to be stuck with a monkey puzzle tree.

A favourite in 1948 was *The Rupert Book,* strange in having a picture, a couplet of poetry underneath, and underneath that two paragraphs of prose which gave the story in more detail. 'The little bear gets quite a fright, when cheeky Jack Frost pops in sight.' 'As Rupert rounds the tree, he pulls up with a start. "Good gracious, who are you?" gasps the little bear. "Wait a minute, I've seen you before! Aren't you Jack Frost?"' And so on.

The alternating picture, prose and poetry was designed to let the reader choose what level was most appropriate for the child being read to. But when I read it myself, it gave a strange feeling of being able to jump from one to another, reading the same story but in different ways, and the mind also makes a jump. I couldn't choose which one I liked the best, all were equally valid tellings of the story, and I would be forced endlessly backwards and forwards between them. I also understood that a story could be simplified down, then simplified even further, and still be the same story. It would be an approach I aimed for as a writer.

Christmas 1948 brought *The Runaway*, the story of a pet rabbit who escapes to freedom: 'Down the hill and through the woodland scampered Sandy free at last, thought no more of Little Michael, and his rabbit-hutchy past!' But Sandy soon discovers that leaving home means he is vulnerable to foxes, who want to kill him (a warning for me, if I had only known). He finally finds safety in the burrow of a friendly wild rabbit. And back home he is already forgotten, as Michael has a new pet rabbit.

At some point about here, early, I learnt to read, and one day when my grandfather came to read to me he was told I could read for myself. 'Cans't boy read?' he said in his Yorkshire accent, astonished and perhaps dismayed. But I enjoyed him reading to me anyway, and would have enjoyed it even more, made more of it, could I have seen the future.

A favourite in February 1952 was *The Old Oak Paddock*, a wonderful idyll of English farm life. 'Jinny stood there perfectly still, remembering things, whilst cocks crowed, and dogs barked, and the moon moved slowly towards Mr Wigg's chimneys.' It was a much-loved work to be read many times. It gained, perhaps even more than it might have done, a place in my mental furniture, coming, as it did, the year my grandfather died. And part of my mental furniture was the story of him, literally on his deathbed in hospital, being addressed, insultingly, as 'Pop' by the nurse, seeing him as an old working-class man of no account, needing no respect. 'Only my son calls me Pop,' he said, rousing himself. 'My name is Mr Young,' he said with pride.

In hindsight, almost all of these books involved animals with human characteristics, and so I developed a feeling for being part of the natural world, and vice versa, and that coloured my approach to zoological research, I think. Got me to focus on the effects of change on individual animals, what happens to a kangaroo or a bird as the climate changes, or a fire burns a forest (perhaps seeing *Bambi* as a child affected me too!), rather than trying to write grand overarching theories. Some of the books also involved history, and those, together with the constant retelling of our family history by my grandmother, gave me the sense of being embedded firmly in time, so that I felt at home there, and that also would colour my approach to the prehistory research work I would one day do.

When I was three or four years old (the year therefore being 1948 or 1949 – halfway between learning to read and going to school, halfway between my father leaving home and my grandfather dying), I had an adventure (or so I am told, because I don't think I remember the adventure itself, but, like so much else in early life, I remember being told about the event). Two somewhat older friends, Trevor Grubenau (later to be my cousin by marriage) and Kenny Vaisey, who lived on opposite sides of the street (Brassey Street, Swanbourne, Western Australia), and I, decided to go to the beach. I have no idea why. We weren't a beach family, being English (I was born Australian, but would speak broad Yorkshire until I went to school, as, much later, my daughters would for a while, and I had the kind of English skin that turns to red crisp if I even see a beach, and the kind of golden hair – 'not red', as my mother insisted – that would later result in endless skin cancers, though not melanomas, as many of my beach-going peers must have suffered) and whose experiences at the tame English beaches, like Scarborough, were much safer than the frightening surf of Australian beaches like West Australian Scarborough.

Anyway, one of us, perhaps Kenny, had decided we would walk to the beach, about three or more miles away. None of us could possibly have known the way, only the general direction (the sun of course sets over the ocean, has to), but off we went. I don't know where we were supposed to be – perhaps playing in the backyard of the Crumps, Trevor's grandparents – but wherever it was, no one noticed for some time that we were no longer there. If you are startled, reading this account in another century and a totally different world, remember that Perth in the 1940s was a pretty small, quiet place where little happened. And each suburb, like Swanbourne, resembled an English village, self-contained and where everyone knew everyone. Children then were quite safe.

Later, in the early 1960s, that would change as a serial killer walked these streets, killing, among others, one of my university classmates. And much later, long after our time, a killer of young women stalked the streets of Claremont, the next suburb, known to us as a place where we went to the library, played cricket, sometimes went to the outdoor picture theatre, and where my grandfather, a Claremont council gardener, would pick up hepatitis A, perhaps in a toilet, and die, horribly, sending our family into crisis.

So we had wandered off unseen. Some time later, the alarm was raised and the families and neighbours were about to start scouring the streets when who should appear but three small boys, me leading and saying to the other two, both distressed, 'Come on, it's all right, I know the way.' No, I don't know how either. Those few streets would later become very familiar to me, being the way to church and Sunday school and Rechabites, the way to music lessons, the way to scouts, the way to my friend Peter's, and the area where my first girl crush lived, where my first girlfriend lived, and where my future wife would live, but in 1948 it must have been as unknown to me as the moon. Perhaps, like a homing salmon, one molecule from the birth stream at a time, I was smelling trees, lawns, the road, gardens, houses, pets, people, the molecules becoming more concentrated as I turned the last corner and headed up the last hill.

Finding my way back, and leading people who didn't, it seemed, know the way, was strange and inexplicable. (You could say I had saved them, in the way that the hero of *Catcher in the Rye*, who I was to identify with some fifteen years later, wanted to: 'I keep picturing all these little kids playing some game in this big field of rye and all. Thousands of little kids, and nobody's around – nobody big, I mean – except me. And I'm standing on the edge of some crazy cliff. What I have to do, I have to catch everybody if they start to go over the cliff – I mean if they're running and they don't look where they're going I have to come out from somewhere and catch them. That's all I do all day. I'd just be the catcher in the rye and all. I know it's crazy, but that's the only thing

I'd really like to be.') Much later in life, I tried to lead people in to understanding things they had failed to understand, so perhaps that tendency started on that faraway day. As did establishing a framework for reality and working out my place in it. But my success in finding my way can only have been a biological imperative, an instinct to know the direction home, the place where my heart was. That far-off day, I was known as the one who led the others to safety. Perhaps as a result I was determined, from then on, not to be a complete unknown (like a rolling stone).

All happy primary school days are alike, each unhappy school is unhappy in its own way. Mine were happy, and so not much more needs saying. Except for a couple of anecdotes, I remember little of school life, though I remember the school and its playground in minute physical detail.

One day during a playground game, someone was hit by a stone thrown by someone unknown. Because the stone had come from my general direction, suspicion turned to me. I was called out of class to the headmaster's office and left to wait outside. There was only one outcome from waiting outside that office – you were caned, the only question being how many 'cuts' you received. I wasn't guilty and I wasn't having that, so I went home. My grandmother came back to the school with me, outraged, I suspect, that her little boy was being falsely accused. She would give that Bert Northam a piece of her mind. I can still remember my alibi – at the time the stone was thrown, I was lying on the ground having been knocked down or tripped and therefore couldn't possibly have thrown a stone. The headmaster, presumably impressed by my bush lawyer work, or my boldness in going home, or my evident distress, or frightened of my grandmother, dismissed the charge. It was the first time in my life I was falsely accused of something, but it wouldn't be the last (though it was the last on which I escaped some kind of punishment), and such events would gradually take on a *Groundhog Day* quality of repeated pattern.

My grandmother, by the way, was not a fierce woman, but she was a woman who stood her ground. At about ten years old, the then Emma Evans had to care for her younger siblings when her father died early, lungs rotted by coal, and she then had to work at a young age in grand houses. But as a servant she was supposed to wear a mob cap, signature of servitude and of inferiority, and this she refused to do.

My mother thought that family was everything (though she had an enormous capacity for long-term friendships), and consequently that genetics were everything: every individual was no more, and no less, than the sum of their genetic inheritance. Whatever trait you exhibited would be the result of taking after someone – if not her (and it often was) then a grandparent or great-grandparent or someone, fancifully, even more distant. There was this image of a cloud of ancestors, extending back hundreds of years, each contributing bits of DNA which would make you, say, good at spelling, or piano playing, or reading, or writing, or cricket; which would not only give you, say, red hair and blue eyes, a good sense of smell and good sight, but would also give you a sore back, a dodgy knee, a wonky elbow, weak lungs. Would result in stubbornness, pride, determination, hard work ethic, getting a job done, not suffering fools gladly, calling no man master, making the most of your talents.

It was an astonishing belief in genetic determinism, a kind of astrology of the body, in the same sense that if you knew the exact position of every star (every ancestor) at the time of birth, you could determine all of the attributes you had brought to the planet and the role they would play during your time upon it. My father, when I finally met him, when I was thirty, thought family was nothing, that you could choose your family (which in essence is what he had done, chosen a new ready-made family to substitute for his own, twice, and had changed his name to his mother's maiden name, Bill Horton pretending to be Bill Baker) but you were stuck with your friends, and consequently blood, genetics, were of no interest at all. If I had inherited all the parts of me, like my mother thought, then what of the parts from my father and his ancestors? I was just like Bill Horton when I was naughty (never specified, but he was said to have been demoted in the army, from sergeant to private, when he stood his ground in the face of an arrogant young lieutenant), but what of all my other traits? And how did one separate nature and nurture? My grandfather, in our brief few years together, had nurtured my love of books. My grandmother had taken care of my environment. How did that relate to the DNA I had acquired from my other, unknown, grandparents (Tom and Ellen Horton), via my father (who carried a single-volume collected works of Shakespeare all through his World War II in North Africa and elsewhere)? Nurture or nature, which was more important?

As a result of my mother teaching me to read and write, and having me reading quite mature books, I completed the first three years of primary school in two years.

In later times, people would say to my mother, 'Did he skip a year?'

'No, no,' she would say, "he completed all the years.' This was important to her, not really sure why. Perhaps skipping a year implied some sort of shady deal, whereas completing years fast implied ability.

Also important to her was my name. 'His name isn't Dave, it's David.' This was a matter of status, I guess, Dave being a child who would later be driving a bus, or working in a factory, David one who was bound for great things.

And finally my hair colour was important. 'It's not ginger (or red) it's golden.' This again I think was a matter of status (at a time of a comic called *Ginger Megs* and a time when redheads were called Blue as in the comic strip *Bluey and Curly*), and uniqueness.

I would wince when I heard these oft-repeated assertions, but was secretly pleased – they were among the things that were part of my identity, and I was trying to establish that as fast as I could.

My mother took great pride in having quickly seen the potential of early computers in the shop where she worked, and got herself trained on these new punchcard machines, rising to supervise the other girls, and later playing the same role in the computer service of the Australian National University. No mere typist she, but a computer operator and a fast and accurate one.

I don't think I was either popular or unpopular in primary school – I doubt that many of my fellow students would have any memory of my existence. The two enormous disadvantages I had were my age and my family circumstances. It didn't matter how many times I ran around the clothes line, or hit a ball against a water tank, or threw a ball against the toilet door to practise marking, I was always a year younger and a year smaller and weaker. I would never be picked other than last on a team, or achieve anything on a team to make me be picked sooner next time. No matter what I did, I was never going to be one of the sporting heroes of the school, and there were no other kind.

My other disadvantage was the lack of a father, a very uncommon thing in those days, and my consequent family home. I called grandmother Mum, because my mother did and by analogy with Dad, but this just left Mummy for my real mother, and no boy has called his mother Mummy since the days of *Brideshead Revisited*. My grandmother worked some afternoons in the greengrocer's and I would go there after school and then come home with her. There really wasn't much opportunity to bring friends home, and if I had, it would have been embarrassing with a grandmother instead of a mother as hostess, and in an old home, when all my father-rich classmates seemed to live in new homes. An old weatherboard home that had no hot water, an outdoor bucket toilet, no carpets, no refrigerator, a wood stove, no car, no TV, no washing machine – we essentially lived in the year 1910.

So almost no socialising at home (except for birthday parties, which my mother loved to hold and show me off). In any case, although I was ostensibly seen as one of the mob, in fact I was a year less sophisticated than my classmates, plus the physical shortfall. Playing with me would have been like playing with kids from the next-lower class, and this was beneath everyone's dignity. On the other hand, I was too mature to play with my own age group, having completed a year's more schooling, and apparently being part of the older boys' network. So it was a no-win situation and with rare exceptions I remember little contact with other boys outside school.

As a result, I spent a lot of time doing things by myself. Like Seneca, I thought, 'Nothing, to my way of thinking, is a better proof of a well ordered mind than a man's ability to stop just where he is and pass some time in his own company.'

One of my favourite places was what we called Butler's Swamp but later was given the more upmarket name of Lake Claremont. It was a relatively untouched place. The swamp/lake was full of the skeletons of dead trees, which seemed odd. Myth had it that some time in the past, Mr Butler had drilled a well, thus puncturing the water table, and he came out the next morning to find the swamp had risen overnight and had flooded his orchard, leaving dead trees in the water. Odd things could happen in this strange country. In hindsight, this was total rubbish, and the contrast between popular belief and scientific investigation was one that I discovered then and made my approach to research and writing. Never mind, it was a place to explore, alone, the natural world, find myself at home in the Australian environment in a way my English family (at least the ones I lived with) had never done, and provide a starting point for my lifelong love affair with, and curiosity about, Australian ecology and its history. There were dense stands of old tea trees, and bullrushes, and the smell, coming from the water and ground, of mud and duck droppings and frogs. A smell rising into the air with clouds of mosquitoes, attracted by my scent and whose bites created red itchy spots.

A final problem I had as a child was the after-effects of measles. I had a severe dose of measles when I was six or seven, and it left me with a punctured eardrum and partial deafness for the rest of my life. The deafness was worst in group situations or inside, though it took a long time for me to realise the extent of it. As a result, I would give the wrong answers to questions or responses to comments, and was seen as having an air of not paying attention or being slightly removed, perhaps even of trying to be superior, none of them attributes likely to result in popularity. Small causes, big consequences in the future.

The ear problem had another very damaging effect. The doctor had given strict instructions that I was not to get water into the ear that had been punctured because it could lead to infection. This almost totally prevented swimming, or rather, it permitted swimming only while wearing a girl's bathing cap to cover my ears, which amounted to the same thing. It prevented me learning to swim properly, if only because I had to keep my head out of the water while swimming. So no swimming carnivals or the beach (except on rare occasions). I could sit on the sand and smell the salt in my nostrils, from afar, but I was insulated from the water and as a result insulated from the major sporting and social activity of West Australian boys during the years when such activities were essential if you were to have a social life.

My mother did her best to create one for me, though. And we did all kinds of things together, some ordinary like the library or a movie, others a little odd. For some reason, for example, we often went to races at the racetrack at the Claremont Showground. We saw both motorcycle and cycle races (perhaps on the same night?), could smell the dust of the dirt track, the fumes from the motors, the sweat of the cyclists. The races were all handicap, as I remember them, so that the weakest rider would be on the start line, the next weakest a yard or two back, then another one at five, ten, fifteen yards, and the best rider would be a long way back, perhaps fifty yards or more. We always supported the back rider, perhaps thinking it unfair that there should be such big handicaps, cheering them on when they overcame the restriction placed on their ability to overtake and beat the ones ahead of them. Perhaps it was a metaphor for later life; perhaps I am investing it with too much significance in hindsight.

We went to the agricultural show every year, with its smells of sheep, and poultry, wheat, tractors, the sideshows. Entered some flower arrangements one year, which seemed natural alongside the sewing my mother entered and the cakes and jam my grandmother entered.

We went to the latest films, including at least one where the audience was issued glasses with a red and blue lens which gave a three-dimensional view.

I consumed enormous quantities of books (at least some involving the kind of school life, or group life, I wasn't having) during my primary school years. many if not all of them were books about England – *Biggles*, *Secret Seven* and *Famous Five*, the William stories, school stories like *Fifth form at St Dominics* and *Jennings Goes To School*. Adventure stories like *Coral Island*. And endless English boys' magazines – *Boys Own Paper*, *Champion*, *Tiger*. But also some better things in the same classes – *Treasure Island*, *Two Years before the Mast*, *Children of the New Forest*, *Tom Brown's Schooldays*, *The Secret Garden*. Books to fantasise about group identity, about belonging – belonging to the fifth form, the Camel Squadron, the Five, the Rovers, the first eleven, the crew, the Cavaliers.

Was there a growing sense of excitement as 1956 proceeded or a sense of fear? It was the last year of childhood, the last year of being safe in a little self-contained world. The primary school was just up the hill. To reach it, I walked just a few hundred yards past houses which had always been there, in which lived people I had known, or known of, all my life. All of the children at school were more or less known by me. My mother and grandmother knew their parents and perhaps grandparents, knew where they lived, knew their histories. I had seen them at Rechabites or in Sunday school, they had been to my birthday parties and I to theirs. Even the teachers were known and some had been to school with my mother. There were no surprises. High school was going to be different – full of strange kids and strange teachers from strange places.

There would be strange new subjects and strange new ideas too. Primary school was cosy, with lessons that matched what I was reading at home. Almost all the history, for example, seemed to be British kings and queens and Robin Hood and burnt cakes and Hereward the Wake and 1066 and all that. There was almost no Australian history that I remember, and what there was related to the west, not the east. Related to European discovery of Australia, not its pre-European past, and to development not to conservation. William Dampier and Dirk Hartog then (not James Cook and Arthur Phillip, neither of whose names I remember hearing at school), and C.Y. O'Connor and Alexander Forrest. And nothing, virtually nothing, about Aborigines, except the occasional story of brave settlers resisting savages who attacked their lonely cabins in the bush.

For Christmas 1956, I received the only book from my childhood that did relate to Australia in any significant way. It was the ABC's *Children's Hour Annual Number 1*. All of us listened to the *Children's Hour* of course, and most of us were Argonauts, though I am ashamed to say I have forgotten my ship's name and oar number. Charles Moses, in his foreword, hoped I 'will keep this book for many years, not only for itself, but because it will remind you of your friends in the *Children's Hour*'. I have, and it does, a bit, with its pictures of Jimmy and Gina, Mac and the Melody Man. But I realised, as I turned the pages the other day, after keeping the book for so long, that nothing jumped out at me as familiar, and I suspect I hardly read it. I am not sure why, but maybe the Australian content put me off (though there was a great deal of non-Australian content) and maybe I was starting to feel a bit too grown-up for the show.

Among things of interest were the preparations for the Melbourne Olympics ('We wish [the Australian team] and all of their fellow competitors – GOOD LUCK'). Another intriguing article records how 'Professor Milgate…told us about the proposed Chair of Australian Literature…at the University of Sydney…we learned what an important thing this was and how it was hoped to make it possible by means of money being raised by public subscription. Professor Milgate ended his talk with these words: "I hope many people will see why those of us who are interested in Australian Literature are so excited about this plan to have a Chair established. It is a great step in the recognition and development of our culture. I am sure that many thousands of Australians will help us to achieve our purpose, and I know all Argonauts will tell people what we are trying to do and will be interested in how we get on. I think we'll succeed and I'm pretty sure that there are some Argonauthors listening to us now whose work will one day be studied by the University. Why not?"'

You couldn't say the *Children's Hour* underestimated its audience. I don't know if I read those words in 1956, and if I did the concept of having a 'Chair established' can have meant absolutely nothing, nor could I have asked anyone I knew what the words might mean. But the idea of having my work studied would have struck a chord, whether I knew what a university was or not.

Of personal interest is some of the names I discovered in the book. Names that meant absolutely nothing to me then, but were to have some significance later. Allen Keast, then at the Australian Museum, had a description of a museum field trip to the north west. Much later, I would study Allen's other work and write papers referring to it and extending it. Allen became a professor (took up a Chair) in Canada, and in 1973 was one of the examiners for my PhD thesis in biogeography. I met him in the Australian Museum and he said I was unlucky in graduating in the 1970s, because when he graduated in the 1950s there were so few Australian graduates in biology: 'if you could sign your name you would get a Chair'. He couldn't help me find a job.

In one of the articles on frogs, there is extensive discussion of the work of Mr John Calaby. When we came back to Australia in 1974, John was one of the first people we met. He helped me enormously in my work on animal bones from archaeological sites over many years, and I was to dedicate one of my books to him. G.K. (Ken) Saunders wrote a story ('Mariners on the Mountains') in the book. Forty years later when I was head of Aboriginal Studies Press, he came to me with a book manuscript with an Aboriginal theme which became the first book for teenagers published by Aboriginal Studies Press. People's lives weave in and out and touch in strange ways.

As I grew through primary school years, my life in one way was like that of boys of my economic level for decades previously, and like that of my contemporaries. I differed from most of them, though, by failing at scouts and succeeding at Rechabites, being unable to swim but reading many books. It was precisely the wrong way to achieve status as a young teenager.

Could I have turned out differently? What if my father had not left? What if my grandfather had not died at sixty-two? What if I had had brothers and sisters? What if I had gone to different schools with different teachers? What if I had not been a year younger than my classmates? What if I hadn't caught measles? So many what-ifs, and yes, they would have made a difference, singly or in total, though underneath it all I would still have had the same nature – ultimately, I think my mother was more right about inheritance than my father was.

But now 1956 was coming to an end. Soon it was New Year's Eve, and then midnight. We had, as a north country family, retained the old country's first foot custom. At the stroke of midnight, a dark-haired man had to knock, hammer perhaps, on the front door and be admitted, welcoming in with him the New Year. Most years, this was done by my dark-haired Uncle Bob, but when he had his own house and new family, I became the 'welcome stranger', but, being golden-haired, it was decided I should carry our male black cat. And so I climbed the wooden steps, knocked on our door, and with me (and the cat) being admitted, we welcomed in this exciting, but scary new year. I had great expectations of 1957 and following years. But I couldn't foresee the changes in friends, school, ideas, achievements, family, sport, travel, housing that were to come. Hell, even the popular music I had known was about to be swamped by rock and roll – behind the green door were Elvis and the Beatles!

2

'Pawn to King 4'

A memoir forces me to stop and remember carefully. It is an exercise in truth. In a memoir, I look at myself, my life, and the people I love the most in the mirror of the blank screen. In a memoir, feelings are more important than facts, and to write honestly, I have to confront my demons.' – Isabel Allende

The new West Australian high school was still being built in 1957. They had taken their first students in, a couple of years earlier, but few classrooms were completed and the 1957 intake of first-year students couldn't be accommodated. Instead, we were to have classes in what had been the old high schools the new one was to replace. There were two schools, Fremantle Boys and Princess May Girls, and they occupied buildings next to each other, the boys' school a single-storey sprawling dark building, the girls' a two-storey compact light building. They had been originally separated by a wall, keeping girls and boys apart, and there were still walls between the schools and the outside world, but the wall between the two had been removed to make a single playground.

The first day (11 February 1957) of my new life began with my mother taking a photograph of me in my brand-new uniform, standing on the front steps (where so many family photographs were taken over thirty-five years), looking off to the north to keep the sun, rising over the blue line of hills, out of my eyes, and looking a little nervous. Then my mother and I hurried up the hill to the railway station and boarded the train for Fremantle.

All the bright keen excited kids from all the primary schools within a radius of several miles turned up on that first day and entered the large hall on the bottom floor of the Princess May building. I was eleven years old. There were 1,250 students in the hall. We had been brought together on the first day in order to be allocated to classes. I assumed that the top students would be put into the top class first, then the next batch and so on down. We were told that there would be classes named alphabetically from 1A down to 1Z. As each new batch of names was completed, a teacher standing out at the front of the hall and then leading off her group of fifty or so, my spirits sank. The numbers remaining in the hall were lower and lower, and it was looking increasingly as if 1Z was to be my fate. If it was, then it was clear I would never be able to go home that night to my ambitious mother.

Finally, there were just fifty kids left, and my fate was sealed. Amazingly, it turned out that we survivors of this horrific lottery were in fact 1A. For whatever reason, the roll call had not been alphabetic but based on some other logic. I think only one other student, Cherry Gribble, from Swanbourne Primary, finished up in the class with me. I guess now there must have been some system of allocating two students, in order of rank, from each primary school to each class, but this is just a guess.

The result was strange anyway, for I had never been top of any primary school class. In the top ten, but never top (frustrating, no doubt, my mother). But many of the kids from primary had gone on to other private or Catholic schools, or high schools elsewhere, or selective high schools, so maybe I was just the top of what remained. Or my teachers had seen potential in me. Or maybe my age had been taken into account in assessing my marks, in something like a weight for age horse race. But, whatever, who cared? I was safely in the top class, status secure, for at least a year.

Attending John Curtin High School (named after Australia's greatest prime pinister, and a West Australian, and one of the first, and largest, of the modern co-educational high schools in WA) was a lucky break for me. Because it was an exciting new educational development (I presume modelled on the English comprehensives which the UK was developing in the 1950s) it seemed to have attracted, or been assigned, some top teachers.

My first year or two at high school were a process of trying to leave behind the world of childhood and present an image of being grown up. Being a year younger than everyone else made it all the more imperative.

Having been allocated, finally, to Class 1A on the first morning of my high school life, we were led out of the hall, across the courtyard, and around the corner into an area with a netball court and a banked row of seats for spectators. There was no netball that morning but we were told to sit on the seats. Perhaps our classroom wasn't ready or we were waiting until the movements of other classes had finished. I was sitting next to another boy, and, as can happen at the age of eleven, we had become best friends for life by the time the teacher got us up and moved us into the classroom.

His name was Peter Leech (a name that was to constantly cause him anguish. I can still hear him now, correcting yet another teacher, 'No sir, that's Leech, L double e c h, not L e a c h'). He had been born in England and had not been long in Australia, though he had attended Mosman Park Primary for a while. He was eighteen months older than me (perhaps because of the move to the Australian school system, he had lost six months; the rest of the class were a year older than me), tall and gangly, very fair skinned, with a shock of hair and glasses, like Roger Bannister or the class swot in an English school story. They were characteristics not likely to endear him to Australian schoolkids, and part of the attraction I guess is that we were both outsiders (when we added two others to our gang, they were also both outsiders: Kevin Rouse, who was going blind, and Ian Bailey, who had to repeat a class and was a year older than most of us, and two older than me). But Peter was very strong and tall, and could bowl a cricket ball very fast, and if there was a fight, he could take care of himself (after taking off his glasses carefully and handing them to me to hold). He also had a father who owned a car repair garage, and Peter knew all about cars. So he quickly gained respect and was not teased as he might have been, and I guess that gave me some cover too.

We would eventually spend a lot of time together throughout high school, particularly once I was permitted to ride a bike all the way to Mosman Park. The family was delightful, Mrs Leech being like a second mother to me, and there was a young sister, Penny. They lived in a rambling old house with a wide veranda. We spent a lot of time playing cricket on weekends or in the holidays in the park down the road, I would arrive with stumps and bat on my bike carrier, and we would play for hours, taking it in turns to bat and bowl.

We were in the same class all through high school, but when university came, Peter was one of the several students from our class who went into medicine. We lost touch with each other, for the lives of medical and science students were very different and inevitably separate. Peter lived in college, handy to the university because of his long hours, and I still lived at home.

I saw little of him after the first couple of years and then I went east while he was still finishing his studies. He got his medical degrees, and then specialised in neurosurgery, and in the early 1970s went off, now married, to Glasgow's Institute of Neurological Sciences to do postgraduate work and training. It was the place to go if you wanted to be the best in neurosurgery, which I am sure Peter did, as I wanted to be best in my career.

When we were in England in 1974, we visited him, catching up late into the night, our two small children long asleep, on all the things that had happened since we had last met some ten years earlier. And talking over days in the old schoolyard. I didn't see much of him the next morning. He lived some distance from the hospital and had an early start, so they left us to have breakfast and get the kids organised and head off by ourselves. He had acquired a little sports car, an MG, the kind of thing we had dreamed about, and drooled over, as teenagers. We broke a glass jar in the street as we were leaving, and had to try to pick up all the fragments. He returned to Perth a few months later, dreams shattered, having been diagnosed with having a brain tumour, and died not long afterwards.

At the end of first-year high school, most of which had been in the Princess May building, was a period of a few days when there were no classes but you were free to bring in board games to play. Cherry Gribble taught me how to play chess, the only productive lesson I had all year, I think, because I can remember nothing else of an educational nature (imitating the sounds of the *Goon Show* with every other boy in the playground didn't count), in between meeting Peter on the first day and learning chess on the last day of school year 1957. My diary, kept for the first half of that year, tells me little except that I was keen on sport, had crushes on a couple of girls, and hated metalwork.

Looking back, Peter was my first introduction to the outside world. Outside Swanbourne, that is. Where a bunch of us kids had all grown up together, went to school together, played together, had parents and often grandparents who knew each other. In the streets, at the shops, on the bus or train, you saw no one you didn't know, who didn't know you and your antecedents. A safe, secure, predictable little world, this 1950s Perth suburb. Going to high school had let me discover that there were other kids out there who had different origins, different lives, were the centres of their own worlds, and that I could begin to explore the world in gradually expanding circles outwards from Swanbourne. And life was full of possibilities.

The report at the end of my first term could have just been copied and recycled, though with some variations, at the end of every term for the next four years – geography 80%, English 76%, arithmetic 75%, history 68%, general science 67%, algebra 64%, geometry 60%, and metalwork (a crooked shoehorn, a bird seed container with hole) and art, both 50%. The note from H. Hoad (first mistress) could also have been recycled over the following years with varying degrees of exasperation – 'Has not worked to capacity, must try hard for scholarship'.

By the end of second term, my marks still ranged from 60 to 79 (and art and metalwork were still 50), which I thought was fair enough, but Miss Hoad was still unhappy: 'Not working to capacity at present' – the future it seemed would never come. And still hadn't come by the end of that year, when my marks ranged from 60 to 86 (astonishingly for algebra) and art and metalwork had crept up to 51 and 52. I had failed nothing and averaged around 70, and was still only twelve years old. Miss Hoad was grudging, though: 'At times attitude to work is casual. Results very fair but could do better.'

My mother was horrified when she saw Hester Hoad's name on my first high school report. Miss Hoad had taught, and terrified, her at Claremont High in 1934 to 1936. She had red curly hair and a red face and looked like she had been born angry. The sort of person you would tiptoe around, hoping not to be noticed. She had a very long and successful teaching career, though, starting as a monitor in 1924, and still teaching as principal in 1970 at John Curtin – forty-six years from monitor to principal.

We returned to school (after a summer playing cricket and chess) for our second year in February 1958, but this time in the new building on the hill, now completed but still looking like a building site, and smelling of paint, plaster, fresh cement. There again seems to have been something of a shake-out, kids recombining in the second-year classes, presumably after evaluation of how they had dealt with the primary school to first year transition. At every transition, primary–secondary, secondary–university, university–postgrad, the performance at the previous level gave very little indication of likely performance at the next. The stars of one level could be the also-rans of the next, and vice versa.

On the first day in this exciting new school, we once again sat outside before lessons started, this time as class 2A, big kids now, not frightened little children. We had been around, we were pretty sophisticated. Not sophisticated enough perhaps. I was sitting next to Bronwen Lewis. She seemed to me the ultimate class sophisticate, and she looked sideways at me and asked if she could squeeze my blackheads. Embarrassing, do you think? I was cool, but rejected the grooming overture. It was something of a sign of things to come, though, which is why I remember it when so much else is forgotten. Bronwen had high cheekbones, wavy hair and bright intelligent eyes, and I was already that morning developing the crush I would later have on her.

Adulthood was beckoning somewhere down the track and we could smell it, our nostrils twitching eagerly. High school was the beginning of our membership of the adult world, and of a change in our relationships with each other and with adults. Until then, the adults you knew had mostly known you from birth or soon after. You would always be, no matter how old you were, grandson, son, nephew in the family, and to those outside the family you would always be Elsie's little boy, or Mrs Young's little grandson, or young David who rides a scooter. You could never be a prophet with honour or have a separate identity.

At high school, though, we were all socially newborn, no history, no memories of scraped knees or runny noses; our lives and identities would be what we chose to make them. We would have new relationships with adults too. The teachers at John Curtin High, which was to turn out to be a very good school, also began to treat us like adults. For the first time, there were older people with whom you could have a conversation which wasn't mediated by the sense of where you had come from.

There was also a sense that we were differentiating from each other, like the first moves in a chess game, that the amorphous, quite uniform group of primary school children, differentiated only by sex and ability with a football or netball, had turned into a collection of individuals each with their own mode of getting through life and their own dreams and their own cloud of cultural and psychological baggage. My first memory of Bronwen Lewis is symbolic of this and she continued to represent to me the smart and sophisticated as we moved through the later years of school.

Don Farner was memorable for being an American, which was a pretty exotic thing to be in a school in WA in 1958. His father (also Don Farner) was a distinguished American ornithologist and was on sabbatical leave at UWA Zoology for six months or perhaps a year. Don junior was a nice chap, who looked like an American student out of a movie. So a rare bird in our classroom. And also notable I think because his father was a scientist (and I doubt anyone else had a scientist parent), and, in hindsight, was working in the Zoology Department, which at that time I had never seen, didn't even know existed, and couldn't have imagined that it would soon play a major part in my life. I wonder what sort of a life Don had after what must have been a culture shock for him in 1958? There were many other interesting students in that 2A class of 1958, and we will discover more of them in what follows.

The existence of this remarkable class was accentuated by the fact that in 1957 and 1958, John Curtin was pulling students from a huge area. I came from about five miles and six suburbs to the north, near the northern rim of the catchment, though others would come from as far as Nedlands, and there were others coming from equal distances to the east and south of Fremantle. It was a melting pot of different socioeconomic origins, parental expectations, primary schooling and so on. There was little variety of ethnicity – there were some Aboriginal kids in the school but none in our class. Only one girl in our class was from migrant (that is, of course, not English migrant, of whom there were quite a few among my friends) background and she was Dutch, but there were many others with other European ancestry (notably Italian) in other classes.

There was some separation between students who lived in the south and east and came to school by bus, and those like me who came by train (a long trip of perhaps an hour including the walk at each end). My gang eventually consisted of Peter, Kevin Rouse and Ian Bailey. We got off the train and then cut through the old woolsheds, at that time still piled high with wool as Australia continued to ride on the sheep's back, so my nostrils were filled with that dusty greasy smell of wool, mixed with the sweet smell of sandalwood, also exported from WA.

From there, we walked through the Fremantle Boys' grounds (full of youngsters now), then past Christian Brothers College. From there, we cut across Fremantle Park, where on sports day we played cricket in summer.

From the park, we headed up a steep hill, following the edge of a high limestone wall which marked one side of what had once been, in colonial times (having first opened its doors in 1864), the Convict Establishment Fremantle Lunatic Asylum and Invalid Depot. Nowadays, in one of those bizarre conversion processes, it is Fremantle Arts Centre. Then we reached the top. In about the year 2000, I revisited the school, and looked, some forty years later, at the route I and my friends had taken to and from school to the railway station. What had been a flat path over hard limestone ground was worn down in a groove perhaps a metre deep. I was reminded of my awe at Chartres Cathedral, seeing paving stones worn down by 900 years of pilgrims' feet.

If I had delusions of approaching adulthood, it was good that my classmates didn't see much of me outside of school. In 1958, I was still reading the *Meccano Magazine* and would be doing so as late as fourth year. And still collecting Dinky toy model cars. The *Meccano Magazine* was really just an extended piece of advertising for Dinky toys, Hornby Dublo model trains and Meccano sets. But it also carried articles and adverts very much like those of the *Boys Own Paper*. The August 1958 issue had ads for traineeships at Metropolitan-Vickers, apprenticeships in the British Army, apprenticeships or 'careers in physics and chemistry', Ilford Films, bicycles, tents, chemistry sets, careers in the RAF and many more. In addition to the articles on the cars, trains and model building, there were others on Dover, stories of northern Nigeria, 'Space Notes' ('The gases to drive a rocket motor along are produced by burning a propellant), '*The Daylight Express*: Australia's Fastest Train', 'Russia's Greatest Designer' (Tupolev), 'Lifeboat Story', 'Railway Notes', 'Air News' ('it is an open secret that BOAC is considering the possibility of opening a transatlantic service next year'), travelling on a freighter, a new post office machine ("ingenious machines for the sorting and handling of letters'), and stamp collecting.

Second year at high school has left little else in my memory (and there is no diary to help). It was, like fourth year, a year of little formal consequence. There was no big exam at the end of it to concentrate the mind, and we all, I think, took it easily, and spent the time trying to work out where we were in this new adult world. My marks went down to abysmal levels in maths (failing two out of three in first term and all three in second – I wasn't used to failing), and while it was embarrassing, there was another sense in which there was plenty of time and no need to worry. But I was only averaging 55% in first term and 58% in second.

Around that time, I was in a fight in the schoolyard, involving our class and, for some reason lost in the mists of my mind, another class. It was a rumble, much like the gang fight in *West Side Story*, but, innocent times, no knives of course, just shoving, but the force of movement was such that I was caught up, helplessly, between the two warring classes, and lifted off the concrete balcony; it then hit my head. Probably the considerable blood flow stopped the ballet. Peter took me down the hill to Fremantle Hospital, where stitches were inserted in my eyebrow. Sixty years later, I still bear the scar, and sinus trouble. Consequences.

I briefly experimented with smoking, getting only as far as a part of a packet of cigarettes, hidden in the garage, lured by the idea that it was a quick way to maturity. Those few cigarettes, possibly in combination with my chemistry experiments with molten sulphur and the like, may be what gave me bronchitis around this time. But maybe it was some genetic weakness I had inherited, or perhaps some environmental factor, or perhaps an infection, rather than a self-inflicted wound. It's always hard to identify the causes of these moments that affect our lives. For over ten years after that, I couldn't sleep at night without taking a tablet to keep my bronchioles open. The nights when I didn't were marked by waking at two a.m. and hearing all the hours strike on the clock in the dining room until, with the first glimmers of dawn, my chest would relax and I could fall asleep for a few minutes before being woken to go to school.

Years later, the bronchitis and my deafness (caused by the childhood measles) would keep me from Vietnam – unanticipated consequences. Living in the high country of Armidale, and later in Canberra eventually, cured me of bronchitis, but the deafness remains and is accentuated by the decay of age, and the smoking left me with lungs permanently damaged by chronic obstructive pulmonary disease – COPD.

Suddenly it was 1959 and I was starting third-year high school – where had the time gone? I was apprehensive. I hadn't covered myself in glory in second year. Would I still be in the A class? Yes, I was – '5 February: went to school and found out that I am in 3A! Phew!'

A popular myth of the day was that if you put a small coin on the rail track, the train running over it would expand it into a bigger and more valuable coin – a halfpenny could become a penny, a threepence could become a sixpence, a sixpence a shilling. I never knew anyone who had done it, never saw a coin so transmuted, never witnessed a transaction in which fake coin was accepted for the higher value. But the belief was enough for a child for whom life was regular and regulated, running on the straight and narrow track, no surprises, no easy sources of wealth or even comfort, the idea that an alchemy, requiring only a coin and a train, and a little derring-do, could result in unearned riches, was always going to be appealing. I would later make it my job to puncture myths.

Until 23 March, my diary records all the same kind of interactions with people it had done two years earlier – sport and movies and games with Peter, Kevin and friends and relatives from my childhood. But that day something changes, and it is that Bronwen Lewis again – '23 March: Lewis sits near me as does [Joan] Hassell [Bronwen's best friend]', then later 'Went to Hall for Musical Appreciation. Lewis asked if she could sit next to me. Wish she could have.' More information needed – was I too embarrassed to sit with a girl? Was it assumed that Peter would sit next to me and I didn't want to disappoint? The diary is silent. But suddenly I am (a) feeling part of the school group and (b) realising I have a crush on Bronwen.

I finally turned fourteen a couple of weeks later, long after everyone else, but at least it was another indication I was maturing. I start recording schoolwork in chemistry and biology, my interest growing as an embryo scientist. Suddenly – '7 April: Wrote note to Lewis'. What could I have possibly said? How embarrassing was it? What did Bronwen think? All lost in the mists of time.

On 20 February, I had recorded 'Play reading at night' (with mention elsewhere of *She Stoops to Conquer*). 11 April was another rehearsal on a Saturday night. It was the start of my involvement in theatre, encouraged by the wonderful Charlotte Bruce, which was also a sign I was moving into the school social circles. As was '13 April: Sat next to Lewis in Biology' (seems my embarrassment had gone).

Then we had a week of term exams. My maths had improved but my average was only 63. Still room for improvement, it seemed. Mr Howieson firmly agreed with Miss Hoad: 'His results would improve if he applied himself more conscientiously to his work.' Fat chance – hockey took over my life and I recorded the results of games religiously in the diary. Play rehearsals continued too. Was I worried about my grades? Seemed not, plenty of time, only June. Or perhaps I was, because the diary stops in mid-July.

Needed to worry because third year was the big one. The Junior came at the end of it, and that was the entry card to adult life, the one that decided where your destiny lay. The teachers put the fear of death into us though there was little need. Whatever you thought about your own intelligence and ability, and however comfortably you were holding down a place in the middle of the top class, there was always a feeling that it might not mean anything. That in the outside world were all these other bright kids in good schools, and maybe all of them were better than we were.

Exams in August and I was still averaging only 62 (and failing physics dismally). Still, Mr Speering (a vicious deputy principal, whose main job seemed to be caning the guys who were lined up outside his office every day; not me, though) said, 'David has a good chance of success in the Junior Certificate Examination.' Easy for him to say, but looking back now, I think it was damning with faint praise – yes, I would pass at some level, but that wasn't enough.

And until thousands of kids all sat down on the same day in hot school halls, seriously supervised by unsmiling teachers, and simultaneously did their best on the same exam papers, there was no way of knowing. Perhaps it would all come to an end, the dream that you were one of the scholars who would continue through school and even, something at the far end of the tunnel, to a complete unknown called university, and then beyond to having your work studied at university.

The Junior was made even more terrifying by the wait (results were not released until January, so once you had left school, there was a period of about seven or eight weeks where you remained in limbo). Perhaps once again bemoaning your failure to answer a question that now seemed in retrospect a piece of cake.

But the time spent waiting for the answer to those nightmares was a new adventure. My mother had spent time working in Foy's department store a few years earlier and still had contacts there. Everybody tried to get a job in the holidays after the Junior – we were old enough for employment, and the Junior being held before the end of normal term meant that there was an extra long period before Christmas when most shops were looking for casual workers.

Either because of my connections, or just by chance, I was put into the mail order section of the store, and it was a marvellous breakthrough. Other students were standing behind single counters all day. I was free to roam the store, and to work from an almost private space in the basement. The mail order section was very important at Christmas time. All over WA there were isolated farms, and those near small country towns, without physical access to shops. They would have an account with a store like Foy's that could supply all their needs from food to clothing and so on.

At Christmas time, they also needed presents and extra special food. It was a bit like children writing to the North Pole (not, of course, the South Pole) and wishing for train sets or dolls. I was one of Santa's helpers. I would head off with a shopping list and a box. Families in the far outback of WA were trusting me, an immature fourteen-year-old, to choose a nice shirt and a tie to match for the husband, or a red dress size ten for the wife, shoes for a six-year-old perhaps, some nice books, a range of foods for the Christmas table, a new train set, and so on. I was filling their Christmas stockings, supplying their clothing needs, putting food on their table, helping their children play and read. It was a great responsibility and I took it as such, wishing that I could see faces when they opened up the parcels I had packed for them.

It was very enjoyable, not like work at all. I wasn't standing behind a counter all day, did a great variety of work, and got to chat up the blonde girl on men's ties (which were a frequent request as a Christmas present) who undoubtedly had no idea that the boy who read *Meccano Magazine*s was trying to chat her up.

And then it was another Christmas, and another New Year, and the days before the Junior results had dwindled down to none. The results were printed in the newspaper, and it was possible to get the morning newspaper late the night before as it began to be delivered. Crowds of people were in Perth streets, standing on street corners, a growing fear in the pit of every student's stomach. Then the sound of a truck engine and the crowd edged forward, surrounding the newspaper seller. A West Australian truck slowed down enough for a man on the back to throw a bundle of papers, tightly tied, onto the pavement. The seller opened them and then we thrust forward, sixpence in hand, reaching out to get the copy that had your fate written on it in fiery letters.

There was your name, so that was the first nightmare disposed of (the prospect that you had done so badly that you had failed to pass a single subject, and your name was therefore left out completely, a non-person, a complete unknown, in the great struggle for existence). Then it was a matter of counting the numbers against your name, and re-counting them and recounting them yet again. There seemed to be eight. It seemed to be all right. You were over the first hurdle of your adult life. Then it was a matter of seeing who else from the class had jumped the hurdle clear with you, looking sideways for the other horses as if in a steeplechase.

Most of us were there and ready to tackle the next moves of the great game. The disadvantage of the Junior, though, was that it was a very blunt tool. You either passed subjects or didn't (later, it would seem inconceivable that anyone you knew would not have passed all eight subjects), but there was no indication of how well you had done in each. So there was no guidance as to where to go next. I had to make up my mind pretty quickly what I was going to do because there was a real choice to be made, Science or the Arts. But first I had earned a prize, one much longed for, and it was time to collect.

3

Working to capacity

'If you look behind every exceptional person there is an exceptional teacher. When each of us thinks about what we can do in life, chances are we can do it because of a teacher.' – Stephen Hawking

My mother had promised me that if I got through all eight subjects, she would buy me a dog. There had been a family dog, Sandy, much loved when I was a child, but he had been run over when he was sixteen years old and I was still very young. He had been my grandparents' dog, and this one would be mine.

We saw an advert in the paper and went off to look. There were two cocker spaniel puppies, a golden roan female and a blue roan male. The male it was, Lilli-Illa Cavalier his stud name, and we would be inseparable for the next five years. I would one day have to leave him, but in 1960 that was inconceivable, just as it was inconceivable that I would ever leave home, or that things would change in any way. It must have seemed just as inconceivable for all the previous generations of the family, about whom I then knew almost nothing. But a family pedigree is not a diagram of a static tree, but of constant change. The tide comes in, washing up children to be part of a family and young forever. Then the tide gradually pulls out as they leave home and then, as the tide goes out even further, they gradually die. Then back in it comes with a new generation of loved children.

Cavalier had a long English pedigree, and I was proud to find, in a book on cocker spaniels, pictures of many of his English ancestors, some standing outside stately homes. But he wasn't the ideal type, having ears too high and a smile too wide. Really he was just a boy's dog, and we ran and walked, and chased, and he swam and sniffed things and went to dog shows (where he never won), and enrolled in gun dog training. He smelled of wet fur and mud after going in the river, of something rotten after rolling on a dead bird. He was much loved and much loving. He was my first dog.

Fourth-year high school after the Junior would involve a reduction from eight subjects to seven, but there was also a change in the form of the maths, social science and science subjects, so that the actual change from third to fourth year was greater than a reduction of one subject might suggest.

There was another complication. Up to third year, the classes were numbered by order of merit, so that there was no doubt you wanted to be in 1A, 2A, 3A, and that those who were not were somewhat less talented. In fourth year, that was about to change, the classes being numbered not entirely by merit but by the choices you had made about what subjects you would be doing (although this was not entirely true; in fact, you had to make certain choices if you intended aiming for university, and in practice the top two classes were still the top in order of merit – 4A and 4B were equal to each other, but with different subject combinations).

I was sailing in new waters here, trying to steer my little ship to a new land. I was the first member of the family in 200 years to be heading into this level of education and there were no navigators for me. In the end, the decision was fairly easy. The choice between the top two classes was one of either doing two sciences and a language and history, or three sciences and geography. I had survived French in the Junior but there was no way I would continue with it. Whatever abilities I might have had didn't include the ability to speak other languages. It is said that there is a very limited period very early in life when your brain is susceptible to the sounds of another language, and if you don't hear them, then you can never be fluent and will always sound like a foreigner. I could communicate with the world in my own language but not in the languages of other people.

Many years later, I was in France for an archaeological conference. As part of the event, we went on a tour of archaeological sites, including one in a cave that had a deposit which clearly had largely come from owls, who regurgitate bones in little pellets after absorbing the nutrients. Trying to show that the fellow from Australia was not only paying attention but knew a thing or two, I asked one of the Frenchmen what the word for 'owl' was in France. The actual word, I know now, is *hibou*, but one of us misunderstood the other and he said something like *huish* – perhaps he was telling me to keep quiet.

After the talk by the cave's excavator, I went up to him and, pointing at the deposit, said, '*Huish? Huish?*'

'Eh?'

'*Huish? Huish?*'

'Eh?'

"*Huish? Huish?*' I said, this time in desperation accompanying the words by holding my arms bent, elbows outwards in the shape of wings, and flapping them. '*Huish? Huish?*' I said again, flapping and smiling and nodding towards the deposit.

He backed away from me, looking haunted and then, gaining speed, turned and ran.

So it was 4B. 'Only 4B,' said my mother. 'Why aren't you in 4A?'

Even after I explained, I don't think she really believed me and harboured a slight sense that I had not quite reached the top level and this was something of an embarrassment. Not only did our family know nothing of education, nor did anyone we knew, and explaining why the supposedly clever son was not in the supposed top class can't have been easy.

It was a good class, in competition with 4A, where much of the rest of 3A (those who knew the word for owl in French) had ended up. Many of the class would go on to university, and about half of us would win Commonwealth scholarships. A significant proportion would have major professional careers, including a GP, a pharmacist, two headmasters, a professor of microbiology, a neurosurgeon, a gastroenterologist, an internationally known biochemist, a botanist, two agricultural scientists, a senior language teacher, and me. And we had good teachers.

Charlotte Bruce had already made an impression the previous year. Her great passion was drama, and she created, through her energy and enthusiasm, a tradition of excellence in drama at the school. She dressed in flowing dresses and skirts, and long scarves, all in pastel colours and floral designs. Her hair was blue-rinsed, the shade varying from time to time. She looked like an artist in Bohemia, and was totally different to anyone I had encountered before. The women I knew were very very conventional. I later discovered that she indeed had a very unconventional early life before returning to school teaching.

She would invite students in her productions to her home and that too was a new experience. The house was light and airy with large windows, and the furnishings were as softly dressed as she was, with cushions on cane furniture, bright rugs on wooden floors and bright curtains hanging to the floor. It was nothing like the dark houses I was used to with their heavy furniture and drab colours. Mrs Bruce's house was both civilised and arty in some indefinable way, and she was opening my mind to such possibilities.

Her productions were set up as a professional company might do them, and done to a standard at which they could be presented to audiences without allowances being made for us being only schoolchildren. She gathered around her students who shared her enthusiasm, and if you couldn't act (and I couldn't) there were always production jobs to learn in stage management, or lighting or scenery painting or costume design.

I had an acting role in *Midsummer Night's Dream* – Snout playing the wall 'and such a wall as I would have you think that had in it a crannied hole or chink (hold your hand out, first and second fingers separated to form chink), through which the lovers, Pyramus and Thisbe, did whisper often, very secretly'. So I was a student pretending to be an actor, pretending to be a rustic, pretending to be an actor, pretending to be a wall.

Other productions I remember included *The Admirable Crichton*, *She Stoops to Conquer* and, most notably, *Toad of Toad Hall*. That was the big one of 1960 and it was brilliant. It starred Brian Hannan, who became a professional actor on leaving school, and he was a real star. My enthusiasm meant I couldn't be left out, but my inability to act made the choice of a role difficult. Finally, Mrs Bruce settled on me being a mouse in the jury. Not a big role – in fact, it only involved saying one word, 'Guilty' – but I thought I could manage that.

Everyone else had quite realistic costumes, but my grandmother had some difficulty deciding what to do at very little cost. Finally, she got a sheet of white calico and turned it into a sort of a bag with a hood, over which was put a brown mouse head. I was the only white mouse, and the role of foreman who said 'Guilty' seemed natural for such an individual-looking creature.

Stan Richards was the next to make an impression. He was the English teacher, thin and wiry with glasses and great energy, who seemed to bound everywhere. He had a passion for education and literature, and a belief in the value of both, and if you shared that with him, he also had a belief in you. He was the first adult who treated me as an adult. He helped to develop my critical appreciation of literature, but most importantly he taught me to write, and taught me to have confidence in my ability to write. He would read anything I wrote, class work or the poetry and short stories I was increasingly writing on my own account. He would provide intelligent feedback, and often read things out to the class. It was the first time, I think, that I had been singled out and given a talent which others could recognise. It was my identity (David Horton is the one who is good at English) which was being developed, and my confidence that I was destined to be a writer, had to be a writer, and I will never forget Stan for that.

Some years later, when I had finished my novel, I sent it to him and he read it and wrote back a two-page letter of serious comments. Won't be published, he said, but don't be disheartened. 'You must keep writing,' he demanded, and I did, and have.

Many, many years later, in 2005, forty-four years after I had last seen him, I was in Mandurah, which he had retired to (after a distinguished education career, and the publication of some children's books he had written), and I phoned him. He claimed to remember me, which was sweet of him, and we compared notes on Aboriginal studies (he knew the *Encyclopaedia*, and his books were about the Aboriginal people of the Mandurah area). I thanked him for inspiring me, and I am glad of that, but I was dealing with my mother's fall, finding a nursing home for her, and selling her unit, and I didn't think I could make the time or effort to visit Stan. One of those great regrets.

Another memorable teacher was Mary Critch, the biology teacher. Small with frizzy hair and a round face with glasses, she looked like an old-fashioned schoolmarm but was anything but. She did two things which were quite remarkable. First, she taught biology as a serious scientific subject. It wasn't just a soft option that girls might do if they wanted to do some science, looking at flowers and birds perhaps, it was a real science to stand alongside physics and chemistry as real, rigorous subjects. So we studied it properly, and took it seriously because she took it seriously.

Second (and in this she matched Richards and the chemistry teacher) she set out in fourth and fifth year to train us for university. But that phrase doesn't quite convey the magic of what was going on and its unusual nature. All three teachers said to us openly that most of the class would go on to university. At university, you wouldn't be spoon-fed and be expected to regurgitate, you would be expected to study and learn for yourself, and be expected to make up your own minds and develop ideas. They would therefore teach us in university style so we would be ready for it.

As a consequence, the lessons and practical classes were conducted like university seminars and tutorials and lectures, not like normal school lessons at all. We thrived on it. The other advantage was that when I reached first-year zoology at university, I had already done the whole course with Miss Critch, and could concentrate on the physics and maths I might otherwise have failed.

The fourth of this quartet of remarkable teachers was Alan Strahan, the chemistry teacher. He was plump with a round face, thick glasses which gave him an owlish appearance, and thinning fair hair. On the first day, we had him, he said to the class, 'Now, at any moment I may collapse on the floor and lie there unconscious and twitching. If it happens, you must make sure I haven't swallowed my tongue, turn me so I am lying on my side, and get help. Don't worry. I will be all right after a while.'

We stared at him open-mouthed. I can't remember what his medical condition was, though it may have been diabetes, perhaps epilepsy. But it was another introduction to adulthood, both because he was being so open about his condition, rather than hiding away serious things, even death, and because he was trusting us to save his life. From that moment, we would do anything for him.

I loved chemistry anyway, having mucked around with it at home for so long. I liked, I think, the idea that new things could be formed by combining other things, and that there was certainty to the process. I had learnt the periodic table off by heart very early, recognising that it was the key to chemistry, and that became another talent – I was the one who knew all the symbols. The chemistry lab was full of all the apparatus I would have loved to have at home, all of the complex paraphernalia that was so appealing. And there were long-term experiments running in containers round the walls. One was crystal growing, chemicals gradually adding to a central core to produce a large visible object that reflected the invisible materials that had been in solution. Another was a huge glass tube. In the bottom had been poured a layer of blue copper sulphate solution. In the top had been poured, somehow, magically without disturbing the bottom layer, a clear liquid. Perhaps just water. There had originally been a clear dividing line between blue and clear, but very slowly, over a long time, you could see that the blue was diffusing into the upper layer. Given an infinite amount of time, the oscillation of molecules would cause the two layers to completely mix and become indistinguishable from each other. Perhaps, sixty years later, that tube still stands in the chemistry lab, silently and slowly mixing itself.

Physics wasn't a favourite, and caused me endless difficulty. But I remember being captivated by a thermostat, the magical, brilliant invention by Andrew Ure that involved simply binding two different metals together. Because the two metals had different reactions to heat, if the temperature was rising or falling, the bimetal strip would bend one way or another, first making connection with one terminal and opening a circuit, then connecting with the opposite terminal and opening a different circuit.

I hadn't been involved much in sport at high school. If you were any good at any sport, you played for the school first eleven (or fifteen or eighteen – a lot of different sports were played). If you weren't, then you just mucked around during sport period, kicking a soccer ball, or playing cricket in a manner no different to that played at primary school an eternity before. I liked to join in, perhaps hoping to be seen by a talent scout for Manchester United, or the state cricket team, but if you were really cool, like Lee Walsh or Robert Paterson (though he was in the school soccer team), you made no attempt to even pretend to play, but sat behind the tree or the toilet block, seriously smoking.

My biggest moment came in early 1961 in athletics. I could run a bit, though I never trained, shouldn't need to. I wasn't fast enough for the 100 and 200 yards, and I didn't have enough stamina for the half-mile or one mile. So the quarter-mile, once around the oval, was my distance. The school had a sports day once a year, pitting the four factions (Red, Blue, Gold and Green) against each other. The winners of each event would then go on to the inter-school sports and potential stardom and fame.

The reason I thought I was in with a chance in 1961 was that the races were of course age-classed. There was a sequence under fourteen, under fifteen, under sixteen, over sixteen. Now, everyone in year five was over sixteen. Except me. So I would be in the under-sixteen race against the kids from fourth year. Now logically this made no difference to anything. I was under sixteen, so were they. But psychologically I was a fifth year and they were fourth years, and that, I thought, gave me an edge in confidence on my part, and inferiority on their part.

My race was after lunch, and it was one of those 'for want of a nail a war was lost' facts. I always ate at exactly twelve thirty. No variation. My race was at one p.m. No problem, just wait for the race, get the accolades for a glorious victory ('Didn't know Horton could run like that,' they would say. 'We like this chap'), eat my lunch. Couldn't wait, though. Stomach empty. Perhaps could eat just one sandwich, relieve hunger pangs, rest later. What harm could it do?

I was soon to find out. Gun fired and we were off, 300 yards all going well, in the lead over those young fourth years. Up to the last bend, ribbon in sight, my faction (Blue? Gold? My memory snaps and fails) massed on that bend, cheering me on, waving our flag. And then the first twinge in my stomach, then another, then I began to slow. Could I push on? More twinges, then cramp, and I had developed a major case of the stitch, guts twisted around that tomato and peanut butter sandwich, so carelessly eaten, so much regretted. My pace slowed, stopped, the cheering stopped in disbelief, and I, bent over to relieve the cramps, felt those puny fourth years race past me to athletic glory. My John Curtin sporting career, never a reality, had come to a crushing end.

Robert Paterson was good at English, and I suspect we saw each other as competition. He had been chosen to write the 4B class account in the yearly school magazine (*The Sentinel*) and so had status I didn't have. On the other hand, in 5B mine was the work Stan often read out to the class. So who was top in English? The Leaving would decide.

I did play sport outside of school. Peter had taken me along to enrol at Claremont-Cottesloe cricket club, and I played under-sixteen cricket in a low grade. At training sessions in the nets, all the grades would mix in together, and we would watch in awe as Graham McKenzie, later Australian fast bowler of great distinction, would bowl a few balls at lightning speed, or have a knowledgable discussion with the first-grade coach. I was never much good, in spite of my love of the game, and my grandfather's genes. Perhaps if he had lived…but there were many sentences that began like that after he had died.

I had also joined the Subiaco hockey club with my other best friend Kevin Rouse. This was a different story eventually. When I first played, I was still very small and slight, and I was on the wing where you were put so as not to do any harm (a sporting Hippocratic oath). But after the first year, I had something of a growth spurt and was a few inches taller. 'We'll try you at fullback,' said the coach, and from then on I had a sport I could be quite good at.

Kevin was good at it too, and in fact played a higher grade than me at first. He was almost completely blind as a result of cataracts by now, and it was a remarkable performance. In his early years playing, he had developed, as good players do, an instinct for the run of play and its ebb and flow. So much so that he would see the vague coloured blobs of players in the distance, get himself ready for the direction the ball must inevitably take, and then listen for the sound of the shot to estimate how fast it was travelling. He could almost inevitably trap the ball and then clear it, and if you didn't know, there was almost no way you could have deduced that he was blind. But just occasionally someone would mishit a ball, and it would fly off the stick in a curve sideways, or upwards, leaving Kevin heading in the wrong direction and unable to readjust. Years later, when I saw the imaginary tennis game in *Blow-Up*, I thought of Kevin and his hockey. It was a remarkable achievement. He played table tennis and badminton the same way.

I seemed to have bounced into 4B successfully. At the end of first term, I was averaging 72 with 86 and 85 for English and biology (thus beginning the endless dilemma I would be faced with for the rest of my life – biologist or writer?), a stunning 76 in maths, and a pass in everything else. Jack Howieson was reduced to calling me a 'good student'. Perhaps he thought I was at last working to capacity.

A rude shock if so. By August, I was down to an average of 62, with no distinctions and bare passes in chemistry and geography. Jack

Howieson had my measure again – ah, yes, that Horton chap, we know about him: 'David has been too erratic in his work to obtain the results expected.' I was only coming eighteenth out of thirty. But what were the 'results expected'? How did he know what they were? Why did everyone think I wasn't working to capacity?

Who was I kidding? I knew I wasn't, but hey, I was now fifteen, there were endless days to play sport, or read books, or develop wistful crushes on older girls. Who cared about physics and maths? December I was still jogging along, fifteenth out of thirty, failing physics, 85 for chemistry, average 64. Mr Howieson was annoyed: 'Passed well in spite of little effort in some subjects.' Yes, yes, OK.

Fourth year came and went far too quickly and fifth year was upon us ready or not. It was the year my family got television. I spent the year doing homework in front of the TV and then studying in front of the TV.

As teenage boys, we were growing all the time, and keeping up with the school uniform as we left small jumpers and trousers behind was difficult, particularly for poor families. If you had finally grown out of your jumper in fifth year, there wasn't much point in buying another one with only a few months of school life to go. So gradually one by one we stopped wearing the school jumper. This began to distress Jack Howieson, and, unusually, a group of us were summoned to his office.

'Now, boys,' he said, 'I know you are all nearly finishing school, and think that the school jumper is a waste of time, but look at it this way, if you buy a jumper for these last few months, you can always use it for a fishing jumper after you leave school. So I'd like to see you all properly dressed in uniform from now on.'

It had absolutely no effect of course. Mr Howieson was keen to maintain the image and identity of this wonderful school he had built, and he was nearing the end of his career. We on the other hand could see our school life and identity fading away day by day, and we had absolutely no interest in refreshing that identity. We were hammering on the door of adulthood.

Not just the school identity was about to fade, but the group identity. After years of seeing people every day in the closest of circumstances, and assuming that they were people you would know for the rest of your life, it seemed inconceivable that you would never see them again. People who were as familiar to you as your own family would become people who you wouldn't recognise if you passed them in the street.

David Robinson made an entrance some time after first term had begun in 1961. His appearance was memorable partly because it was after term had begun, partly because he had an orange in one hand, and mainly because he had come from South Australia. Eastern staters (as I would be memorably called by a Customs man when I returned from England in 1974) were as rare as Americans in Perth in 1961. I had never met anyone from another state, and I doubt if many of us had. Suddenly here was such an exotic creature.

It would have been daunting for me (as it was when I arrived at the institute in 1974), arriving from another world, clutching an orange, faced with a classroom, walls dripping with IQ condensate, full of mostly striking individuals determined to go places. But David managed it, seemingly with ease, and, apparently within a day or so, it seemed as if he had been part of the group ever since that education D-Day, 11 February 1957, when Miss Hoad had announced the composition of class 1A.

I drifted on as if in a dream. I enjoyed school, but more for the companionship than the work. Life was too short, I thought, to spend it grinding away at books in the way that a number of my friends, much more aware than me of the importance of results, were doing. Looking back, I suspect I thought that, like Jack Howieson, everyone knew I had ability, so what was written down on paper was not important.

By May, I was back down to an average of 61, and failing maths and physics. Mr Howieson seemed to have given up on me, or else he had confused me with someone else:– 'Has worked conscientiously with good results except in maths and physics.' Oh, come on, that isn't right. I got a shock I guess because by August I was averaging 71 with astonishing distinctions in maths and physics! But not in English and biology. Mr Howieson could at last relax; he had got me to the finishing line without a stitch. 'Good prospects of Leaving Certificate,' he said, much relieved.

I don't know if Jack Howieson knew who I was. I saw him as a remote Olympian figure of an incredibly ancient age (I think he must have been sixty-one!) but recently I have discovered that he mentored some students.

The Leaving exam of 1961 was the really terrifying one. Not only were there the results themselves, but there were Commonwealth scholarships hanging on the results. Without a scholarship, there was no way I could go to university. I kept watching TV, but much more nervously as the exams approached.

The results were announced in the same way as the Junior results had been. So once again it was into Perth at night to listen for the sound of the tumbrils approaching. For the Leaving, there were also grades, so that you either got a pass or a distinction, or a fail. I opened the paper nervously. All seven subjects, with two of the magic Ds in brackets behind English and biology. Peter had four Ds, and most of my friends had similar results. Stephen Graves had worked heroically hard all that year, and it had paid off with five distinctions, one of the best results in the state (there were usually one or two in the state who got seven Ds, and a handful with six).

But two distinctions was enough, just enough, to get a scholarship, so I had scraped in yet again. Now there was one more question. How good were the marks for the distinctions? The actual marks were posted out to students, and I guess came a short time after the newspaper announcements. I went round to Peter's house clutching my bit of paper. English 78, biology 76 and chemistry, irritatingly, 72. So I had just missed out on the third distinction, and might have got it without TV, or with more strength of character. The school motto was 'Persevere and Advance' but few except Stephen had heeded it. Not very high for English, but was it high enough to make me top of the school and retain my mark of identity – 'Oh yes, he came top in English.' Only one other student had a distinction in English, Robert Paterson, working, or trying, harder than his image suggested. Peter and I started ringing around (there may have been other queries as to how Peter had done relative to others, or where I stood in biology) and eventually reached Robert. It was like playing poker, and we both knew the stakes.

'What did you get for English?' I asked.

'Oh. 79, or something silly like that' was the usual languid, casual reply, perhaps hiding a nervousness as to whether I was holding a full house.

But I wasn't.

The results had failed to sort out a big dilemma for me. Was I a science student or an arts student? I had scored a distinction in English and biology. I couldn't choose both, so which one was I meant to have a career in?

My uncle saw himself, I think, as head of the family in the absence of both my grandfather and my father. Now that I had passed the Leaving, my schooling, in his view, was complete. It was time I got a job, and the only question really was whether I was to go into a factory or perhaps an office. His belief, I think, was that any time spent at school past the Junior was a waste. That given our family economic circumstances, I should have been put out to work as soon as I legally could be, in order to bring a few more pounds a week into the household.

It wasn't that he was against education as such. He saw himself as a self-educated man. He subscribed to magazines like *Reader's Digest,* and *National Geographic,* and obtained his knowledge of the world from them. That was the way people of our class did educate themselves. In a more general sense, though he would not have said it like that, he saw us, people like us, as having fixed roles. In that, he would have agreed with Uncle Len, and Len's father Charles, back in Yorkshire. If your family were farmers, then you became a farmer, and if you broke away from that role (as my great-grandfather did), then you were rejecting the family and its history and all its values.

Now that our branch of the Youngs had broken away from the farming life that Uncles Len and Tom and Nick and John had so faithfully followed, our options were in the world of mining or factories, or working behind the counter in shops, or, if you managed to get a bit more education, you could aspire to be perhaps a clerk or a bank teller. Uncle Bob himself had gone to work in factories and had trained to become a welder, so he had a trade. You could have aspirations, you didn't have to be a labourer, but the aspirations would be circumscribed within factory or office life.

In an even more general sense, both Uncle Len and Uncle Bob would have seen the family as being bounded within the great hierarchy from God (though neither, I suspect, were religious men) through the royal family, the aristocracy, the professionals, the tradesmen and the working classes. We were clearly working class, but you could have aspirations to acquire a trade or, as a farmer, you could stay in that trade.

A consideration of anything else meant you were getting above yourself, and there was a major row between my uncle and my mother. She had a smart son, and by God he was going to get as much education as he could. She had missed out, her father had missed out, her son wasn't going to miss out. He had got a scholarship so there was a bit of money coming in (about four pounds a week as I recall) and she would keep working. Eventually, he washed his hands of the whole thing. I don't know how he felt about it in later life.

I had finished school, and I wasn't yet at university. I was sixteen and I thought myself pretty unique. But how was that uniqueness to manifest itself? How was I to make it clear to the world that David Robert Horton was someone who was going to make a splash? Ah, I was only sixteen, and I had just come second top in the school in English. I would write a novel. I would become the youngest person in the world ever to write a novel. I got a large notebook and a pen, and sat under the mulberry tree and started to write. I don't want to make fun, sixty years on, of my sixteen-year-old self under the tree, writing a novel. It was a valiant attempt. It told the story of a sixteen-year-old boy and his thoughts and dreams. What else could it do? I called it *The Night is Open*, the idea being that in the daytime the hero had to be conventional but at night, in his dreams or imaginings, he was free to be extraordinary. I started on the first page of the book with the first day of the story and then wrote it in real time, as it were, in sequence. After a few weeks, I had managed to fill the first large notebook and calculated that I had half the novel written.

It was at that stage I must have told someone what I was doing, or perhaps I happened to pick up a newspaper, and discovered that Françoise Sagan had just published a novel at the age of sixteen. Bugger it. I was clearly going to be seventeen by the time I finished, and in any case there wasn't much point in being the second person to publish a novel at sixteen. So I stopped and put the manuscript away somewhere. I later finished the second half of the manuscript when I was living in Melbourne aged twenty-one, which must make for a big disjunction between the two halves, if I could ever bear to read it again, which I can't.

So I was going to have to make my mark at university. Perhaps I could become the youngest biologist in history. Or should I study English? Or chemistry? Or history? Who knew? The rest of the class who had got scholarships seemed to know what they were doing (Peter, for example, had never doubted he was going to do medicine), had, in most cases, it seemed, family backgrounds that gave them a context for study and career. But I had no one from whom I could seek advice, so what the hell was I going to do at university?

4

Thrown out of the nest

'How these curiosities would be quite forgot, did not such idle fellows as I am put them down.' – John Aubrey

There was only one university in Perth in 1962, so the University of WA was where you went. I entered at the age of sixteen, having, as the youngest entrant that year (and indeed for most years, though I presume there have been younger ones since), to get special permission and undertake additional tests including aptitude and psychological evaluation. I guess I was considered able to cope. My choice was either arts or science, but there was no career guidance in those days, and a family background that had absolutely no experience of making such choices. But among the many tests I did was a Rorschach test – and I just saw animal pictures. So biology right choice, yes?

When I set off, aged sixteen, for my first day at university, I was dressed for it. Well dressed. My mother and grandmother had little concept of what a university was, seeing it, I guess, as a kind of third, but very fancy, level of school. Just as high school was much grander than our little local primary school, university was grander again. It was a place where the upper classes went and became doctors and lawyers, I suppose, and when I began there, I was among some of the first few poor students who could take advantage of the new scholarship system to get into those hallowed halls.

All of that being the case, while I (and others) might have got a bit sloppy in clothing towards the end of high school, there was no room for sloppiness here and my family was determined I would look the part, fit in. So I had been bought a new very smart blue blazer, and my mother had acquired somehow the crest of the university in a cloth form suitable for sewing on to the pocket, which my grandmother did. Just like the high school blazer, here was the university blazer. I would belong. Oh, and they got me a smart, and shiny, briefcase. It was an ugly orange-brown colour and much too big, but it was a briefcase, and that is what you would need for university.

I was carrying a briefcase, on a bus, on the first morning, wearing my university blazer, and smart new trousers and shoes. I got off at the front entrance to discover of course, to my horror, that I was the only university student in the universe to be wearing a blazer with a crest on the pocket and that, while one or two others might have had briefcases, they were nothing like mine. If I had once been underdressed for scouts, I was overdressed for university.

But I was there and could try to be inconspicuous while I figured out where to go, what to do. First step was enrolment in the Winthrop Hall. I had no sense of how to proceed with it. My gut feeling was that if I was at the university with the big kids, I needed to show them I belonged, was right up there with the best and brightest, and the obvious way to do so was not just to enrol in science, but to enrol in the four hardest subjects and at the highest level of each – a hand with four aces, no bluff there. So it was not just zoology 1A, but chemistry 1A, physics 1A, maths 1A. Ah, if only I could go back and give my naive young self a bit of a nudge. But still, the university, like the school, had a motto – in this case, 'Seek Wisdom'. So all I had to do was combine the two – if I persevered in seeking wisdom, I would surely advance. We shall see.

Back to my enrolment. The zoology was fine but the other three, especially maths and physics, were nightmares. They were all designed for, respectively, students intending to major in each of those subjects, and they were hard. They were held in the main part of the campus, in dusty old laboratories and lecture rooms, and it all felt like being back at school. I struggled, and struggled, and struggled, and hated every moment of every course for the year, and at the end of it just scraped through those three subjects.

But all that time, the zoology department was like a shining beacon. It was in what had once been an old mansion, up on the hill, next to Kings Park. And whenever I was slaving away at incomprehensible equations, or conducting experiments that never worked, my eyes looked up the hill.

When the exams were over at the end of first year in 1962, I happened to bump into Julie Robins in the coffee shop. It was my first view of the coffee shop and perhaps I had gone out of curiosity. As a science student, there was very little free time for coffee during the course of a week, with five mornings full of lectures and four afternoons with practical classes, and the fifth afternoon spent in the library preparing an essay.

The reason I was there at all was that I had made a vow early in first year not to buy or read books except textbooks until I had got through the year. It would have been extremely embarrassing to get so far, full of promise, and get an end of year report saying 'not working to capacity'. In any case, I had no idea what level of work would be required. School and I had reached an equilibrium where the teachers knew how much work I would do and I knew how much was required and we settled on the deal. Until I had got through a year at university, I wouldn't know whether the bar was set higher or not. Anyway, I had made a pact with myself on the books (though not on TV) and now it was time for my reward. I had saved a few pounds from my scholarship and I had a list of the classic books that I hadn't yet read but knew that I should (Tolstoy and Dostoyevsky, Sartre and Mann, Forster and Balzac, Zola and Stendhal, Bennett and Butler). I was going to wallow in the luxury of buying a pile of books that had nothing at all to do with science and taking them home and reading them.

Julie was also a science student. She had been in my class at John Curtin and although I didn't know her well, there was a feeling that she was one of the core group of interesting and intelligent people in the class. People outside the common run. Julie had blonde hair and grey-green (she told me recently) eyes and didn't suffer fools gladly, I think. She seemed to consider me to be OK.

In the coffee shop, she thrust a book towards me and said, 'Have you read this yet?'

'This' was *Catcher in the Rye* and I had never heard of it, let alone read it. I read the first few pages, and when Holden Caulfield's teacher picked his nose in the second chapter, a blinding light hit me. There was this whole range of modern books that were potentially relevant to my life, and they were waiting for me to read them. I had read Dickens and Galsworthy and Bronte and the like at school. They were English classics, and they were clearly great books, but they were of a time and places and people far removed from me. The new European classics on my list would be the same. That was what literature was, that was how you recognised it. Suddenly here was someone who also loved literature, showing me that there were authors like Salinger who were great authors but also directly relevant to a teenager in the 60s. It felt like the start of my real education, and Salinger was added to my pile, and later Mc-Cullers, and Braine, and Amis and Mailer and Golding. My heart sang at the thought of just how much there was still to read.

During my university undergraduate years, I did vacation work in hospitals. It was through a Rechabite friend of my grandfather's, who was now very high in the Public Service, that I had managed to get work. He had been told (you'll like this chap) by my mother that I was doing science, and therefore would have the skills to work in the public health laboratories, which of course was nowhere near true.

The first year, I worked in the histopathology laboratory. For some reason, this was based in the Repatriation Hospital, quite separate to the other laboratories, and therefore had something of a secret society feeling about it. The boss, Keith, was a Seventh Day Adventist. He gave me a book to read by creation scientists John Whitcomb and Henry Morris, *The Genesis Flood*. Published in 1961, this book was aimed at convincing Seventh Day Adventists about a young Earth with no evolution, and then more widely. In fact, Keith was advanced in his backwardness. This book was the beginning of all the young earth creationist nonsense in Australia and then in America. It was my first contact with the sort of religious belief that is so strong as to completely overturn common sense. I came in each morning trying, without success, to explain to Keith why each chapter of the book was wrong. Ah, if only I had been more convincing, maybe I could have stopped all this nonsense in its tracks!

The other senior man in the lab, deputy to the abysmal Keith, was Harry (I have forgotten both surnames), quite a different fellow. He was mature, I guess in his forties, and he was my supervisor and teacher. He became, I suppose, something of a father figure to me. I had never really felt the lack of a father, or indeed a grandfather, growing up, although of course being brought up without one was seen then as a bad thing. As it is now – I get angry when I hear religious fundamentalists railing about how bad it is for two lesbians to be bringing up a child. I was brought up by two women. So what? Consequently, I had never acquired a father figure, as cliché would have had me do.

My Uncle Bob didn't fill that role, although he might have to some extent seen himself in it. Nor had any of my teachers through school. So Harry was the first. He was plain-spoken, straightforward and confident in himself. His job included attending post-mortems in order to parcel up specimens removed in the autopsy and bring them back for sectioning. He told me that seeing women cut up during an autopsy had badly affected his sex life. I saw him a year or two later. He had got out of pathology and started his own business in making concrete building blocks. He had also acquired a young wife, and I had the impression his sex life had improved.

It was interesting work in the lab, though, and I was taught how to carry out all the processes professionally, which was later useful in my science career. Tissue samples came to the laboratory from either post-mortems or biopsies. Each sample was impregnated with wax in a vacuum flask, then placed in a wax tray (like an ice block tray) on top of a label, then wax poured in, carefully avoiding bubbles, and the whole tray allowed to set. Each block of wax in turn was then trimmed to remove excess wax, and attached to a chuck with some melted wax.

The chuck was placed in a guillotine, the block carefully lined up, and then thin sections cut by winding a handle, rather like a salami slicer, click, click, click, click. You might turn the handle ten or fifteen times, making sure that you had reached into the main part of the sample and away from the edge. The result was a chain of wax, which you carefully lifted off from the edge of the guillotine blade with a small paintbrush and gently laid it on to the surface of the water in a water bath kept slightly warm. Like magic, the warmth expanded the wax, unfolding the wrinkles, and producing a long transparent strip just like a piece of movie film. Each 'frame' contained a piece of the tissue, the sequence unfolding like a person's life.

You would have a look at the sequence, pick out the best one or two sections, detach them from the rest with the brush and carefully lay them on to a glass slide. The slide was then placed on a hot plate, long enough to evaporate the wax and leave the tissue attached to the glass. The slide was then run through a series of chemicals (varying according to tissue type and nature of disease) for differing periods to stain the cells. They were dried, a glass cover slip put on top and glued in place (avoiding bubbles, which might have to be teased out around the edge by angling the slide and gently squeezing with the blunt end of the paint brush). Then they were dried in an oven, labelled and placed in a rack.

The slides would go to the pathologist or doctor for diagnoses. We were just the technicians, but the senior men had many years's experience and knew what they were looking at, and taught me how to recognise cancer and other abnormalities. It suddenly jumped from being the practice of a technique you were trying to perfect, to a slice of someone's life, because the case notes would give information like 'breast lump from forty-year-old mother of three' and the cells you had so carefully stained clearly showed malignancy, secretly growing inside that mother.

The laboratory smelled of hot wax and the staining chemicals, of alcohol, of cleaning liquids, and vaguely of the hospital laundry which was next door.

After second-year university studies, I reported for work again. This time (there was a policy of rotation) I was attached to the virology laboratories, which unlike histopath were near the centre of Perth, and close to the children's hospital, where a lot of our work came from. The ethos was quite different. In histopath, there was a great sense of urgency. Life and death could hang on the result of a slide, and samples were processed as soon as they came in and turned around within hours – faster if necessary. You felt part of a medical team, trying to help save people, as I was later saved.

Virology was quite different. We were looking not at visible lumps but at invisible agents in the human body. It was impossible to get a quick result, and many analyses could take weeks. We joked that by the time we could work out what the virus was, the patient was either recovered or dead. The atmosphere then was more like a research institute. There was time, and what we were trying to do was to see if there was an epidemic of a particular virus, or whether some new strain had emerged, or work out better ways for detection. The work involved live tissues, of necessity. There was an incubator for hen's eggs, which I was responsible for maintaining. The eggs moved through a sequence of shelves, so that there were always some available at each of the required incubation periods. I would later learn how to drill a hole into the air space and insert viral material. After more incubation, the chicken cells would be extracted and examined.

There were laboratory mice too, which I was also responsible for. I loved looking after them and maintaining the breeding stock, but injecting the babies with viral material was enormously cruel and I hated it. That and then killing the mice for autopsy was not a job, like my grandfather in the butcher's shop, that I should have been doing.

The third method of testing for viruses was the human cell lines. There were two: one I have forgotten, the other was HeLa, named from an abbreviation of the name of the woman (Henrietta Lacks) from whom the cells had originally come. She recently became famous following a biography, but at the time nothing was known of her; she had her name and identity stolen from her, as I would much later. I was told her name was Helen Lane. She had died twelve years before, but all over the world she lived on through her cells, which continued to grow and reproduce. I had to maintain them too. They grew in flat jars, in a red culture medium. When they had covered the lower surface of the jar, a chemical was added to detach them and break them up, then they were centrifuged and added to a whole new tray of bottles where they would begin to divide again.

When a test was needed, I would supply the number of jars and a drop of the viral sample added to the jar and the bottle placed in another incubator. After some days, the bottle would be placed under a microscope to see what, if anything, had happened to the cells, different damage being the signature of different viruses.

There might have been no urgency, but on the other hand there was a strong need for perfect laboratory techniques and disease control measures. Because the viruses of necessity remained alive, there was a constant danger of catching any one of them. In histopath, there was no real risk of catching anything; in virology, there was a risk of catching everything. I learnt to wash my hands the way surgeons did, we wore gowns all the time, all equipment and clothing was sterilised, and I learnt to remove a cap of a jar with my little finger, while holding a pipette in the same hand and the jar with the other hand, then putting the lid back on with the little finger, all the time wearing a surgical mask.

The laboratory smelled of mice, and eggs, and the sweet culture medium, and the steam when the autoclave was opened after sterilising a new batch of bottles and gowns.

At the end of third year (1964), I was assigned to haematology. The laboratory, because of the urgency of blood tests, was housed in Charles Gairdner Hospital. I was fine for a while, learnt to centrifuge blood, measure hematocrit, make blood smears and do white cell counts, test for blood chemistry. But then came the crunch. I was sent off with one of the senior technicians to learn how to take the blood samples.

Up we went in the lift, through all the hospital smells I was to later be familiar with – poor quality food, floor wash, sick people. There in a bed was an extremely old, very grey and very pale woman. The skin of her arms was wrinkled, the arms thin. The technician began to try to find a vein, telling me to pay close attention. After several unsuccessful attempts, she seemed to have no blood left in her, and I was feeling very sick. As we stood up, I nearly fainted, turning as pale as the old woman. I was asked to have a try myself but refused, and went back downstairs, telling the boss that I just couldn't get blood from old people (impossible to imagine that fifty-five years later I would be an old person who was hard to get blood from).

I was quickly sent back to the histopath lab, and spent the rest of the vacation there. But the atmosphere was different this time, because the brand new lab was now also in Charles Gairdner and the people were different. Perhaps for the first, but not the last, time I learned that you should never return to a place left behind.

But back to my university career. Getting to the end of first year without failing those three subjects felt like I had climbed a mountain and lived to tell the tale. So now the department on the hill could become a home, and it quickly became obvious that it would be. When you began second-year zoology, it was assumed that you were serious about the subject, were intending a career, and you were treated accordingly. It began with a field trip, how wonderful, to Rottnest Island. It was the first time I had been away from home without family, and it felt like a giant leap forward to adulthood. And what a place. Rottnest in those days was a tourist resort, but the tourism was very strictly kept to one part of the island, the rest being a nature reserve. And a reserve in which the zoology department undertook research.

One purpose of the field camp was described as follows: 'No matter how friendly the atmosphere of a university department, there is always an inherent barrier between staff and students. The idea of the camp is to lower this barrier so that there can be an easy flow of knowledge between these two groups of people, and so that during their studies students will freely discuss problems with the staff without "teacher-student" tensions.' I was to discover three years later that this ideal would be anathema in zoology at Melbourne University

We arrived on a ferry (MV *Islander*) on the Wednesday morning and drove in a bus across the island heading for another light on the hill. This was the Rottnest lighthouse. Once fully manned, it was now automated, which meant that the lighthouse and associated buildings had been made available for use by the zoology people.

We piled out on to the sand and into the lighthouse, which had several floors for use as a male dormitory (the female students would use the main house), each with several old metal and wire bunk beds of the kind that might have been used to harden up army recruits in the war. But it all seemed like magic as we claimed a bed, slung our bag on it and then went outside to begin the adventure.

Some staff went along on the trip, and a few doctoral students (including, unusually for those days, an American PhD student, Paul Licht, and fifty-eight years later I wrote to him, thanking him for being something of an inspiration to me when he gave a talk on reptiles), who would show us, over the next few days, field techniques like mark and recapture, and surveys, and marine collecting techniques. I think this was the first occasion where I suddenly became aware of what research was about and that it was possible for young people like me to be involved. It all felt like being out of the dusty old textbooks and in to the cutting edge of science where new things were being discovered, old ideas overturned, and we were foot soldiers, recruited to the cause.

Camp was five days in total in March 1963. There were sessions on reef fauna, catching quokkas, night plankton collecting, sandy shore fauna, salt lake fauna. Talks on marine animals, reptile thermoregulation, quokka research. By the last night, we were all buggered and somewhat emotional. But we were on our way, apprentice zoologists at last, part of a club. By the time we had returned home, we had all happily enlisted in Harry Waring's army, and the command post on the hill would be, we hoped, where we would be based for many years to come.

We got back from Rottnest Island, shook the sand from our shoes and got down to work. The field trip had been a smorgasbord, a sampling of some of the many research activities going on in the zoology department in WA. The state was Zoology Incognita, and the genius of Professor Waring, arriving from the industrial wasteland of post-war Birmingham, was to set in motion a great wave that would sweep all before it.

Zoology at Uni WA had many advantages, but the major one was that, for both research and teaching, nature was never far away. The department was on the edge of the amazing Kings Park, and neither the ocean in one direction, nor the blue hills (Ranges) in the other, nor even the desert to the east and the great forests to the south, were very far from the building on the hill.

Another advantage, I guess, was that the state was isolated from the rest of Australia. Different now that flying is cheap and frequent, but in those far-off times of the fifties and sixties, even Adelaide was two days on a slow train, or several days in a car bouncing over a goat track littered with wrecks and ruined tyres. Just as far in the other direction of course.

West Australians were the poor cousins (in those days before the minerals of the north began to be dug up in huge quantities) of the country, looked down on when they weren't being ignored, and consequently a chip on the shoulder was part of our birthright. So in zoology we were on our own, studying a unique (also the product of a much older isolation) fauna and flora in our own way, and to hell with everyone else. It was an effective ethos and soon the first PhDs from Harry's program began to fan out across the country taking up senior university positions.

And in a microcosm of all this, up on the hill, us second years were also isolated from the rest of the campus, a band of brothers and sisters who had seen the light, and, if truth be told, pitied those down below whose destiny hadn't been to be in Harry's army. Ah, bliss was it in that dawn to be alive, but to be young was very heaven!

The sense of being part of a glorious endeavour was heightened by the linkages between undergraduates, postgraduates and staff. Unlike the rigid hierarchy I was later to experience, disastrously, there was a sense here that it was one for all and all for one. That the second-year student was just a larva soon to pupate and then to burst out into a glorious butterfly. Possibly.

Anyway, as students we worked hard and late in the department, begrudging any time away down in the valley, where, of necessity, other subjects had to be done. I had, with some recognition of my first year near-disaster, picked biochemistry and physiology, and a lower level second-year chemistry. They were also bad choices, as it would turn out. Staff and postgrad students also worked hard and late, toiling away on fascinating projects. Our laboratory lights burning midnight oil, and the smell of coffee, attracted thirsty postgrads, who would drop in to take advantage of our coffee supply and repay us with tales of derring-do in the study of marsupial rumens, or desert reptiles, or marine molluscs. As would staff, including, not infrequently, Harry Waring himself, constant pipe drooping out of his mouth spilling ash as he accepted a strong brew and regaled us with tales of past, present and future of the world of zoology, our world. He had been a student of the almost mythological Hogben in Aberdeen, and then an associate of his in Birmingham, and so he linked us almost back to times when modern zoology began. We were part of the great endeavour, scientists now, no longer students.

The second-year zoology class was big in 1963, and we were divided up (alphabetically) into two halves for practical classes. While we knew the people in our own half, those in the other half were only familiar faces in the lecture hall. It was the time when a serial killer was loose in Perth suburban streets. We were all aware of it, but they were things that happened to other people not to people we knew. Shirley McLeod probably felt the same way.

She was babysitting near the campus, her way of earning some money to help her through university, when Eric Cooke shot her through the window and killed her. I don't remember her well – she was in the other half of the practical class – but I do remember a fair-haired pleasant girl, always smiling and friendly, delighted to be at university, with plans for the way her life would be. For all of us, I think it was our first taste of violent death in someone we knew, the first sense that, even in Perth, life was potentially as much about nastiness and evil, coming without warning through a window, as about happiness, working hard, and succeeding. Shirley was studying when she was shot.

By the time we got to third year, it was like the end of a marathon, the last few stayers struggling on towards the end. Those who were majoring in botany or geology or chemistry had moved on out, and many of those who were left were the ones who wanted careers in zoology if only they could do well enough.

There wasn't much room for outside interests, but I had continued to play hockey and had taken up badminton. Third-year zoology work was at a much higher level. We were acquiring skills like statistics that we would need, learning the details of embryology, ecology, nutrition, physiology, gaining more intense knowledge of fossils and evolution.

But I had made a big mistake. If there was a general overarching philosophy in zoology in WA, it was that the subject's future lay in being linked to physiology. Harry was a physiologist himself, but it was more than that, it was a feeling that to study these unique animals, in this unique and often harsh environment, meant studying their physiology, understanding how they had evolved and adapted to, say, desert conditions. Hence my physiology in second year seemed only natural.

But now it was third year and I needed a second subject to go with zoology. It would have been life-changing if someone, Harry himself perhaps, or any of the others, had taken me aside at this point and advised me. Had said, 'Look, you are going to be a zoologist, so you need to put all your strength into third-year zoology and pave the way for honours and postgraduate work. Whatever you do, don't do a second major' (that is, a second third-year subject, since third-year subjects, majors, were designed for those going on in that subject and were extremely testing and packed full of work for that reason).

This mythical person might have explored my particular interests and, discovering that they were more along the lines of evolution and ecology than physiology or nutrition, should have said, 'How about you do a first-year geology or botany as your second subject? You should really have done them before, both of them, given the way I foresee your career going, but better late than never.'

But such an imaginary conversation never happened. Instead, I had funnelled myself towards physiology. It would undoubtedly be a plus in a Waring zoology department, and then there was a clincher. I knew – one of those pieces of information that circulate in hothouses – that only one person had ever attempted the double major of zoology and physiology, which loomed like Twin Peaks. That person was the star postgraduate student (who would later succeed Waring as professor), Don Bradshaw. So, rather in the way I had chosen the hardest topics on that long-ago first day, now it seemed obvious that I should shine as the second person to attempt this mighty feat. I would show that I was a star, and my achievements would later be spoken of in hushed tones like those of Don. Done.

A terrible mistake. Second-year physiology had been pleasant enough, third-year was unpleasant and hard. I hated every minute of it. And what was worse, because it was so demanding, it sucked my mental energy away from zoology. Couldn't afford to fail this albatross hanging around my neck, otherwise I was stuffed, would have to do another year, and there was no scholarship money for that. So I ground on, managed to pass it all right, but at some cost. And it was to have another unforeseen consequence later.

A final field trip to Rottnest, bookending my zoology undergraduate life, and there we all were, likely lads and lasses, on the hill again for one last time as a group. Exams, and the weight of physiology, had pulled me back to third in the zoology class. Enough to let me go on to honours, thank goodness, but not enough to go into honours perceived as a rising star.

So a final vacation filled with working in the hospital laboratories as usual and then it was back to the hill for the honours year of 1965. The structure had changed recently, and we were the first year to try a new, experimental zoology honours year. There were four of us doing it under the supervision of Don Bradshaw, his first teaching role as he completed his PhD. The idea was that rather than narrow down to a single topic and thesis at this stage, honours would be seen as a continuation of undergraduate life, and we would continue to receive a broad zoological education, before finally making a choice in the postgraduate years. The result was that we worked as a team on four different projects during the year. The projects involved ecology, behaviour, physiology, nutrition. We all worked together, but for each project, one person wrote up the work and presented the seminar, while each of us wrote up particular aspects we had personally done. It was a good idea, but I find it hard to know now whether I would have been better with a single long project.

We were a reasonably close group, survivors of all those years of school and university, all of those kids who had started out on the journey had boiled down to just four. We were on the verge of scientific careers. We had to do well to be allowed to go on to a PhD, and, in my case at least (the others were from wealthy families), well enough to get a postgraduate scholarship.

We had our own honours laboratory – for three years, we had watched other students in there and now others would be watching us. We worked together, for example on all-night stints observing quokka behaviour from a hide in the yards. And we had many field trips together. On one, I remember riding in Mike's old Volkswagen, hearing as we travelled early one morning along St George's Terrace, Tom Jones singing 'What's New Pussycat?' on the radio (so it must have been about July 1965). What's new? We were new, brand-new scientists, on our way to starting a brand-new life blissful life as research zoologists. February the following year, Tom Jones, on tour, would be in Perth, but by then I would be on the other side of the continent, my brand-new life as a scientist having taken a wrong turning.

We four students, I think, assumed that we were working at the same level, we were working together as a team, and I guess if we had thought about it, we would have agreed that we would all be assessed as equal. There was no apparent way for the staff to distinguish between us, other than the individual bits we did, which were a small component in the overall scheme. It came as a great shock when two of the group were awarded first class, the other two, one of whom was me, not even upper second, but lower second. It was devastating and I think, even after all these years, unjust. It can have only been based on perceptions, expectations.

Fifty years later, Don Bradshaw told me, 'I actually tried out a so-called objective system of grading on you four at the end of the year and Harry then got me to write it up on the boat to England (we left for Sheffield in December 1965). Years later, I pulled out the manuscript and cringed somewhat at its naive attempt to quantify what cannot be measured (ability to think laterally, capacity to withstand uncertainty et cetera). All the marks were based of course on my subjective prejudices and this is why I think it is important to have more than one person involved in assessment and more than a single task.' That explained that, half a century on. Leaves a bad taste, knowing the whole course of your future life had been decided by a naive, arbitrary, invented system. It would have made a huge difference to my life, and made for a much easier one, had I got a first. Still, I got through it. As Macbeth says, 'Come what may, time and the hour runs through the roughest day' (a thought I would need very often in the next fifty-five years).

Part of my shock was that I had thought that we had all been accepted into the zoology club. That these superhuman characters like Harry Waring and Bert Main, gatekeepers, had agreed to let us come into their world. I had hammered on the door of science, but it had stayed closed. I hadn't been allowed to belong, was not one of those who would pick up the torch of learning and carry on. They hadn't accepted me as being one of them. My cosy little gang had been punctured. But still, in the words of Dani Shapiro, 'To be fully alive, fully human, and completely awake is to be continually thrown out of the nest. To live fully is to be always in no-man's-land.'

OK, being thrown out of the nest was philosophically a good thing, but the implications for my future were bleak. Honours 2b meant I couldn't go straight into a PhD, and the future, which had seemed clearcut, was suddenly very murky. What the hell was I going to do now?

5

'He's (not) a physiologist

Nicholas Emir Brunsengett's notion of "natural disruptors". These are individuals whose mere presence…profoundly disrupts their environment. Brunsengett believes natural disruptors interfere with normal patterns of causation, radically changing the status quo in ways totally counter to the intentions of all those involved. These are people who aren't even trying. In fact, they often react to their powers by trying not to be disruptive. But they can't help it, it's almost supernatural: wherever they go they disrupt the status quo.'
– Christopher Shevlin

Not being able to go directly into the WA PhD program with a scholarship (which the two firsts of our group did; Mike Gray, the other second, was also okay, he decided to work on spiders, and that got him into an ongoing project which he could take part in and earn a Masters, so I was the only one out on my ear), there was only one avenue available if I was to continue on to become a zoologist. Not that there was any 'if' about it: I was going to become a zoologist, a top zoologist, and if the zoology staff hadn't had the sense to recognise that, then it was their loss.

But bravado could only take you so far. In real terms, there was only one other pathway and that was to enrol for a Masters as a stepping stone towards the doctorate, and to do it while employed as what was called a demonstrator (a very old title) or a teaching fellow (more newfangled). Since zoology (and botany) involved very large weekly practical classes, lecturers couldn't deal with showing students how to dissect, say, an earthworm, and needed numbers of zoology graduates to do the hands-on teaching. Sometimes, they might be female graduates who just wanted to earn a bit of extra money, but generally the work was allocated to postgrad students without a scholarship, who could survive on a pittance, and squeeze in research work on a Masters or PhD in the evenings or the odd morning with no classes.

At the time when I was cast adrift from the promised land, there were two universities advertising for a zoology demonstrator with opportunity for postgraduate enrolment – Melbourne and New England. Knowing nothing of either, and having no preference really, except a mild tendency towards the rural university, I sent off applications and waited, hopefully. In what seemed a short time, back came, in February 1966, pleasingly, a job offer from Melbourne. I accepted, instantly, in case they changed their mind. Only to find in the letter box, by the old front gate, a day or two later, an offer from New England. Bugger, I was in demand. Why couldn't they have come in reverse order? Too bad, I had accepted Melbourne, my word was my bond, and it never occurred to me to go back on it and reject Melbourne and accept UNE. My bed was made, my path was set, I was off to Victoria, it would be an adventure.

I said goodbye, quite happily, to mother and grandmother. Was I an ungrateful wretch? Yes, I was. Did I understand how heartbroken they were? No, I didn't, and wouldn't until many years later, as an older and marginally wiser man. All I saw was that I was leaving home, no longer a child, gaining independence, in a big city on the other side of the country. Getting away from being looked after as a twenty-year-old man was a positive, it seemed. Unlike leaving my little dog behind, which was heart-rending for both of us.

Board a plane (itself an adventure, having only ever flown once before, on a DC4 doing a cargo run to and from Rottnest, which we hitched a ride on as honours students), and some hours later, ears blocked and very painful, land in the big city. I arrived at the front door of the zoology department in a taxi, clutching a suitcase in my hand. 'Uunsophisticated suburban boy from small town arrives in Big Smoke ready to go through door to a new career' was the caption if anyone was watching. The department was awe-inspiring, brand-new, two storeys, pale brick, big glass windows, a feel of a modern office about it, not the rabbit warren of dark small rooms I was used to back in the house on the hill. I entered the big glass doors nervously, but it was a very warm and cordial welcome inside. Professor Geoffrey Burnstock assigned Wendy, his personal secretary, to settle me in, and quickly this nice woman got me a bedsit in Toorak, introduced me to her husband who was a big wheel in St Kilda hockey club, showed me around the department, and got me set up in a very nice brand-new office with extensive laboratory space. Hey hey, this was something like it. They appreciated me here, anyway. What I didn't know was why.

During the tour of the building, it had become obvious that there was something unusual about its structure. What I hadn't realised was that the imposing building I had arrived at was something like the false facade in a cowboy movie. The tour began in this glossy part, physiologists downstairs, geneticists upstairs (where are the zoologists? I began to wonder), modern laboratories, nice offices, bright young things in white lab coats searching for glittering prizes. But there was another part to the building, as I discovered as we walked through the teaching laboratories and into the old part of the building, which was just like what I had left behind in Perth. And here were the zoologists, rooms crammed with zoological specimens, piles of reprints and old books, enough space to fit a chair and a desk. Rarely has a building so accurately reflected, not just form and function but form and status, and form and history.

Burnstock had been appointed as professor of zoology straight from the nearby physiology department. Where Waring was a zoological physiologist, Burnstock was a pure physiologist. He brought with him several physiologists from his old department. The addition of the new wing, the facade, symbolised, and made concrete, a desire to leave the old zoology department behind. The way of the future was physiology and genetics (which had its own professor), and the rump of the old zoology (where there were still specimens collected and labelled by Baldwin Spencer, the first professor, some sixty years earlier) could be left to wither and die.

I don't know whether Waring was aware of all of this, but he would have known that Burnstock's field was in pure physiology. So when he wrote the letter of recommendation which got me the job, he included the phrase which he must have known would be a clincher: 'You'll like this chap, he's a physiologist.' Hence the warm welcome. I was unaware of this introduction until a little later, and had thought I had been appointed, on merit, as a zoologist to a zoology department, and it was only as the first few days went by (days that included my twenty-first birthday, celebrated by looking at the cards from my mother and grandmother which sat on the smooth white painted shelf in my laboratory – leaving home wasn't necessarily all beer and skittles, it seemed) that, heart sinking, I came to understand that they thought Waring's comment was literally true, that I had majored in physiology, and after a brief wrong turning in zoology honours, I was ready to be welcomed back into the world of pure physiology.

Could I do this? No I couldn't. Third-year physiology had been a misery; there was no way I could spend several years doing postgrad work in the subject. So I mulled and I mulled and finally told myself not to be silly. I was a zoologist, this was a zoology department, what could they do to me? It would be fine. So, summoning sinews et cetera, I made an appointment with Burnstock and let him know that I really really really didn't want to do a physiology Masters, but would quite like, please sir, to work on the taxonomy-evolution-biogeography of a group of lizards (a group suggested to me by one of the zoology PhDs, Peter Rawlinson, a nice fellow, who worked on snakes, but knew, it seemed, everything about the reptiles of Victoria). Can't remember how the conversation went – frosty, I imagine – but anyway, it was done, weight lifted off my shoulders, could get on with research in zoology now.

Had barely got back to my room when the message came that, since

I was no longer doing physiology, it was no longer a suitable room for me. There was another room available, in the old dark zoology wing. And indeed there was, in a bit chopped off the second-year laboratory with plywood partition which had been used as a windowless cupboard by the cleaners, but now, mops and brooms removed, chair and small desk inserted, would be my future home. Somewhat noisy whenever there was a laboratory class on the other side of the barely head-high plywood, but can't have everything, right. Oh, and by the way, you know how we said research funds were available for your research? Sorry, we meant to say there were physiology research funds available. As a zoology researcher, you wouldn't need money, stands to reason.

Bugger them, I thought, you won't stop me, I'll just get on with it. My PhD student friend told me not to worry, I would need to sort out the taxonomy first (the group had hardly been studied since the 1880s, and indeed one major reference I used dated from the 1830s) and that could be done with preserved specimens. He himself had lots of jars full of my lizards which I was welcome to examine and measure, and there would be plenty more in the museum (then called the National Museum, in competition with the Australian Museum based in Sydney – the old colonial rivalry was never far away). So I trotted down into town, met Joan Dixon the curator of vertebrates, who took a liking to me (she didn't always, it seemed) and we would be friends for years. 'Yes, of course, here's a table [in the old catacomb-like collection storage area under the building], light, microscope. Come whenever you like.'

So I was on my way. Doing a lot of practical teaching with the big second-year class, spending the time in between getting to know the lizards. But there was more to life than work, wasn't there? Apparently not (except for hockey, once a week), since I knew no one, had no family, no support network of any kind in Melbourne. The three-way division of the zoology department resulted in three separate groups of staff and postgrads who socialised as separate groups. In addition, and very much unlike WA zoology, there was a complete division between staff and postgrads on one hand, and undergraduates on the other. Oh, and then there was me – I had rejected physiology, was not a geneticist, was not seen, having come from outside, as one of the under-siege tight-knit zoology crew.

Something of an outsider elsewhere too. After my first game for St Kilda hockey club, the secretary's husband took me with the boys for an after-game beer. I was too embarrassed to say I didn't drink (Rechabite culture ingrained), but in any case, before I could speak, he had ordered without asking. So for the next hour a full glass (middy? schooner?) of beer sat on the counter of a mobile beer shop caravan. Where were we? In the beer garden of a pub? Was it some kind of hockey club facility? Dunno, doesn't matter. What did matter was that undrunk glass of beer, bought for me as a matter of course, by the husband of the departmental secretary who had been my sponsor into the St Kilda hockey club where he was a senior player. I wasn't one of the sporting boys, so there were no more invitations of that kind. I wasn't invited to anyone's house either during my time in Melbourne. If there were parties the staff were having, they weren't telling me. I went home to a one room bedsit each night. Come on, this was the swinging 60s, I was twenty-one, where was the FUN?

If I wasn't having fun with staff (although, to be fair, a geneticist, Vin Stangio, and a zoology Masters student, David Woodruff, were friendly during daylight hours and would invite me at work for a cup of coffee and a chat about research), then that just left students. The ones I knew came from the large second-year class I was supervising, and that was my only involvement with them. I had no role in marking or grading. I overlapped in age with them (many were older), and I was treating them, during classes, as if they were human beings and not some kind of lower orders, behaving, in fact, like the postgrads in WA had behaved towards me. The result was that some of them might join me for coffee when they saw me drinking alone in the university café. Might mention that there was a party on, friends of friends, in Carlton, Friday night, turn up if you like, might be fun. So I did, and it was, and there were often parties, and it was better than drinking alone (which I had now started doing, at last leaving my Rechabite heritage behind).

My work was going well. The museum collection was letting me sort out the taxonomy, the specimens the PhD student had collected gave me more detail for Victoria, better idea of variation within species. I kept going back to him – would you mind if I checked out species x again, need to do some additional measurements, check that colour pattern, get started on this other group, record the habitats in more detail. I was feeling my way, not sure what was useful, what wasn't. I had no real supervisor. The person who would have had that role (Murray Littlejohn, an early emigrant from Waring's department) was away on sabbatical for a year, and I was nominally on the books of another PhD student, Angus Martin.

After some months of this, I became embarrassed at disturbing my PhD friend, knocking on his door, disrupting his work. So I began going late in the day, when he was just finishing, so I could work without disturbing him. I knew his collection of my lizards as well as he did now so I didn't need help to find things. And eventually when that routine was okay, I would sometimes go after work so I could do measurements unobtrusively and not annoy him at all. I thought I was being very considerate. It seemed not. Like a bolt out of the blue, late in the year, I was told he had made a complaint about me using his collection without permission in his absence. Didn't talk to me about it, drop a hint, a quiet word. No, a formal complaint.

I was devastated and wasn't sure what to do next. Not long to think about it. I was called in by Professor Burnstock, who had his own complaint about my behaviour – I was too friendly with the students. It wasn't permitted. If I was seen on casual terms with any student again, I was going to be sacked. I stumbled out of his office, out through the big glass doors, and, as it happened, bumped straight into the group of the students I knew (one of whom, Max King, was interested in research on reptiles and genetics, and would later go on to do that; a second, Don Gartside, also later did reptile research – I had, it seemed, helped to inspire them to distinguished professional careers in zoology). Seeing my distress, they said hey, come to the café, you need a cup of coffee. I hadn't thought too much about it, but our meeting, and subsequent joint travel towards the café, had taken place right under Burnstock's office window.

I arrived back after the coffee (and an agreement that in future I would have to keep my distance from all students, interested in reptiles or not) only to get a message that Burnstock wanted me in his office, NOW. He told me that I had disobeyed his instruction, immediately after he had given it, and that was that, I was out on my ear, pack your bags, you're gone. Melbourne was meant to have been a lifeline for a chap who wanted to be a zoologist. Instead, it was a dead end – no protests from the physiologists, cause I wasn't one; and no protests from the zoologists – wasn't clear perhaps what I had done, but must have done something outside the code of zoologists, stood to reason really, otherwise there wouldn't have been a complaint.

I packed up my few belongings in my car, and set off for Perth. It was a long way. My career in science was over, before it began. Where could I possibly go from here?

6

Farewell to New England forever

'Paul, though he did not know it, had been acting in his few days in England as an animated question mark, a living question which had been hurled at various people, and according to their natures, eliciting entirely unrelated reactions. He had passed from one person to another and annoyed or delighted or worried or exasperated them in turn. All of them remembered him for different reasons.'
– Victor Canning

When I got back to Perth, I pretended to be the sophisticate, at home in a big city, experienced in all the fabulous activities of the 60s. The first disco had just opened in Perth, and I took my former honours comrades (now a year into their postgraduate work, with no roadblocks – Kent Williams later had a career working in ecology in CSIRO; Bob Henzell went on to work on feral goats; Mike Gray later had a career as arachnologist at the Australian Museum) along to show them what it was all about, I had, after all, once been, briefly, and to be honest, rather boringly, to one in Melbourne.

But it was a hard image to maintain, and mostly I just sat, as before, in a deckchair under the old mulberry tree. I sat in the shade, smelling the old familiar scents of mulberries, and roses, and dog, and chickens, reading books, mostly waiting, I suppose, for something to turn up, although I had reluctantly (not my university home any more) gone into the zoology department to see if they knew of anything I might try. There was a research job going with WA Fisheries on crayfish, said Bert Main, but that was as little to my interest or capability as physiology. But if I didn't want to work on crayfish, what next? With the help of the family friend, back to the hospital. I had a biology degree now so could be slotted into a more significant position. Research. In my case, it was to get involved in work on folic acid and its role in pregnancy. It wasn't too far-fetched – I had after all done zoology, physiology, biochemistry and chemistry, and I knew how to do research. I sat down in the hospital library and started reading everything published so far on folic acid. Not much, I remember; the work was in early stages. I could have gone on with it, I guess, but I was seeing it very much as a task, a job, work, and what I wanted was zoology, a career, a vocation, a love.

And, like magic, something did turn up in early 1967. The University of New England wanted to know if I was still interested in the job I had been awarded a year earlier. The second choice who had then filled it had moved on, and there was again a vacancy. If I wanted it, I better get myself to Melbourne to be interviewed by the professor (Tony O'Farrell), who would be there in mid-January for a conference (ANZAAS). I put the blood chemistry books back on the library shelf, packed the car and was on the road again, retracing my steps all the way back to Melbourne.

The interview was conducted in Tony O'Farrell's motel room, and Alex Stock (who had a personal chair) also took part. Being interviewed by two full professors in the circumstances I was in should have been daunting, but somehow wasn't. I hit it off with Tony immediately (not at all with Professor Stock and never did), but I also had a feeling that the tape of my life had been rewound to where I knocked back their offer a year earlier, only this time the *Sliding Doors* script would have me accepting it as if the awful year in Melbourne had never happened. So I had the job; there was just one proviso, one condition. There were to be no politics. Sure, fine, whatever you say, no politics (I didn't say it like that). But inside, my mind was saying, 'No politics. What does that mean, no politics? What on earth is he on about?'

It was later, much later, that I managed to piece together what it was all about. Curious and concerned about the reason I was on the loose again after only a year in Melbourne, Tony had, it seemed, asked someone on the Melbourne zoology staff what had happened. Whoever it was (perhaps my acting supervisor) had said, 'Oh, no big problem, it was just politics.' They had clearly meant the departmental politics of physiology versus zoology and my being got rid of to make room for a physiologist when I hadn't played the game. Tony, however, seemed to have heard it not as 'small p' departmental politics, but as 'big P' Politics. It was the time, early 1967, when anger about, and opposition to, the Vietnam War was beginning to gain momentum. There had been protests in Melbourne over LBJ's visit the year before, and both Monash and Melbourne universities were seen as being much more left wing than campuses elsewhere. Tony, I imagine, thought that he had here a bit of a radical, perhaps a socialist, perhaps even, heaven forbid, a communist, and there would be none of that sort of stuff in his conservative department in a conservative university in a very conservative country town.

The irony was that at the time I was politically somewhere just right of centre. In the Melbourne tea room, where, yes indeed, there were one or two staff members who were strongly opposed to the war, I was likely to argue with them that it was necessary, a judgement I based on my reading of *Time Magazine* and *Newsweek*, media outlets I still, in those days, thought were objective and factual sources of information. I had even told my grandmother in 1961 that she should vote for Menzies because I didn't see Arthur Calwell as being of prime ministerial quality. I still shudder in embarrassment years later at the memory.

Anyway, O'Farrell was happy to employ me on the basis that I was okay except for suspect Politics which he would need to keep an eye on in case I erupted in some kind of spontaneous demonstration in the main street, and I was happy to be employed on any conditions really. Further irony, though, I would become more left wing in Armidale, joining a moratorium march (down Beardy Street) for example, and going to a talk by the great Jim Cairns.

I filled up the back seat of my old Volkswagen with the stuff I had left stored (unsure of where I would be heading) in Melbourne – clothes, bedding, books, odds and ends – and was heading north. It was, as it would turn out, the best move I could have made. I should have done it one year earlier.

Over the next six years or so in Armidale, I would go to a lot of parties, play a lot of sport (including for UNE, in the inter-varsity hockey team in Hobart and Canberra, the inter-varsity badminton team in Sydney), get married, have two children, buy a house, make lifelong friends (but later, sadly, lose touch with some), complete three extra degrees to add to the honours degree, gain a qualification and a referee which would lead to my major career, and have a lot of fun. After the awfulness of the honours result, and the year in Melbourne, Armidale provided emotional well-being.

It also provided intellectual stimulation, The group of six teaching fellows I was part of was top class. Rod Simpson, an expert on intertidal ecology, was the only person I ever heard of whose Master's thesis was so good it was converted to a PhD, and who later became professor of zoology in the department. Veronica Parry, who I briefly shared an office with, was an ornithologist who wrote the book on kookaburra behaviour. Rob Pidgeon was one of the best ecologists I ever knew; an expert on galah ecology, he later switched to his first love, freshwater ecology. Bob Hardie became an expert on the enigmatic peripatus. And John Veron, who I briefly shared a house with, later became one of the leading Australian experts on coral reefs.

The university had been established, uniquely, as a result of community pressure and politicking and fund raising, the people of New England sick of having their children having to go away to Sydney or Brisbane for university education, and seeing a great opportunity to have a university focused on rural research in the rich farming area of the northern tablelands of NSW.

But it also proved to be, like the University of WA, and unlike Melbourne, ideally situated for biological research. Within a few minutes, you were in open farming land, and within an easy drive east, you were on the rugged edge of the Great Dividing Range, falling steeply to the coastal plain. An easy drive west took you to semi-arid country. A couple of hours had you on the coast with an interesting marine environment, and a few hours north took you into subtropical Queensland. I was heading towards an idyllic place to do zoology (although it took me a while to adjust to the rural side, remarking, on my first drive around the countryside outside Armidale, 'Wow, look at those big brown sheep.' They were, of course, cows).

I was also, as it turned out, heading to a department that was undergoing a great expansion and ferment. The year before I arrived, O'Farrell had appointed, an undoubtedly courageous decision, a brash and energetic young American zoologist. Hal Heatwole had interests and expertise in ecology, herpetology, marine biology, tropical ecology. He was an inspiring lecturer and an inspirational postgrad supervisor. His arrival had stimulated a flurry of new postgraduate students beginning research work, of which I was to be one.

His teaching style took me back to the environment I had been used to in WA. Here was a lecturer who was friendly with undergraduate students and encouraged his demonstrators to be the same. He held parties at his house, almost weekly, to which staff, visitors, postgrads, and undergraduates were all invited and came. Not an approach that would have been appreciated, or permitted, in Melbourne, but the result was that a rather staid even stagnant department with little research program was quickly transformed into one where undergraduates were clamouring to do research work, and those who completed higher degrees were beginning to expand out and fill posts in various institutions around the country. It was all very exciting.

I continued work on the lizards (taxonomy, and with biogeography ideas based on Bert Main's work with frogs) and in 1968 I finished the Masters (as well as teaching four full afternoons of practical classes, and also teaching in the holidays in the university's then unique external student program, a first for Australia) I had begun in Melbourne, so could now enrol for a PhD – I was back on the road again towards a career in science. I got my research underway and then had a kind of mid-postgrad crisis.

I had never really resolved the split between my interests in science and the arts. Instead, I had just got onto the science highway, and in spite of a few bumps and detours in the road, had stayed there ever since. But I didn't want to die wondering whether I should have gone into arts instead. So I quietly went off after enrolling in the PhD and enrolled in an arts degree simultaneously. I could get some credits from my science degree to count towards an arts degree, but I would have to do at least five new subjects, including a major.

So it was English and ancient history. I had an interest in Roman and Greek history, so the latter was obvious, but the New England course began, somewhat unusually, with Australian archaeology, taught by another newcomer to the university, Isabel McBryde (also an inspiring figure, and one of the nicest people in Australian archaeology). I discovered, to my surprise, knowing nothing about it previously, that Australian archaeology was very interesting (and was also about to flower vigorously as a discipline), so I continued into the second-year course (there was no third year, although you could do the course as either a second- or third-year component of a degree).

Isabel discovered that I was also doing a PhD in zoology and asked if I would be willing to teach my fellow archaeology students about bone identification (bones being often present in sites and revealing much information about diet and environment). I did, with great pleasure – it was to prove an important decision.

I was enjoying the English literature course too. My tutor was Ken Stewart. Most of our tutorials involved Ken and me discussing the collected works of Dickens, or Lawrence (Ken's PhD subject), the other students in the tutorial group having never read anything except the single set text, if that. I was there after already a lifetime of reading everything I could lay my hands on. At some point, I told him I had written a novel. I guess it was the first time one of his students had ever said this. He was excited and helpful. Thomas Keneally happened to be a guest writer in residence in the department that year, and Ken invited me to the pub to have a beer with Tom and himself and talk about my novel.

Tom was just thirty-seven years old but had seven novels and three plays under his belt, and two Miles Franklin awards, and had been nominated for a Booker Prize, but he treated me as if I was a fellow novelist, just a little down on my luck in the publishing game. He wrote to his publisher, Angus and Robertson in Sydney, and the next time I was there I went to the office of A&R, manuscript clutched in hand, a publishing door opened by a major author. So they gave it serious consideration and then equally seriously rejected it. I would remain a novelist manqué, but never forgot Tom Keneally's kindness.

My first published work was a short story in my high school magazine in 1961. I had written a lot of poetry and many short stories that year, and my English teacher, Stan Richards, must have decided this one was good enough to reach a wider audience and to last through time. I guess it was of some interest in having a trick, or surprise, ending, not what the reader expected. Much of my career was like that, I suppose.

My next public work, a science research publication, was eleven years away, and would be something quite different! Before that day came, though, I had to resolve a dilemma. In WA zoology, I had been taught that publication was a last resort. That the research was the thing, and that you kept working away, gathering data, until you could produce the single perfect form of a paper. Then, if you had timed it right and avoided fatal illnesses, you might work towards a second paper that would turn the zoological world upside down. Charles Darwin was the ideal example. Working away for twenty years, never happy he was finished, he wouldn't have published then except Wallace was about to beat him. Then intervals before publishing other major works.

But then I went to New England zoology, where my supervisor had exactly the opposite belief. In his view, the publication was what mattered, so you got them out as fast as possible. Finish a piece of research, publish, repeat every few months. Get the work out to other researchers; it was useless just sitting in your notebooks. It had another big advantage – in this brave new world, you would only get a job on the basis of numerous publications. WA zoology was still mentally living in the age when, as one of my examiners, Allen Keast, told me, university graduates were still so scarce that, if you could sign your name, you got a professorship.

So publication it would be, but I wouldn't rush. I finished my Masters in 1968, so I now had material to publish. But I had to get going on the PhD (no jobs for basic degrees any more), and start the arts degree. It was frustrating, though. I had dreamt of being a published author since the school magazine, and my attempt, thwarted by Françoise Sagan, of becoming the world's youngest ever novelist. I should be publishing, I thought, Master's degree safely in my back pocket, PhD baton in my rucksack.

My two major papers were burbling along through the refereeing process, but slow, slow. Then a discovery – collecting lizards around Armidale and realising that they were a completely new species. Hooray, I was on my way – a quick short paper and a new species would be my introduction to the discipline as a professional zoologist. Elation, work starting, my fellow postgrads happy for me. Then down. I discovered somehow, perhaps directly, that Glen Storr at the WA Museum had found some specimens of *my* lizard in a museum collection and was about to describe them.

Now I liked Glen. But he was established, I was desperately trying to get a foot on the ladder. I had no money for research. All I could do was work on museum specimens and do a bit of local collecting around Armidale. Finding a new species was a lucky fluke. But it was not to be. Glen had got there first. Stiff upper lip, no use crying over spilt formalin, grin and bear it, et cetera. I would just knuckle down to analysing the whole genus, something that hadn't been done since 1887 (and before that, 1845).

But Roni, who I shared an office with, had heard my exclamation of disappointment, asked me what had happened, and then went off and discussed it with the other postgrads. She decided that they would come to my 'rescue' by publishing my find in the local newspaper (the *Armidale Express,* nicknamed the 'Armidale Distress'), thus giving me priority before Glen could get his description published in a scientific journal. None of them were taxonomists, so they had no idea that this was a bad thing to do; they saw it as a bit of a joke. They called the new species *E.* 'brownei' (which was my nickname for it since it was related to *E. whitei*, and was brown) and took a picture of a specimen while I wasn't in my room, wrote a description of my find and rushed off to the newspaper office.

Hal discovered what was going on very late in the day and was of course horrified, seeing the implications. It was too late to get the article withdrawn, but he did insist that they changed the joke name to the name I had picked for it originally (*E. geophana*), and the newspaper inserted the new name (if you look at the article, you can see the change). The newspaper appeared and my friends hurried to show me, smiling at their achievement, certain I would be pleased. I was horrified and angry. There was nothing I could do. There it was in print. I wrote to Glen to apologise, his formal description appearing soon after.

Back to work, measuring specimens. Embarrassing episode over. Except it wasn't. Two leading Australian herpetologists (Alan Greer and Harold Cogger) strongly criticised me for publishing a new species in such a way and for the resulting confusion as to the proper name. Once again, I was seen as guilty of something of which I was innocent. I wrote to the chaps concerned, explaining what had happened, mistake by others, not my fault, et cetera. No reply from either of them. I was clearly persona non grata among the close-knit Australian herpetology community. Forget about a career. Whatever you do in future can't make up for this. Can't be helped, just get on with it.

I started on PhD research on a related and, in hindsight, unsuitable topic. It involved a lizard genus occurring over the whole southern hemisphere (except Australia where the previous genus I had worked on was, I thought, its representative). There was no money available for travel and field work or anatomy or genetics, so it all had to be done by describing museum specimens. The museums of the world were wonderful (in hindsight amazingly so, being asked for specimens by a totally unknown postgrad student from a tiny rural university in Australia), and packages began arriving from the Smithsonian, the American Museum of Natural History, and museums in Hamburg, Los Angeles, Jerusalem, South West Africa, and many many more.

I had the smell of alcohol and formalin in my nostrils every day. The former gave me a hangover without the preceding pleasure, the latter, so unpleasant, may have planted seeds in my bone marrow, to germinate years later.

It was important to get the PhD done and publish the earlier work when I could get down to it. It was complicated because, oddly, the PhD thesis couldn't include published work (you'd think the opposite would be true), so I had to time publishing new work carefully to not appear until the thesis was submitted (which was aimed for 1973).

Publication finally began in 1972, my name in lights, attached to work from my Masters. Oh, and something extra on bird evolution that had come to me inspired. I was on my way. I quickly followed the first publications with new ones from the thesis work. At last I was a scientist with publications, part of the academic community in spite of the slings and arrows that outrageous fortune had thrown at me since 1964.

I had reached third year arts as I was approaching what looked like being the last year or so of the PhD. I had timed it so that I wouldn't be trying to write up a thesis while continuing the undergraduate work. At that point, someone in university administration happened to notice that what they thought (I guess) was two people with the same name doing a PhD and an arts degree respectively was the same person.

Consternation. Hal, who knew I was doing both, asked if I was managing okay, and when I said yes he reported back to administration that everything was fine. So I was allowed to complete the arts degree, but the university quickly changed its laws to prevent dual enrolment. I guess I will remain unique in having done two degrees simultaneously (take that, Françoise Sagan).

Anyway, while an amusing diversion, that didn't get a PhD finished, and a career in zoology required one. Suddenly, what had seemed like a steady jog to the finish line became increasingly frantic. Almost at the moment that I took up my pen and wrote the heading 'Chapter 1', Hal announced that he was off on a year's sabbatical (at that time, every seven years for permanent staff), not somewhere close by but in Tunisia. So for the next twelve months I would complete a chapter, send it off in a parcel to Tunisia by camel train, wait for comments to come back, make corrections, send back, each parcel taking, each way, a week or two. At the same time, with one eye on what the hell I was going to do when I finished the thesis, my friend Rod, reading the massive *Guide to academic scholarships and post-doc fellowships*, saw something ideal for both of us in England. One that would suit his marine biology interests in Newcastle, one that would suit my biogeography research in York. Even better, the scholarships, based on a fund donated by a Victorian-era soap millionaire with a desire to do good, were so obscure that no one else seemed likely to apply for them. So we applied successfully and were given a starting date of the following October (the beginning of the UK university year), a few months away – I would be heading even further north. However, the success was contingent on me having a PhD, which meant finishing the damn thing, and getting it examined and passed, in a very short time indeed.

With quick work from Hal in Tunisia, quick work by me (and friends who collated it), the thesis was submitted and sent off to three referees, one in England, one Canada, one Australia, with a heartfelt plea from Hal to get the examining done quickly in order to then get it through the UNE bureaucracy. But now it was October 1973. I had to sell our house, store furniture, get packed and head off to England, leaving our poor dog behind, all the time knowing that the thesis was not yet approved. But, after buying a second-hand camper van from returning Australians in Bristol, and a brief stop to meet, for the first time, my father's relatives on the way, I discovered on arriving in York that the examiners had been approving. I was indeed Doctor Horton, and I would start being paid a salary. Phew!

I had, in a way, completed the return home that my grandparents, feeling they had failed out in the jungle, were never able to do. I had gone back to York with a university career and future under my belt. Would I be welcomed with open arms, or what?

The University of York in 1973 when I arrived was only ten years old, many of its buildings much less. It was part of a new wave of 'concrete' universities, following the red-brick campuses of earlier times, and of course the hallowed ancient halls of Oxbridge.

The biological sciences (none of this old-fashioned zoology) were in a long concrete and glass structure with light airy laboratories and offices set along very long halls – no dreaming spires on this campus proudly 1973, not 1173. There was, inside, something of the Melbourne division between the modern biological sciences involving chemicals and test tubes, the smells more like those of a hospital than a zoology department, and the ecologists, all beards and corduroys. Whereas Melbourne zoology didn't really want to know you unless you were a Melbourne graduate, York was much more broad-minded, being equally happy with a degree from either Oxford or Edinburgh.

I didn't know whether Hal had written a reference saying 'You'll like this chap, he's a biogeographer', but that seemed to have been the attraction to Professor Mark Williamson, Oxford graduate and lecturer at Edinburgh before being appointed as professor at York, whose research interest was also biogeography/evolution. So, all good. There was some tutoring to be done each week, but otherwise I was free to follow up some publications from my thesis, do a lot of reading in evolution and the history of science in the university library (catching up on the general reading in biology that there hadn't been time for in the last few years of specialised thesis work), and begin work on some new theoretical ideas about biogeography.

It was also great to be able at long last to get to know the ancient stamping grounds of Youngs and Carters, and to get to know my father's relatives in the Midlands. For someone used to the huge distances of Australia, the idea of driving for an hour or two, apparently unheard of for most English people at that time, was nothing. I could go to Coventry for a weekend, where we were made welcome by aunt and cousins.

Not so welcome in the department, though. Years later, I read Manning Clark's memoirs about going to Oxford as an Australian, and his experience that as a colonial he was not just being set an exam for acceptance, but an exam it was impossible for an Australian to pass. I knew how he felt. The ecologists were friendly at morning tea, the others not so much. I was once invited to a general staff/postgrad party at a lecturer's house (where oddly we all played board games), so that was one more than in Melbourne, but only one. I was seen, and referred to openly, like Clark, as a wild colonial boy ('You colonials' began one conversation to me, going on to detail some sin of omission or commission), an expression I thought might have been dead and buried fifty years earlier. There was no getting around it, I had an Australian accent.

Once at a cricket match, halfway through the year, and fancying myself to have a fairly neutral, if not blending-in English accent, I was asked by a man selling hot dogs where I was from. Hah, I thought, he is wondering if I am from Yorkshire or further south.

'Where do you think I'm from?'

'Well, I know you're from Australia. I was wondering which part. I have a cousin in Sydney I thought you might know.'

I wasn't an Oxford graduate, and in the great scheme of things, the best of the Australian universities were perceived as being another rung down the ladder from even the worst of the English ones. Old habits die hard, it seems. I could hammer on the door of English academia as hard as I liked, it wasn't going to be opened.

We had an area of new-built semi-detached. houses at the end of a cul-de-sac, and on the edge of campus, on the banks of the central lake, smelling of Canada geese and various ducks. It was a beautiful campus.

I made friends among the other visiting postgrads from other colonial outposts like South Africa, London, red-brick English universities, who all seemed to have a similar lack of acceptance. And I got on with my research in biogeography. The fellowship was only a year, and I needed to try to establish academic credentials beyond the thesis. Most of what I was sending off for publication was on the reptile group I had studied for my PhD, and that was fair enough, but I did need to broaden my publications a bit.

And then one of those light bulb moments, not that frequent in science, in spite of popular perceptions, and all the more welcome when they do come. I had been reading up on some of the new ideas about mathematical modelling in biogeography, which was getting the subject away from a kind of naturalist approach of mere description about what had gone where when, and into a more scientific basis for explaining how the fauna and flora composition of, say, islands, was determined.

There was a major book on island biogeography that had come out a few years earlier and it was all the rage, the American authors instantly becoming leading figures in biology. And suddenly I, little me, saw a way to slightly modify, adapt, one of their ideas and apply it in a new way. YES! You ripper (as us colonials might say). I was about to make a bit of a name for myself. I drew some graphs illustrating the model, wrote it up, and sent it off to the professor, sure that he would be delighted, but also thinking maybe I had missed something, or needed to expand on something, and looking forward to getting comments back (as I was used to from Hal), modifying my draft and sending it off to a journal.

I waited and waited and got no response for several days. Odd, but perhaps he was busy, perhaps my breakthrough wasn't as important as I thought. Still, I was disappointed, having thought that this was the point at which I had proved my worth to the department, had indeed been the chap who was a biogeographer. Then came the summons to the professor's room.

Far from enthusiastic, he was grim-faced and clearly restraining his anger. 'What do you mean by this?' he asked. 'Are you suggesting a joint paper with me?'

No, I wasn't, it was my idea, but maybe this was how things worked here. But I was puzzled by the anger. Had I broken a convention by not immediately suggesting a joint paper myself?

Then all was explained. 'You were at my seminar last week,' he said, 'you heard me present this hypothesis. Why are you writing it up as if it's your idea when you got it from me?'

I sat stunned – I had graduated, it seemed, from stealing lizards to stealing a professor's ideas (had I again lost the art of making sure perceptions of me matched reality?). There was just one problem, and I pointed it out (on the ground when the stone was thrown) – 'I wasn't at your seminar.' I can't remember why not now. Perhaps I had been sick, or one of the children had been, but whatever, I hadn't been there, nor did I have any idea in general what he was working on – we had rarely even exchanged good mornings since I arrived, let alone discussed biogeography. We had, it seemed – great minds and all that – come up with basically the same idea (though using different data) independently at exactly the same moment.

I doubt he believed me, but whatever the truth, I had a black mark against my name which wasn't going to be erased. Not a team player. Couldn't expect a colonial to be a gentleman, I suppose. So I went away, joint publication abandoned. I sent it off as my paper, which it was. It got published and sank without a trace, being, as it turned out, really just a very minor idea after all. The dream of being either the new Macarthur or Wilson was over.

That was my card marked, the black ball placed in the hat at the gentlemen's club, and any slight hopes I had had that maybe there might have been a job or a continuing fellowship of some kind at York, were gone. And the year was coming to an end. Things were getting a bit frantic; applications began to fly off to Canada, America, Australia, all to no avail. I was on the same wave of PhD graduation as many another baby boomer, and competition for any zoology job was fierce. Would my publication record make me stand out from the other new doctors? But the publications didn't help me get a job. It turned out I couldn't get one in the areas I had published in (by 1974, there were thousands of people available who could sign their names).

And then, as I began to settle into the slough of despond, one day, plopping through the letter box (oh, I was going to miss the arrival of mail and the *Guardian*, delivered to the door every day), a postcard from the wonderful Isabel McBryde, recently moved to the Australian National University from Armidale. Attached to the card, a tiny slip from a newspaper, just a couple of brief lines, blink and you would miss it (almost as if they didn't want applications), was an advert for a palaeoecologist at the Australian Institute of Aboriginal Studies. Isabel thought, diffidently, as was her style, that I might like to apply.

When I was studying archaeology with Isabel, she had once included as an exam question (Discuss) a famous quote from Mortimer Wheeler: 'As for archaeology, I do not even know whether it is to be considered an art or a science.' It could have been applied to me – 'As for Horton, I do not know whether he is to be considered to be in arts or science.' And now here was a job that resolved the question by combining both disciplines. Getting the job would depend on me having done both zoology and archaeology. Isabel could write a reference saying 'You'll like this chap, he's an archaeologist', while Hal could write, 'You'll like this chap, he's a zoologist.'

I sent off my application. In the meantime, the professor in York, knowing my time was running out (and it is possible I dreamt this), surprisingly asked tentatively if he could explore some options for me staying on temporarily. If there had been a question about whether I was English or Australian, it was resolved at this point. We were migrating, with the bairns, back to Australia, back to the jungle of Canberra (as Uncle Len had said to my grandfather in 1929).

But then an oddity. A letter saying, in effect, that I had the job but asking ('I need to ask you what will seem a strange question') whether I would prefer to have the institute job or a very similar position at ANU. This came under the same kind of heading as 'Of course you will have to stay out of politics.' Why did these imponderable questions keep recurring?

Chewing my fingernails, and pencil stub, desperately anxious not to mess up (must be a trick question, right, trying to assess my level of dedication?) and lose this fabulous-sounding job, I composed a reply of the kind that a politician, faced with a question about beating his wife, would have been proud. On the one hand, I was absolutely delighted to be employed by the institute, and although I didn't know much about it, I was really looking forward to contributing: on the other hand of course, ANU was a magnificent university and if it was decided to employ me there, I would be very proud indeed, blah, blah. There, that had everything covered.

So back came the firm offer, I was going to work for the institute. It wasn't until months later that I discovered what was behind all this last-minute mystery. But there wasn't time to worry now. Sell the camper van, goodbye to the cul de sac, goodbye to family in Coventry, and on a plane for Australia. The last piece of unfinished family business in my wallet, a letter from the Salvation Army (who I had approached as a neutral party) saying that yes indeed, if I cared to call in, my father would see me. We landed in Perth. Took the train to Adelaide, had a meeting which was a strain for me, but also, as I only years later realised, as great a strain for him, a sixty-six-year-old man meeting a thirty-year-old son for the first time (I would only meet him once more, when he came to stay with us for a couple of weeks, also a strain, and he died a year or two later). And then on to a plane for the last lap travelling east, landing in Canberra after a tumultuous couple of years, hoping to settle.

7

A room with a view

'A memoir is my version of events. My perspective. I choose what to tell and what to omit. I choose the adjectives to describe a situation, and in that sense, I'm creating a form of fiction.' – Isabel Allende

When I turned up, right on the dot of nine a.m. (door open, no need to hammer), in early October 1974, for my first day at the Australian Institute of Aboriginal Studies, I had no idea what to expect of any aspect of this strange new job I was beginning. But if I had been expecting, spoiled by the beauties of the campuses of York and New England universities, an attractive building in pleasant surroundings, I would have been sadly disappointed.

The institute was housed in one of the defined commercial/light industrial areas (in this case largely devoted to cars) on the edge of the CBD of this very planned city. The building had originally been a shop or some other retail or service operation, with offices upstairs and an open-plan ground floor. It was next door to a discount tyre service, surrounded by petrol garages, spare parts outlets, another tyre centre, fast food joints, new and second-hand car sales yards, car repair workshops, and so on. The smell in my nostrils as I arrived was car exhaust, and tyres, and petrol, and bitumen, and the distant scent of hamburgers.

Inside the main glass entrance doors was a reception desk, and then the rest of the ground floor (not a huge space) was occupied by the institute library. You walked through the library to the other end of the building, where a wooden staircase took you up to the top floor, and at the end of the corridor there was the office of the principal, he who had asked the odd question before appointing me.

Not knowing anything about the institute, I had turned up wearing smart trousers, a business shirt and tie, and my smart new sports jacket. There wasn't a cloth pocket badge version of the institute logo, but even if there had been, I am almost sure that, being twenty-nine and a half years old, and having had a fair bit of experience of the world by now, I wouldn't have put it on my jacket.

At the end of the corridor, after all, was Peter Ucko. I did know who he was because his book, co-authored with Andree Rosenfeld (academic and domestic partner), *Palaeolithic Cave Art*, published in 1967, had taken the world of archaeology by storm and had been one of our set textbooks in archaeology in Armidale. It was one of those major works (like Macarthur and Wilson's *Island Biogeography*, published the same year) that change an academic discipline forever and become instant classics. So walking down a corridor to meet Peter Ucko was no small deal, and my mouth was dry, my stomach a little uneasy with a potential to become very uneasy. Did I really deserve this job? Would the great man instantly see through me as someone with rubbish qualifications who had been mistakenly employed because he was thought to be an archaeologist/zoologist?

Whatever I had been expecting, it wasn't what I found. Behind the desk was a very youthful fellow (he was still only in his early thirties, just a few years older than me, this enfant terrible) with a shock of unruly dark hair like an English schoolboy, a quizzical expression, and eyes that were clearly assessing me instantly and accurately. He was very casually dressed (if not quite as casually as Harry Waring) with no tie (he only owned one scruffy op-shop kind of tie which he would hastily and inexpertly put on if he had to go to Parliament House, I would later discover), a crumpled white shirt, ill-fitting wrinkled trousers. He might have wandered in from his real job selling petrol over the road. I would not wear a jacket and tie again at the institute after the clothing embarrassment of that first day except on essential public occasions.

There was no time to think about how to make a good impression, just blurt out whatever came to mind first. 'You are much younger than I thought.' Oh God, no, don't say that.

He glanced quickly down at my job application on the desk in front of him, looked up and said, 'So are you.'

It was fine; we were going to get on. But I wasn't out of the woods yet.

'I've managed to do a really great thing for you,' he said, leading me back downstairs and out to the rear of the building. Flinging open a door he said, 'There, how about that?'

'That' was an almost empty room except for a small desk and chair, some boxes piled in a corner, with scruffy old linoleum on the floor, and a view out into the institute car park behind the building.

I must have not looked quite astonished and grateful enough, because he pointed to the corner of the room behind me and said, 'There, there, I managed to get you a room with a sink!'

I discovered a little later that he had achieved this amazing feat (I had never thought about needing a sink, and didn't really, but Peter had assumed that since he was hiring a scientist, scientists needed a laboratory, and while he couldn't manage that in the building we had to make do with, he had, by a miracle, managed to get me a room with a sink, which was a huge gesture towards a proper laboratory) by throwing out the coffee-making facilities and chairs of what had been originally the tea room. From then on, people drank coffee at their desks, as was often pointed out to me.

'So what do you need?' he asked, recognising my underwhelmed expression, and sensing that the room was a bit lacking in scientific accoutrements once you had got past the sink.

I had absolutely no idea, searching desperately for something to say as he stood there notebook in hand, waiting to take down the list of astonishingly arcane scientific equipment his new star recruit was going to want.

'Um, a filing cabinet?' I said. 'Is that possible?'

He looked a little disappointed but wrote it down.

'Some shelving, a table perhaps?'

Yep, seemed I wasn't beyond the realm of possibility yet.

Oh, of course, silly me. 'A microscope?' (I had, in my defence, never before been in a place in which microscopes weren't part of the standard equipment.)

Yes, of course, but I would have to order that myself, work out exactly what I wanted.

That was that. I had exhausted my imagination about how a palaeoecology laboratory might be outfitted, never having seen such a thing.

'So what would you like to do now?' he said, needing to get back upstairs.

'I'll get to work,' I said.

This seemed a little surprising to him, perhaps thinking that a scientist would need to warm up like a tennis player (which he had once been). 'OK,' he said, 'there's your first job,' pointing to the pile of boxes I hadn't paid attention to in the corner.

'It's Andree Rosenfeld's excavation in Cape York, very important project, those are the bones for you to analyse.'

Uh oh, here was the real test. Not some anonymous break-you-in-gently kind of project to do while I worked out what on earth this job involved, but straight into a major excavation and by the boss's partner. I was so screwed.

As Peter left the room, and his sink, he called out, over his shoulder, 'Oh, and you should go and visit Jeanette Hope pretty soon.'

I would soon find out why, but in the meanwhile I sat on the chair, picked a box off the pile, put it on the desk and opened it up with a sense of trepidation. But mixed with exhilaration. I had landed by chance and a lot of luck in a place (and with a boss) with a supportive atmosphere in which the future seemed limitless, the possibilities for me to achieve things endless. That remained true for many years. And then it wasn't.

Having been told to go and see Jeanette as a matter of priority, I made an appointment (the result of a short and chilly phone call) and off I went. I knew who she was in the sense that I knew of one or two of her publications, and knew that she was doing, at ANU (for ANU researchers), the kind of work I would be doing at the institute. So, plenty of room for cooperation, sharing of experiences and ideas, perhaps an opportunity to begin making friends in this new environment.

Sadly, not. The frostiness of the phone call continued into the meeting in person. Jeanette had a crowded office (filing cabinets, shelves) and an adjacent large laboratory (microscopes, sinks et cetera) which she shared with Alan Thorne, who worked on human bones and was beginning to become known for his work at Mungo and Kow Swamp. He was friendly and would remain so through life. The building which housed their department of prehistory was new (the whole of ANU was quite new) and part of the Research School (of Pacific Studies in this case) system very distinct from the School of General Studies, which was the part of ANU where undergraduate teaching took place. The two halves of the university duplicated many departments (SGS had a department of prehistory and anthropology, which was where Isabel McBryde had moved from UNE). ANU campus, like UNE and York, was idyllic, with trees and gardens and rolling lawns, set on the edge of the lake, and within walking distance of the centre of Canberra. All a huge contrast to the current institute location, although we would be moving nearby, and just as idyllically, within the year.

Anyway, that"s where we were. Cup of coffee, some chit-chat about what she was working on, what I was going to be working on, and then suddenly the mystery was solved.

'Did you know I had written the job advertisement for the job you got?' she said. 'Peter Ucko asked me to.'

Had asked her to because she, as the first and at the time only Australian palaeoecologist, was the only one who knew what the qualifications and job description should be. And she had, therefore, written the advertisement precisely for herself, apparently desiring a move to a more permanent job. Written it for herself in the sure and certain knowledge that there was no one else in Australia who was qualified for such a job, couldn't be, she would have known them. But, just like Malcolm Fraser calling an election he thought he could win against Bill Hayden, only to discover that at precisely the same moment the Labor Party had switched to the unbeatable Bob Hawke, so I had suddenly popped out of the woodwork, thanks to Isabel, and applied for the job from the distant jungle of York.

Even then, it had been a very near-run thing. As I later discovered, the selection committee was split down the middle, and most of them thought that either one of us could do the job. It was a debate between someone just with a zoology degree and (uniquely) experience in zooarchaeology; and someone (uniquely) with degrees in both zoology and archaeology, and no experience in palaeoecology but obvious potential.

And so the strange question that Peter had put to me about choosing. If Jeanette had been appointed to the institute, then her ANU job would be available, and I was the only other suitable person for that. Or vice versa. The archaeologists on the selection panel were determined that both jobs would continue, part of the growing ferment and development in the discipline, as more and more scientific techniques became applied to archaeological questions. The discipline no longer an art but definitely a science.

So Jeanette felt betrayed by Peter and, by association, me. Years later I understood this, just as I understood the professor in York – positions reversed, in both cases, I would have felt and acted the same way. But at the time, hard done by, you demand more saintly performances from those who misunderstand you. And members of the department and profession who liked Jeanette also felt she had been hard done by and that I had stolen her job. Not the act of a gentleman. So we never became friends, and people who I might have worked with made a decision about me, sight unseen, that would affect my relationships for decades.

In addition, this Sophie's Choice was in a way symbolic of much larger forces beginning to swirl around like an incoming tide, and big waves and subtle undercurrents were also to set directions and determine outcomes in quite unpredictable ways. The major factor was the election of the reforming and progressive Labor government of Gough Whitlam in 1972 after twenty-three years of conservative rule during which the politics of social, cultural, environmental issues had ground to a complete halt. Whitlam, among many other changes, had initiated a massive increase in university activity (including free admission for students) in Australia, and was undoing years of neglect on Aboriginal matters by introducing land rights and recognising the value of Aboriginal culture. The institute was benefiting from these moves in a massive increase in funding (hence my job, among many other jobs and research fellowships). On the other hand, it was also to feel the effect of Aboriginal people finding a public voice and expressing a desire to determine their own futures.

The institute hadn't come into being as a result of these developments; quite the opposite. It had been formed during the Menzies era some ten years before I arrived as a result of considerable willpower and effort from a most unlikely source. Bill Wentworth was an extremely conservative (we would now say culture warrior) member of the very conservative Menzies government. He was descended from, and named for, a very prominent member of the first British colony in Australia William Charles Wentworth, one of the trio who famously crossed the Blue Mountains in 1813 and discovered the potentially rich farming country of the slopes and plains inland from Sydney. The family had been wealthy and well-connected and involved in politics ever since.

Billy Wentworth, perhaps as a result of some lingering guilt feelings over the role of his famous ancestor in the initial disruption and dispossession of the Aboriginal people of inland New South Wales, and concerned at what he saw as the approaching end point of a 200-year process of the destruction of Aboriginal culture and society, demanded the establishment of the institute, and nagged Prime Minister Menzies until it happened. Wentworth saw the loss of Aboriginal society as inevitable, but unlike Daisy Bates some sixty years earlier, who merely wanted to soothe the dying pillow of the Aboriginal people, making them comfortable as they faced their inevitable end, Wentworth wanted to urgently get hold of all the remaining vestiges of Aboriginal culture – language, kinship, music, art – record them for posterity and store the results in a library or archive. That was to be the role of the institute, supervised by the senior figures in each discipline from the Australian universities, which would carry out the work. The sole function of the institute was to hand out research money, coordinate (for example, through specialist committees and conferences), publish, and store the results safely. The work was to be concerned only with traditional Aborigines (that is, from the north and centre). Neither Wentworth, nor the university people, had any interest in what they saw as degraded remnants of culture in the south and east of the country. He couldn't foresee that the institute would begin to form a major focal point for all Aboriginal people, emphatically not dying out and into reviving culture in a big way, in the 1970s and beyond. That indeed, totally unpredicted, Aboriginal people would begin to take a major role in running the institute and determining where its efforts should be directed and what should be done with the results.

However wrong-headed, in some ways, his reasoning was, there was no questioning Wentworth's sincerity, nor can it be argued that if he hadn't acted (no one else was) then much more would have been lost. And his institute, much in the way a child can turn out in a quite unexpected way, must have exceeded, in its first three decades, all expectations of its father. And in spite of his horrible politics, and against my expectations, when I met Billy Wentworth, I quite liked him. It was hard not to.

Anyway, for most of its first decade, under Principal Fred McCarthy (pioneer archaeologist, museum man, scholar and gentleman) the institute did no more and no less than its founder had prescribed. And then, a courageous appointment (an archaeologist, Richard Wright, associated with the institute had seen him organising a major conference and been mighty impressed), along came Peter Ucko. Nothing would be the same at the institute again, and I was arriving at just the moment when the change began to gather force (rather as I had done with Hal Heatwole).

When Peter Ucko began as principal at the Australian Institute of Aboriginal Studies in 1972, he had a vision of what the place could be. Instead of a tiny, passive organisation that handed out money to universities to conduct esoteric research on Aborigines and then store the results, Peter saw it as becoming a major research organisation which would conduct research itself. In doing so, it would be in a position to set the agenda and ensure that work that needed to be done on Aboriginal culture and society would be done, instead of leaving it to the whims and personal interests of a few professors in universities.

So he organised a major conference in 1974, which both set the tone and showed where the knowledge gaps were (and there were many), and then he set about filling them by employing staff who would directly conduct research themselves, and employing research fellows to fill a particular knowledge or geographic gap.

He immediately ran into strong resistance, which would continue, from the university people who thought that all the available money should go to them, and the institute should not conduct its own research, or indeed employ staff other than for archiving and accounting purposes.

While those battle lines were being drawn and the first shots fired, a second front opened up. All of the work by the institute to that point, and the dreams and visions for its future, had been conducted as if Aboriginal people were merely passive subjects to be studied in the way, that, say, a zoologist might study a kangaroo. It had always been that way. What was worse was that all the research was of a purely esoteric nature, examining the curiosities that were Aboriginal languages or kinship structures or song cycles. And making this still worse was that the research was all directed at those Aboriginal groups seen as having maintained a purely traditional lifestyle. Absolutely nothing for the tens of thousands of Aboriginal people from Tasmania, or Victoria, or living in the big cities of Australia, or indeed on cattle stations or missions.

In all of the developing Aboriginal protest movement (begun in its then form by Charles Perkins in 1965), the institute was a relatively minor issue, but it was potentially important, it was noticed, and a group of Aboriginal people wrote a manifesto demanding that the institute also change. Peter Ucko may not have been expecting this, in his vision for an Australian Smithsonian on Lake Burley Griffin, but he seems to have quickly become aware of the justice of the demands, and set about changing things.

Aboriginal people were brought into membership, appointed to the committees, mechanisms used to get them on to the governing council, plans developed for staff positions (one of the first was a research assistant for me – at first this meant short-term visits of a few months by Aboriginal people wanting some experience in the institute. Peter Yu, for example, later a major figure in Aboriginal politics, came for three months – but later Brian Blurton and Richard Wright, a name that was to cause confusion with the other Richard Wright, came permanently, and I got him involved in research and helped him publish a paper on skin cloaks). Stan Grant began working at the institute in this period, and many more Aboriginal people were to follow their lead. I continued to be involved with that when I moved to publishing, by bringing in Aboriginal people who wanted to get some experience in editing and design work for their careers.

For example, Hannah McGlade, later a successful barrister, came to us for a few months, followed by Robyne Bancroft, who would become a vital part of the *Encyclopaedia* project. In addition, there was a marked move to get the institute working in non-traditional communities in addition to traditional ones, and to start research work in areas such as health and education which were of potential direct benefit to Aboriginal people.

All good, and from the point of view of Aboriginal people it couldn't happen fast enough. Trouble was, from the point of view of many of the university-based academics with links to the institute, it was all happening too damn fast. Some saw the inclusion of non-academic Aboriginal people on committees, and of research funding in non-traditional communities, and in applied research work, as diluting the standards of the institute, which they thought had always been high. It also further reduced (added to the reduction resulting from the institute carrying out its own work) the funding going directly into, say, departments of linguistics or anthropology in universities. The interplay between these conflicting forces was to continue over the next few decades, and I had a room with a view of some of it.

My involvement wasn't particularly central, although almost everyone employed by the institute at that time to a greater or lesser extent shared the vision of excellent research and of involving Aboriginal people in it. Peter Ucko had instituted a 'happy hour' once a fortnight where not just staff but all kinds of people involved in the institute would turn up, drink, and have fiery discussions about Aboriginal politics, or social issues, or the latest in rock art research. Late-night debates were intense. Staff meetings much the same. Ad hoc committees were set up, and discussion groups. We all had a strong mental and emotional investment in the good ship AIAS.

A significant development I led was converting the old physical anthropology committee (measuring skulls, the genetics of blood samples, neither activity any longer sanctioned by Aboriginal people) into a health committee. Bringing in significant people like Fred Hollows (briefly in his case – he thought being on a committee a waste of time and was impatient to get back to saving eyesight), Max Kamien (good fellow, who once told me I was the only sane person in the institute), Jack Waterford (later *Canberra Times* editor), Tom Gavranic (later to be my GP briefly, in halcyon days when I didn't need a GP), Jan Reid and Trevor Cutter, to set priorities in health research.

The problem I thought the institute was ideally placed to deal with was that research in Aboriginal health was scattered and piecemeal. I wanted the committee to advise on where there were gaps and proceed to fund research, but also to compile a central database where people could see what had already been done, compare results, look for further problems to address.

I got agreement to employ a research fellow (the admirable Neil Thompson, a GP from Perth who wanted to widen his experience and make a more general contribution) who would continue what I had started and put together the reference sources and act as an adviser to the committee and to people in the field. This preceded, by some years, the establishment of the Australian Institute of Health and Welfare, which would later take the same approach I had developed and carry it out more generally (and in doing so take over Neil).

At the institute, you would suddenly find yourself, out of the blue, involved in something interesting outside your normal work. Sometime late in the 1970s, someone who had visited the Australian Institute of Anatomy complained to my institute about an exhibit they had seen there.

The Institute of Anatomy was an odd place. It lived in a beautiful old Art Deco style building, one of the first buildings in Canberra (as was Acton House, which my institute now occupied), just over the road from my office. I forget now why it existed – some enthusiastic anatomist had convinced some politician, I guess. But Canberra had no museum in the 1970s, and the Institute of Anatomy had defaulted into that role for tourists and locals who were convinced that they needed a museum experience in Canberra.

The Institute of Anatomy had many skeletons, and skulls, which brought me to the purpose of my first visit. There was a display case containing three skulls, carefully labelled and intended to show the sequence of human evolution. On the left, the skull of a baboon, on the right a modern European, and in the middle an Aboriginal skull, plainly suggesting it as a missing link not fully evolved like Europeans. No one it seemed, among staff and visitors, had seen a problem with this in the forty years or so from its beginnings to my arrival. I pointed out the problem. They agreed. The exhibit was removed.

Apart from such diversions, I was busy working on animal bones from archaeological sites from one end of the country to another. Which made it ironic that fifteen to twenty years later, the *Encyclopaedia* I was editing made me the focus of all of the accumulated anger in Aboriginal studies academia that the institute was no longer as it had been under Fred McCarthy (who was also an archaeologist).

That was a long way in the future, though, and in the meantime the institute in the late 1970s was an exciting place to work. You could find yourself talking to Kim Beasley senior or Bill Wentworth at a happy hour; returning the skeleton of a community leader (stolen, as so many were over a long period, it was one of the things that had made the Aboriginal backlash against physical anthropology so strong) to Groote Eylandt after finding it by clever detective work – it was the first return of human remains to an Aboriginal community; visiting a minister for Aboriginal affairs (a Liberal government now, but Peter Baume was a good fellow; unfortunately, he thought I had 'developed an index' which would measure Aboriginal health status in communities, instead of a reference system for published work); having dinner with Dick Roughsey, an Aboriginal elder from Cape York.

Listening to wonderful Bill Stanner (one of Australia's greatest Anthropologists), seen each day in my corridor, describe how as a young man he had met an old man who when young had met someone who had fought in the Battle of Waterloo – including me, that meant four degrees of separation between 1815 and 2022!

Dear Jane Hubert drawing cartoons of me at work with bones. Setting up an archaeozoology laboratory in Victoria for Peter Coutts; somewhat unusually we got on well. Working with legendary Faith Bandler on her book. Drinks with the equally legendary Bobbi Sykes in the ANU staff club. Walking through Arnhem Land bush with a group of Yolngu people helping search for a lost child. Chatting to Paul Martin around a camp fire on the Liverpool Plains. Many different mental images that somehow make a coherent picture in my memory.

Every new day was exciting, challenging, and I would rush in happily, eager to see what it would bring, and work late into the evening most days. It was a totally different environment to that of a university department (although it did have something of the feel of WA zoology in the 1960s, but on a bigger and faster scale) – we saw ourselves engaged in good things for a good purpose. My emotional well-being levels were building again. Couldn't last? No, couldn't last.

When I sat down and opened, with trepidation, the first box of bones from the Andree Rosenfeld excavation of the important rock art and archaeological site at Laura, in Cape York, it marked the start of a long career for me in palaeoecology. But having seen the tiny bits and pieces of bone, sometimes burnt, I realised I had better step back a pace, take a deep breath and get myself mentally organised.

So I set about reading everything I could find on the topic in the institute library, and also visited John Calaby. I had met John within a day or so of arriving in Canberra, at a welcoming dinner party thoughtfully organised by Isabel McBryde. He was a senior scientist in CSIRO, and had a long, distinguished career, beginning in WA as it happened, in many aspects of wildlife biology. He had a tiny office which was packed to overflowing with books and manuscripts and journals and correspondence, as was his desk, at which he was almost invisible behind the piles. He was one of the nicest people I have met in academic life in over forty years (I later dedicated a book to him). Always pleasant, always supportive, never competitive or begrudging of help. The initial help I needed from him was to make use of reference specimens of mammal bones to try to identify the material from Laura. He was happy to oblige, having an interest in archaeology and Aboriginal studies generally, so that was one support in place. I would have to gradually build up my own reference collection, but in the meantime, access to the CSIRO collection was essential.

Having read a great deal of Australian archaeology (which was then beginning to see a great expansion in people and ideas) I made a decision about my approach. I dropped in on Peter Ucko and said, 'I have decided that I am not going to be an appendix.' By this decision I was breaking away from the accepted format. In Australia and elsewhere, the archaeologist on a site had absolute primacy, and his or her report was the central defining publication about a site. Any other consultants who had been brought in to analyse carbon, pollen, soils, bones, any of the increasingly long list of scientific analyses that could be applied to an archaeological site, were seen as second order to the analysis of stone tools and their stratigraphic context. Indeed, it was often the case that specialists in other disciplines not only were not involved in excavating a site, but might not even visit it (I, for example, never saw Laura, excavated before I arrived at the institute, or my second site, Louisa Bay, likewise excavated earlier).

I thought that all specialists should be involved in excavation, so they could fully understand the context, and be involved in discussions as the dig proceeded, and that when the final report was produced, it should be an integrated document, not archaeology with appendixes tacked on almost as afterthoughts. Peter, who had a similar view that the institute would no longer be an appendix to the universities, although he hadn't put it like that, instantly agreed. I had also decided that I would begin developing the discipline of palaeoecology in Australia, along lines that were being explored overseas, and no longer be content with supplying a mere laundry list of species present as a faunal report, but begin to explore taphonomy (the science of how a site was formed) and to see how much biological information (such as age and sex and seasonality) could be extracted from the bones. All of it would add to our understanding of how people had lived in the past. I had a philosophy, and an agenda, and I was about to find a site, and a colleague, where I could put them into practice.

But first, a second pile of bone boxes had arrived in my office shortly after I began. It was from Ron Vanderwal, and my first two sites couldn't have been more different (except they were both L words) – one from the far north, one the very far south; one inland, one coastal; one from a complex art site of Cape York, the other a set of simple open camp sites in Tasmania. Quite a challenge to do both, but both were completed in a year or so and written up as joint publications (the Louisa Bay one completely integrated), both, as it happened, in the same journal series. But I was still wanting to get involved in a site from the beginning, be an equal partner, and suddenly there was Lancefield Swamp (and I began joking I could only work on sites beginning with L).

Lancefield was a very unprepossessing little swamp in a small town about an hour's drive north of Melbourne. It had, briefly, been known in palaeontological circles in the mid-nineteenth century as one of the very first sites at which the fossil bones of giant extinct animals had been unearthed (by a farmer digging a well) in Australia, and then it had been instantly forgotten again. Until in 1973 a geologist happened to come across the reference to it in that early publication, and decided it would be fun to take a group of his geological friends out for a few days, have a picnic, see if there was anything to see. So they did, dug up a few bones, came back the following year and did a more serious test pit excavation in which they made two amazing discoveries.

The first was that the site was a massive bone source, a layer a foot or so thick full of tightly packed and beautifully preserved (though disarticulated and broken) fossils of giant animals. Second, and even more astonishing, as they began digging, they came to a large piece of stone, inserted solidly among the bones, and which proved to be, when brought up and cleaned, a hand axe of the type Aborigines once made. They were excited and shaken, and knew they had to bring in the experts – this was a site with enormous potential.

To understand why, we need to go back in time to the mid-nineteenth century, when a debate began about these giant animals (seen as being analogous to, but of course unrelated to, the giant extinct animals of Europe like mammoths) and what had happened to them. There were two theories (three really; Ludwig Leichhardt expected to find some still alive in inland Australia, but he was to be sadly disappointed in this as in so much else): either climate change had caused the extinction, or humans had hunted them to extinction. The debate continued for 150 years, continues today, in fact, because it seemed impossible to even find evidence that the animals had overlapped in time with Aborigines arriving in Australia, let alone that Aborigines had ever had any interaction with them at all. And suddenly, here were giant animals, with a hand axe of the type you might use to chop up a large beast. The end of the debate seemed nigh.

Phones started ringing, and a team came together which consisted of me, Richard Wright (an archaeologist from Sydney University, plus wife Sonia, an indispensable part of the team for any fieldwork), Tom Rich (curator of fossils at the National Museum of Victoria) and Philip Ladd (pollen specialist from Melbourne University). The original group of geologists who had rediscovered the site mostly drifted away, not wanting to be involved in a major excavation outside their areas of interest. The one who stayed, and became an essential part of the team, was Phil Macumber, a geomorphologist with a strong interest in archaeology. It was undoubtedly the strongest multidisciplinary team ever assembled to that time to tackle an archaeological site in Australia.

If I was the specialist bone man, I didn't get off to an auspicious start when we all began assembling in Lancefield in January 1975. I had a long arduous journey to get there – plane to Melbourne, train to middle of nowhere (Clarkfield), bus from there on country roads to Lancefield, then a long walk, lugging my suitcase on a hot day, from bus stop down through the recreation oval and into the swamp area. There was Tom Rich (whom I had never met), specimen tent (the museum's role was to curate all specimens recovered) already set up, sitting at a portable desk on which were various bones which he was looking at in a puzzled way. I ducked under the tent flap and said hello.

'Can you identify kangaroo species from toe bones?' was Tom's reply.

'No,' I said.

He looked relieved, perhaps appreciating honesty, perhaps glad that I couldn't do what he had failed to do. We were to get on well. He was a dinosaur man, and had no interest in the late Pleistocene material from Lancefield, which he, perhaps jokingly, described as being the scum that real palaeontologists removed to get at the proper fossils.

In fact, we were all to get on well as it turned out, adding greatly to the enjoyment and success of the work. I had a particular rapport, professionally and personally, with Richard. We approached excavation and archaeology in general in very similar ways, and sparked ideas from each other, and we shared a similar sense of humour and world view. January 1975 would turn out to be the start of a long and productive working relationship and friendship, not ending until over fifteen years later when we both moved on to other kinds of projects. Lancefield changed both our careers in significant ways. And Lancefield was to become a very important site in Australian archaeology, still argued over and debated today, half a century later. It may not have provided the answers that looked so likely when that stone axe was first unearthed, but it has provided many questions and ways of working, and has served as a litmus test for the battle of ideologies over how to interpret Australia's past and the place of Aborigines in it. My theoretical contribution, in brief, was the idea that the site had been the last source of water in a drying climate in the late Pleistocene, and animals had accumulated there and then died.

But all of this was just a distant dream as we left the museum tent and walked down to the swamp, in stifling heat, to begin digging the sticky clay of Lancefield Swamp. Five years of digging there lay ahead. Years of smelling stagnant swamp water, and clay, and fumes from the petrol pump removing water. And then I got involved in other sites, discovered I was good at excavating and site interpretation. I had made the switch from science to the arts, was becoming more of an archaeologist than a zoologist, though it was not so much a switch as a gradual fade-in/fade-out.

8

Picking up the pieces

'These days, when in the circumstances I am not getting much done, well-wishers think to comfort one by instancing what one has done already. This is no reassurance. One's back-catalogue is more of a tribunal. One is arraigned before it and current work (or lack of it) judged.' – Alan Bennett

I once knew a man who, at the age of eighteen, after getting his first job, planned his financial arrangements for the rest of his life in order to finish up in the best possible position when he retired half a century later. It involved staying in the same job throughout his working life and putting away a lot of money each year. I didn't. Easy to laugh, but if I was advising my young self, I would advise something similar not in relation to money (although, now I think of it...) but in relation to careers.

'Listen young fellow,' I would say, 'choose a field of research and stick to it all your life, publishing as you go. Don't be all over the shop, researching this, investigating that, analysing the other. Successful academics stick to their last.'

I did the opposite. The first lane switch was unavoidable given the need for a job. But it meant that my first dozen papers, and nine years of my career were irrelevant, of no further use, full stop, might as well have been written by some other David Horton. Start all over again in a completely different discipline.

So how was I to do that? As I'd said to Peter Ucko, I wasn't going to be an appendix. I had no interest in doing this work unless it could be fully integrated with the main report. It would be much better for the understanding of the site.

So the archaeologists I worked with were happy with this, and my work was usually published in joint papers. There was a corollary – if I was accepted as being involved in considering the implications of a site for the prehistory of the area, then I could also be involved in discussing the big picture issues of Australian prehistory in general. I had little (no!) interest in stone tools, but was very interested in issues like Aboriginal interaction with the environment (extinctions, fire); patterns of occupation of the continent; the unusual features of Tasmanian prehistory; and so on. And all that in turn also gave me an interest in the history of Australian archaeology.

These were all big questions, and they had therefore all been tackled by some of the biggest big guns in Australian archaeology. In tackling these issues then, I was in the position of the young lieutenant, pistol in hand, climbing over the lip of the trench and into the withering machine gun fire, or mustard gas cloud.

Except that, when I got up there, the machine guns were silent, the gas blown away. Seemed me and my pistol were no threat and would simply be ignored. To the archaeologists I was a zoologist, while to the zoologists I was an archaeologist; in neither case was I perceived as being part of the club. Therefore, I had no right to be writing about the big issues, and so whatever I wrote would not be seen as legitimate debate but as cheek.

And I wasn't concentrating on just one subject; the whole field was too interesting. Oh, hey, look at this, and now that, oh, and what is that over there, picking up pieces of prehistory. Finally, I only had less than ten years of more or less full-time research. In 1984, I took over institute book publishing and became the editor of the institute journal. It was still possible to do some short pieces of writing but field research was no longer possible. And then that position evolved into the *Encyclopaedia* and I spent some eight years doing that full time before being tossed out on my ear.

So a short and interrupted research and publishing career. No chance to establish a dominant academic position, no chance to gain public/media exposure. And therefore (among other reasons) the massive *Encyclopaedia* project could be largely ignored in academia and the media, and my later book, *Pure State of Nature*, suffered the same fate. But I am getting ahead of myself.

The old shop among car repair shops was inadequate with the expansion Peter Ucko had set moving. In early 1975, the old Acton House, which for fifty years had provided temporary accomodation for workers arriving in Canberra, and was no longer needed for that purpose, was made available to the institute. A wonderful sprawling old two-storey building with endless corridors, bedrooms suitable for offices (all with sinks!), and wonderful grounds with old trees, extending down to the lake. Heaven. Room to grow. I had room to spread bones being analysed, and an office, and rooms for a reference collection. More generally, there were plenty of rooms for the growing staff numbers, and research fellows from all over the world, and rooms for visiting distinguished scholars who needed an office. In my corridor, for example, I was able to greet each day Bill Stanner and Charles Rowley (another leading anthropologist). Suddenly we were in a university atmosphere not a tyre depot.

The ten years from 1975 were to see me working solidly in archaeology/palaeoecology, cooperating with different archaeologists, working on a number of sites the full length of eastern Australia, developing contributions to a number of theoretical questions in Australian prehistory, and, at the end of it, shifting careers. All of this against a background of some turmoil, and three principals, within the institute. In describing much of this period, the adage 'If you can't say something nice about someone, don't say anything at all' will be my guide. At least not by name, but I can say guilty, like the mouse.

For the first five years, fieldwork was at Lancefield with Richard and Sonia and the team (and 100 or more students in that time; Richard used the site as a practical teaching class, and many good young archaeologists went through Lancefield and on to later careers). Twice a year, January and May, boiling hot or cold enough to freeze water in buckets.

Digging through sticky mud as trenches wound through the swamp, as if on the Somme, water constantly draining in and the sound of pumps removing it, picking up pieces of bone. Thankfully, much of the dig was in the shade of willows.

Bones, hundreds of them, coming back to the institute in Canberra from the museum after treatment, and me measuring and describing them. The task seemed never ending, and the fieldwork the same, since I spent a total of close to a year in the field over those five years. And then it was off to the Liverpool Plains in northern NSW with Sonia and Richard, who had been contacted about the finding of a whole diprotodon skeleton, and that leading in turn to sites with artefacts.

Another four years of similar conditions but quite different site contents. And different social contexts. The village of Tambar Springs, which became our base, began advertising itself as being Diprotodon Country with tourist trinkets. On the other hand, as we travelled around looking for sites, we came across farmers with boxes full of Aboriginal artefacts ploughed up from the paddocks and kept secret in case someone wanted to protect a site. In one country pub, we asked if there were any local Aboriginal people who we could consult with and were told, 'No, we got rid of them 150 years ago,' and realised that the Myall Creek Massacre was being proudly referred to.

At the same time, though, I was taking up other invitations – with Graham Connah elsewhere in northern NSW (where I discovered that apparently similar sites can be quite different, one way and another); with John Campbell in inland Cape York (where I discovered that caves, and limestone outcrops, aren't as much fun to explore as they seem); in northern Cape York with John Beaton (where I discovered that a tropical paradise can be full of sandflies); with Peter Murray in northern Tasmania (where I discovered an extinct species of wallaby not previously known from Tassie).

It was varied and interesting, and I was seeing a lot of the country. And a lot of data. And giving it a lot of thought. When I began studying Australian prehistory, and then working in the field, the discipline was undergoing a philosophical change. Aborigines had, from the time they were first seen by various European explorers, been viewed as, in one much later famous phrase, intelligent parasites.

In the 50s and 60s, first Norman Tindale, and then Rhys Jones, turned this idea on its head, and began presenting Aborigines as active agents, very early farmers down under, who had moulded the whole landscape (including causing many extinctions) of the continent in ways (as Sylvia Hallam later suggested) that had enormously benefited the white settlers. All of this fitted with developments elsewhere in linguistics, anthropology, art, music, suggesting that far from being primitive stone age people (the popular view, and a rationale for taking the continent, being wasted, from them) Aboriginal society and culture were highly complex and advanced.

So I absorbed all this, and it seemed pretty good. The work I was doing, I thought, would help to flesh out the picture even more. But the more I dug, and analysed, and thought, and wrote, the less comfortable I became with the Tindale-Hallam-Jones theory (later to be successfully popularised in a best-selling book by Tim Flannery, and then in turn by Bill Gammage and Bruce Pascoe). In particular, I came to the conclusion that Aborigines hadn't modified the environment by the use of fire (the mechanism hypothesised) and hadn't caused the extinction of the giant animals (the megafauna – giant species of kangaroos, and wombat-like creatures, and emus, et cetera – now all extinct), the two critical components of the idea that Tindale had set rolling.

Incidentally, I had, and still have, a lot of admiration for Norman Tindale, which developed when I began to share with him the experience of being the only two researchers who had created a map of tribal groups in Aboriginal Australia (as well as a history of starting research careers as zoologists). On the other hand, it wasn't an uncritical admiration, since I thought everything he had believed and written was wrong. I once happened to be sitting behind him at an institute conference in the mid-1970s. He, distinguished white-haired gentleman, as old as the century, was sitting with another distinguished white-haired gentleman of the same vintage and prestige, whose identity I have forgotten. It was a time when the significant involvement of Aboriginal people in determining the future direction of the institute was accelerating, and one of the leading Aboriginal figures, chairing the session, got up to speak to the audience.

Tindale leaned over closer to his friend and said, 'Octoroon, do you think?' and I was transported back to another age. An age when the amount of Aboriginal blood an individual possessed (full-blood, half-caste, quarter-caste, octoroon) would determine exactly what rights, if any, they had, where they lived, who they could marry, whether they could keep their children or not. And an age when researchers debated the importance of such divisions, as Tindale indeed had done. There we were, in the late 1970s, and the Aboriginal academic, viewing themselves (rightly of course) as being the equal of anyone in the audience, and as having a role in determining what this institute would be doing in future, was, to Tindale, just an object for classification. *Plus ça change, plus c'est la même chose.*

Anyway, I began to write about Aboriginal fire use, and extinction, and how the Aborigines had originally colonised the continent, and what had happened to the Tasmanians (the latter two topics of popular interest and relevant to the overall philosophy), and was instantly, it seemed, viewed as mad, bad and dangerous to know. These theories were, it seemed, unquestionable, set in stone for all time (when I much later told someone I was writing a book which totally contradicted Flannery's popularised account of this Tindale-Jones-Hallam theory, I was looked at in astonishment, and the question asked, 'How could you possibly do that?'), and to query them, suggest that the emperor's theories had no clothes, was to be put beyond the pale, not a gentleman, nor a colonial boy, I suppose, but wild.

While all that was going on, and just at the time my work with Richard was switching from Lancefield to the Liverpool Plains, there was a sudden major change at the institute – Peter Ucko announced that he had tendered his resignation. I was horrified, could see that everything we had all worked for at the institute was in danger of being lost, and I wasn't sure that the governing council of the institute was fully aware of the importance of Peter to what had been done.

So I wrote to the then chairman, the wonderful Les Hiatt, nice anthropologist, carefully explaining all that, and my concern (though he was very very deaf, I knew he would hear me). But almost immediately after sending that letter, somebody told me that there were personal factors involved in Peter's decision (I seem to have been uniquely unaware of this, having, as always, being totally deaf to any relationships, or changes in relationships, between people in and around the institute – ignorance that could quite often be embarrassing). So when Les took me aside for a little chat, with something of the air of a father about to tell his son the facts of life, in his always reticent and awkward sort of way, I told him it was okay, I understood the situation. It didn't make it any better, but I understood.

And so I had my first change of principal at the institute. And everything indeed did change (rather in the way that an election result changes a country). I remember little about him, but one of the things I do remember, vividly, was the sound of his voice one day as he came around the corner into the research wing of the institute. My room, where I had been working so hard for the previous six years, happened to be closest to the corner, and my door, as always, was open, so I clearly heard the words with which our new principal introduced the area to some distinguished visitor who was being given the grand tour. 'This is the research wing, or, as we like to call it, the sheltered workshop.' That derogatory statement was a foretaste of what the institute environment was going to be over the next five years. The knowledge and ideas I had were no longer valued or wanted, so I put my head down below the trench and concentrated on being a pure palaeoecologist.

Not good enough, though. A little later, I had a phone call from the principal saying that one of the professors at ANU wanted to see me and had an interesting job offer for me. Not someone I knew (geography) so I was a bit puzzled but off I went. Pleasant chit-chat with a nice professor and one of the geographers I did know, but chit-chat going nowhere.

Eventually, as topics of conversation dried up, I said, 'Look, this is nice, but was there a particular reason you wanted to see me?'

The other two looked at each other and said, 'But you wanted to see us, to ask whether we could find you a job over here, you wanted to join us.'

'No, no,' I said, 'you wanted to see me, offer me a job.'

The meeting ended in some embarrassment, and as Geoff Hope was showing me out he said, 'You'd better hurry back, make sure your chair is still there.'

I agreed. I knew the feeling of being forced out of a department because your position was wanted for someone else, and I was determined it wasn't going to happen again.

Fortunately, before I could arrive one day and find my chair missing, the principal announced he was moving onward and upward. i didn't write a letter of protest to council this time. Deputy principal Warwick Dix (a very nice man, and another West Australian) asked me to take over as editor of the institute journal, launched a couple of years earlier, with the then principal as editor. Only one issue had ever been produced, and its role as institute research flagship was sinking and very embarrassing.

I took it on and got it moving. To do that, given the circumstances in the neglected and moribund and politically sensitive publishing area, I had to do the lot -- chase contributions, write stuff myself, edit, do the layout (in those days before computerised page make-up, this involved physically pasting, with wax, typeset galleys on to a page with layout guidelines), organise photos, take to printers, distribute. I learnt a lot.

Enough so that when the director of publishing left, worn out with the struggle of an impossible job, at about the time Warwick was appointed as principal, he asked me to take on an acting role in publishing until they could find a permanent replacement, and bingo, I had a new career, although it was more complicated than that. Warwick being principal meant there was now a vacancy for deputy principal, which would take some time to fill. He asked me if I would be acting deputy principal. I said yes, but there was a consideration. I knew that two of us from the research area were intending to apply for the deputy principal's job.

I said to Warwick, 'Look, it wouldn't be fair to just let me be acting DP. It would give me an unfair advantage in the application. How about you make us both half time in the position?'

'Okay,' he said, 'in that case, would you take on responsibility for publishing as your special interest in your half deputy principal role?'

They appointed an outsider, so it was a futile gesture. I wouldn't do it again.

So I took on publishing, got the logjam moving. Two books in particular had been delayed for many years, causing much aggravation to the authors and questions in council. The first day I took up the job, I asked the designer where the manuscript of one of the books was, so I could get it moving. She pointed down, and I realised that I was standing, in her large room, on a carpet of typed pages, photographs, diagrams, spread all over the floor like mulch on a garden bed. My first couple of days were spent sitting on her floor, picking up pieces of paper, trying to match pages up with illustrations, put chapters together in order. Then, manuscript reassembled, get the typesetting done, and do the layout for the book, sending it off to the printers some weeks later. 'About time,' is all I remember the authors saying.

The other manuscript was sitting in the typesetter's cupboard. It was a book about music, and the complexity of the content and author corrections had baffled the typesetter. Piece by piece, I got corrections done, down to personally adding some full stops by pen, did the layout, off to the printers. Not sure there was any comment from that author.

I started to pick up and sort out all the other problems that neglect and interference and interpersonal problems had caused over many years. Then the marvellous Frank Thompson (formerly head of University Queensland Press, which I had a dream of modelling institute publishing on, and enormously experienced) agreed to take the job of running publishing. I stayed on to guide him through the political and philosophical questions he had to deal with, and he taught me much about professional publishing. Sadly, he only stayed a year or so in the job, and I was back in the hot seat, at first temporarily, then permanently, when Warwick, relieved to see the publishing arm being sorted out, agreed I should shift my job. I had a new career.

But then an intermission. I had the journal up to date (after personally laying out four issues in one year) and the backlog of books was under control, many systems put into place. Peter Ucko turned up at the institute. He was now Professor of Archaeology at University of Southampton. Not content with that, he had taken on the organising and running of the World Archaeological Congress for that year. He wanted institute input, and he wanted me to attend and give a paper.

Normally, there would have been an instant refusal by the institute. But I had recently been elected as the Australian representative on the International Council of Archaeozoology, and they met every two years, plus a conference, and in 1986 it would be in Bordeaux the two weeks before WAC, so I could attend both for one fare. In addition, as I said to Warwick, I could visit university bookshops in England, let them know that institute publishing was back in the game, and get them to sell some of our exciting new books. Done deal. I was allowed to go on my one and only institute-sponsored overseas trip (I had no such thing as a sabbatical system available to my peers in universities). So I was off to Bordeaux and Southampton, had papers to write, material to get organised for bookshops, travel to plan.

9

'I come from a land down under'

It is said that every life has its roses and thorns; there seemed, however, to have been a misadventure or mistake in Stephen's case, whereby somebody else had become possessed of his roses, and he had become possessed of the same somebody else's thorns in addition to his own.' – Charles Dickens

Everything organised, it was 16 August 1986, and I had my air ticket in hand and was boarding my Lufthansa flight.

'*Guten morgen,*' I said to the hostess, having practised for my cosmopolitan adventure, and '*Danke schön*' as she gave me headphones.

My accent, based on a blend of *Hogan's Heroes* and old British war movies was apparently impeccable because she, pleased to welcome a returning fellow countryman, burst into an excited few sentences in German.

Embarrassed, I had to hold up my hand and say, 'Sorry, I don't speak German.'

At which she instantly, and with a cross expression on her face, said in English, 'Well, don't you ever dare pretend you can again.'

I slunk to my seat, conscious of having committed a terrible international faux pas. This cosmopolitanism wasn't going to be as easy as I had thought.

Nor was travel, as I arrived at Charles de Gaulle airport late in the evening, and stood forlornly at the carousel as bag after bag was removed by excited travellers, eventually leaving just one lone bag, circling round and round, which wasn't mine. Not a good start with no spare clothes, and, perhaps more importantly, no copies of my prepared lectures. I reported the loss sadly, and caught the airport train into Paris, reached my hotel and slumped wearily into bed. Up the next morning. Breakfast *café complet* (never in trouble for attempting French, it just never got me far, French Resistance movies apparently having given me the wrong accent, and mostly I just pointed at things I wanted). I was in Paris! Paris! Now, if only I had some clean clothes. They arrived later that day, efficiently delivered to the hotel. I was back in the business of appearing human and being able to give a lecture.

Next day, out to Versailles on a bus. We had decided it was best if I picked up my hire car out there rather than attempt the nightmare of Paris traffic and spending my entire trip driving around the central roundabout unable to escape.

I was in Versailles! Versailles! And there was the palace, greatest ever monument built by rulers to thumb their nose at the peasants. Into a little car, and off I went, each fifty metres punctuated by a bang as I bounced off the kerb, and then corrected, and then bang again. Driving on the right-hand side was not as easy as I thought it would be – like trying to trim eyebrows with scissors while looking in mirror. Eventually, I escaped the narrow roads of the forest of Versailles, which I had entered by mistake, and then I was travelling south. Through France!

It was a challenge to drive alone from Paris to Bordeaux, but at the same time relaxing – after over two years of frantic publishing work, I was out of reach of the phone with its endless impossible demands from authors and council members and printers. Out of reach of the constant arrival of people in my office wanting instant decisions on complex matters of design, or cost, or promotion, or timing, or some impossible to resolve conflict between two staff members.

Surprisingly, I made my way successfully, and alive, to Bordeaux, and the conference was good. Truly international, with another Australian, Iain Davidson, who I knew from Armidale, and a couple of New Zealanders, and British and Swedes, and so on. The last day saw a splendid outing. On a bus out to view some famous archaeological sites – including one where Neanderthals had been excavated. There it was, just an ordinary-looking rock shelter by the side of the road in a French village, but occupied 25,000 years earlier.

In the evening, we reached the Chateau Malrome, which had been the home of Toulouse-Lautrec, now a vineyard and restaurant-convention centre. A splendid evening as we all let our hair down, revelled in being famous palaeoecologists in France. Toasted our hosts, toasted each other, celebrated birthdays, gave impromptu speeches in various accents. This was life, this was being cosmopolitan.

Unfortunately, at the end of the evening, I failed to take into account the likely effect of so much good French wine, and forgot to go to the toilet before boarding bus. The journey, over what seemed excessively bumpy roads, took, apparently, some seventeen hours longer than the outward trip, and by the time we arrived back at the student accommodation we were using, I could only hobble painfully towards the door – six metres, five, four... *Bon soir* everyone! *Bon soir!*

And then it was train back to Paris, then to Cherbourg, then ferry across the Channel, then taxi, shared with Iain Davidson, to Southampton.

The World Archaeological Congress of 1986 planning had begun some years earlier as if for just another conference of the world's Western archaeologists, but a funny thing happened on the way to the Southampton lecture halls.

Just as the institute in 1974 had experienced protest from Aboriginal people about their lack of involvement in its research, so by the mid-1980s there was a worldwide protest from Indigenous people everywhere about the way archaeology was being practised.

Archaeology had always been presented as a kind of pure, value-free, description of the facts about the past (apart from a few recognised anomalies like Hitler's use of it), and therefore those whose ancestors were being studied in Australia, the Americas, Asia and Africa, could have no possible objection to the work being done by white folk. Indeed, I remember one white archaeologist's comment to the effect that it was much better, more objective, for the work to be done by outsiders!

Indigenous people all over the world had finally had enough of this nonsense. If you are going to talk about us, they were saying in effect, at least have the courtesy not to do it behind our backs. And by the way, we've had enough of the removal of our artefacts to Western museums, and the excavation and removal of human bones. Give 'em back. Oh, and don't pretend that archaeology is so pure and far above the ordinary world of politics and human rights that we can welcome white South Africans to a conference like this. We want them banned.

Just as in the institute context, many of the white academics erupted in outrage over these propositions. Peter Ucko was facing not just damage to the conference but a split in the whole world of archaeology. He dealt with it: the South Africans were banned (a popular song of the day was 'Free Nelson Mandela' – it was sung loudly at the final conference party), Indigenous people from around the world invited, sessions added. We voted in plenary sessions for noble resolutions. The times they were a-changin'. Archaeology would never be the same again.

And that was something. Oh, we were realists. Knew, in those heady days of 1986 that Maggie Thatcher would be prime minister for ever, that Apartheid would last for a thousand years, that the Berlin Wall was a permanent blot on the landscape. Couldn't really do much about those things (banning South Africans from an archaeology conference was unlikely to have the same impact on South African public opinion as banning their rugby and cricket teams), but at least we could get our own small corner in order. Make sure that archaeologists behaved ethically and that archaeology was no longer part of the colonial process. It seemed to me that what was going on back in the institute had anticipated this movement by a long way (the skeleton I had returned to Groote Eylandt ten years earlier, and my changes to the human biology committee, being just two straws in the wind) but that now we needed to keep the process going. Having anticipated the rest of the world, we now needed to keep up with it.

After another day or two, the conference was over. There was a final raucous party in the university convention centre, where the Aussies present, always louder than their numbers suggested, endlessly demanded that the DJ play, over and over again, 'I come from a land down under', each time singing along, and drunkenly dancing, just as enthusiastically as the time before. Beer flowing and men chundering was appropriate for the night. But given the events of the last week, and the radical changes envisaged for the discipline we all shared, the chorus perhaps sounded a warning: 'Do you come from a land down under? Where women glow and men plunder? Can't you hear, can't you hear the thunder? You better run, you better take cover.'

Next morning, badly hungover, we all departed in buses that took us to London for a visit to the British Museum. I came out to look for a hotel nearby, and walking along a street I saw heading towards me that familiar figure of Les Hiatt. 'Small world,' I said.

After that' the time flew. I had a few pleasant days staying with a friend's family in Hereford and in Coventry with my father's family. Then to Southampton to stay with Peter Ucko and Jane Hubert. Jane arrived back with Olivia (her daughter), who was going off to France the next day and buying stuff for her trip. Peter rang to say he was feeling very sick and would be late. He got there about three o'clock, saying he'd had blood in his urine. We persuaded him to reluctantly (!) see a doctor straight away. As he was making the appointment, Jane said, 'You haven't been eating beetroot have you?' Yes, he had but we persuaded him to go anyway. The urine test showed massive amounts of sugar. Yes, he had diabetes.

I spent twenty-four hours with Jane talking to him about it. I didn't realise until after he had complained about having to do things like not drink much, eat regularly and sleep occasionally – life wouldn't be worth living (he'd also have to lose weight and get some exercise!) – that what he was really worried about was that he had it so severely and would have to inject himself, since he was even more frightened of needles than I was then. He was very depressed and nervous. I asked if they would like me to stay on for a few days (I had planned to go to London to stay the next day). I was reluctant to impose, but they were happy to have me as a result of Peter's news. We had a pleasant relaxing time including a trip to the Isle of Wight. Then it was all over and I was boarding a plane at Heathrow. This time I didn't say '*Guten morgen*'. I had learnt my lesson. Anyway, this time I was flying Qantas.

After I returned from my brief taste of living the life of an international academic, it was back into the publishing wing (B block) of Acton House, where I was now settled in as director of publishing. It wasn't a move I had made with eyes closed. As Frank had said to me, publishing at the institute by the mid-1980s was beset with every problem it was possible for a publishing house to have, plus a number of unique problems of its own. But I thought I could make a difference. A major, perhaps the fundamental, problem besetting the area was that it fell in the intersection between academia and publishing. Since I was an academic who now had considerable experience in the reality of publishing, I thought I could possibly rationalise the conflict and reduce it.

In addition, there were three changes that clearly needed to be made. The first was that we needed to be much more involved in publishing works by Aboriginal people – if the institute wasn't the place where an unknown Aboriginal author could turn to, then we weren't doing our job. The second was that we really needed to be producing at least some works that reached out to the public and helped to inform, educate, inspire them. And finally we needed to begin taking into account a likely readership. It cost just about as much to produce a book that 300 people (or indeed thirty) wanted to read as to produce one that would reach 3,000 (or 30,000). That didn't mean you should never produce books for a tiny audience if they were important (say for the purposes of a particular area of scholarship, or for the interests of an Aboriginal community), but that given rising publishing costs and limited resources, such decisions needed to be faced (and had never previously been faced). There was strong and bitter resistance from Aboriginal studies academia to all three propositions.

In 1984, Ken Colbung had become the first Aboriginal chairman of the institute (from then on, all would be Aboriginal). Ken was something of a controversial figure in the wider world of Aboriginal politics, but I liked him very much and always found him immensely supportive and helpful. He had the same approach as Warwick Dix, both believing that the roles of chair and principal were to support, facilitate, provide the foundation for, the work of the skilled and professional staff in key positions. With both Warwick and Ken having that approach, and with both of them liking and having confidence in this chap, anything seemed possible. (When that approach was totally reversed, under a different pair of people, though I had remained unchanged, nothing was possible, or nothing that didn't come at immense personal cost.)

A great deal was achieved with the support of Warwick and Ken (and the magnificent Diane Barwick as chair of the publishing committee until her shocking untimely death, at work in the institute library, her great friend, and mine, Nancy Williams by her side, in May 1986). Diane was a good friend and an indomitable supporter of institute publishing in general, and of myself in particular. She was a wonderful woman. Perhaps if she had lived… But there were many sentences that began like that after she died. Many things would have been different over the following decade with her support for me personally and for the press and *Encyclopedia*.

The publishing committee was reconstituted in a more professional form (Frank Thompson coming on to it after leaving the institute); the critically important position of senior editor was introduced, and held, even more importantly, first by the superb Robyn Lincoln, and then by the equally superb Stephanie Haygarth; I developed a computer program to keep track of publishing costs on each title, and another one to track sales figures; set a production goal (there had never been one, but usually only four or five new books appeared each year) of one new title a month; obtained the services of first CUP and much later Peribo to provide professional distribution services; brought in Apple computers for staff and upgraded typesetting equipment; introduced the name Aboriginal Studies Press, to give institute publishing an identity; created a new logo for institute and press; added barcodes to book covers before most other publishers; improved promotion (including creating an attractive illustrated catalogue); and made sure the press was seen as an integral part of the Australian publishing industry.

They were all basic and obvious changes, and even just to list them gives some idea of the parlous state of institute publishing before 1985. Sales began to improve rapidly, our profile lifted, reviews appeared in newspapers, books appeared in bookshops. As a result, we began to attract new authors with sales potential, seeing us as a first resort instead of a last. It was coming up to Australia's bicentennial year in 1988, and there was clearly going to be an increase in interest in Aboriginal material in that year and hopefully beyond.

In particular, I had set out to attract Aboriginal authors. I had in mind Bill Stanner's essay in 1968 about the 'Great Australian Silence' (the invisibility of Aboriginal people and culture and history in Australian culture and history) and was determined to help correct it. There was the elderly and stately Tasmanian, Ida West, who turned up with a shoebox full of scribbled bits of paper, and things written on the backs of envelopes. As things about her personal story, and that of her people, had occurred to her, she had written them down in handwriting curiously (given they had developed at opposite ends of the Earth) like my grandmother's. 'There you are,' she said, 'there's my book.' And there, after a huge amount of my work assembling the jigsaw, it was.

Oh, and then there were the senior men from Yuendumu, concerned about what was happening to the children of the community, who had painted the doors of the local school, each door painted with a different Dreaming story, each story told. That was a book of dreams. I learnt enough Warlpiri to relate stories to labelled paintings.

Other books of dreams began to flood in – children's books from Aboriginal communities in NSW, books from the Torres Strait, the biography of an old Aboriginal boxer, teenagers in Walgett, old-timers in South Australia. And on and on. They were Aboriginal people who had not previously been give an outlet for their stories and ideas and histories, and they relished it (a big regret was that Sally Morgan didn't offer *My Place* to us – it would have provided us with the impetus it was to give FACP. But so it goes, and we had plenty of good Aboriginal authors anyway – including Jackie Huggins, who I encouraged and published her *Aunty Rita*).

I also encouraged non-Aboriginal authors somewhat outside academia. On one memorable day, I had Judith Wright and Nugget Coombs both in my office, while I tried to conduct a conversation with two distinguished Australians who I greatly admired, but who were both, not to put too fine a point on it, as deaf as posts. With goodwill and much mutual respect, we managed. I did publish Judith's essays, and later still she wrote the foreword to my own book.

While all this was going on, we hadn't neglected the academic side, and books on music and anthropology and linguistics, and all the rest, kept appearing regularly too. And got better promotion and sales than would once have been the case. The response from the institute members was swift.

First the white academics, who had, in many cases been associated with the institute since the time it began, or not long afterwards. They were outraged that things like children's books, or the autobiography of an old man in northern NSW, were being published, partly because they saw them as being of very low standard – not academic, and the institute should publish only academic books – and partly because they saw them as crowding out worthy academic books. It was in vain to point out that the latter wasn't true, that since I had nearly trebled the production rate, there was enough room for both, as our catalogue showed. In vain to say that in fact very few academic books had been rejected, and that any that had been were rejected because their sales potential was so low as to make publication unviable. In vain because to these people *no* book should ever have been rejected. If a university academic had been good enough to send a manuscript in, then I should have been leaping on it with glad cries and publishing it instantly, no questions asked. Particularly no questions about this new-fangled notion of sales potential. To these academics, the lower the sales in fact the better because it would be a sign of how pure the research was – an ideal book, I sometimes thought, with not a hint of exaggeration, would have been one that sold only one copy.

But at another level this wasn't what these academics believed at all. There were many who had never had a book published by the institute because they had never submitted one to it. There were others who had published an unsaleable work of data with the institute, but whose main, popular work, aimed, say, at the general public or at university textbook status, was sent off without a thought to the big commercial publishers with the aim of getting big sales, publicity, promotion. But they wanted to be sure that when they sent off a manuscript of, say, lists of kinship terms to the institute, having published the major work on Aboriginal society with, say, Penguin, it would still be accepted instantly.

And there was more. My academic status, such as it was, rather than being a reassurance was a big negative. Memories of Peter Ucko, who had set all this Aboriginalisation in motion were still fresh. He had betrayed them, as they saw it, betrayed academia, sold them out. And I, with a few others, were seen as being Peter's boys – supporters who had helped him in such treacherous activity.

Furthermore, the academic status I had in Aboriginal studies was seen as phoney. I had been employed not by a university but by the institute and so was illegitimate; no researcher should have been employed by the institute. So whatever status you think you have won't wash with us, Dave, and you have absolutely no right to be passing judgement, accepting or rejecting the manuscripts of real academics (and useless to point out that the acceptance and rejection was done not by me but by a well-credentialled committee).

It was, with little exaggeration, similar to the attitude Charles II had to those who had dared to try his father and condemn him to death. I escaped being hung, drawn and quartered, I suppose. Well, physically anyway.

'But,' I hear you ask plaintively, 'all that may be so, but by now you had a council consisting of a big majority of Aboriginal people. There had already been one Aboriginal principal and after Warwick all subsequent ones would be, and all chairpersons were now Aboriginal. Those white academics could whinge all they liked, but with Aboriginal people in positions of power, their delight in what you were doing must have been overwhelming at times.'

In fact, no. A number of the Aboriginal people who had come into positions of importance with the institute either had university degrees or an equivalent kind of status. Some may have felt a little insecure in dealing with very senior people in anthropology, say, professors and the like, and therefore, perhaps needing to be more Catholic than the Pope to establish their academic bona fides, were very critical of the kinds of things I had been publishing in the way of autobiographies or children's books. They saw these kind of books as being, perhaps, a little demeaning for Aboriginal people. Whatever they thought, and I don't know for sure, because it was never discussed with me, the outcome was the same as from the white academics – I was doing the wrong thing.

So, the more demand there was from Aboriginal communities or individuals for publication of their books, the more pleasure they got from seeing their work in print, being present when it was launched (one community group drove all the way in a van from far western NSW to Sydney for their launch by Gary Foley, for example, and I managed to get the elders who had painted the Yuendumu doors all the way into the Stanner Room at the institute for their launch) or being nicely reviewed, the more damning was the evidence that I was letting institute standards fall.

Publish Aboriginal works and you were letting some Aboriginal people down, don't publish them and you were letting down others. Publish autobiographies and you were demeaning Aboriginal culture, don't and you were just another racist not recognising Aboriginal self-determination and the right to publish what they chose. Publishing Aboriginal works was also a sign to white academics that I was letting the side down – neither a gentleman nor a scholar.

On the other hand, publishing white academic works was also a crime because I had no right to be passing judgement on university academics (even if that decision was to publish) – they were the gatekeepers of each discipline, and only they could decide what it was valid to publish. It was all reminiscent of the classic trial by ordeal in water for a wizard – if you sank and drowned, you were not guilty, if you floated you were guilty and would be killed. But that isn't quite the right analogy – those wizards had it easy.

Jumping ahead a little here, the situation as it applied to the *Encyclopaedia of Aboriginal Australia* encapsulated all of the attacks that were being made on the press as a whole. The small numbers of people who were critical of the *Encyclopaedia* were critical in totally contradictory ways.

There were Aboriginal people who thought no one writing the *Encyclopaedia*, least of all its editor, should be white (one threatened to spear me). There were white academics who thought there should be no Aboriginal involvement of any kind in writing the *Encyclopaedia*. There were Aboriginal academics who wanted no involvement by some other Aboriginal people, likewise white academics who wanted to specify particular Aboriginal authors and not others as being suitable.

One white academic wanted any Aboriginal contributions marked by being set aside in particular coloured boxes (I thought this one symbolised all that was wrong in what they were demanding). Some white academics thought the project was too much like an encyclopaedia, others that it wasn't enough like their vision of what an encyclopaedia of anthropology should be. There were white academics who blasted and denigrated the contributions of other distinguished academics.

And so on. You would think, I thought, that what I was doing was producing a work that would make all these competing and contradictory complaints superfluous. That by creating a mix of modern and traditional, of purely academic work and more personal writing, of Aboriginal and white authors, and so on, that everyone would be happy. What I hadn't counted on in this ducking stool process was that it made none of the critics happy. Whatever I did in including Aboriginal authors meant that I had in fact included some, but on the other hand it wasn't 100% Aboriginal authorship, so both lots of critics kept pounding away, not having achieved their aim. The same with traditional and non-traditional, the same with every other dichotomy. The same with the dichotomy between the 99.9% of people (Aboriginal and non-Aboriginal) who loved what I was doing and the 0.1% who didn't – the more I met the wishes and needs of the great majority, the angrier and more determined became the 0.1%. Aiming for a happy medium was evidence of witchcraft, achieving the aim was certain proof. Some ducking stool.

The institute had recognised and remembered the great Bill Stanner, who I had once shared a corridor with, by naming the meeting room (where I had once heard him speak about time depth) the Stanner Room and by instituting a Stanner award for published contributions to Aboriginal studies. But when it came to what I was trying to do to help end the Great Silence by publishing books by Aboriginal authors, and ultimately by publishing the *Encyclopaedia*, it seemed I was the worst person in the world, and it also seemed few if any people in senior institute positions shared Bill Stanner's (and my) desire to end the Great Silence.

Oh, it was all sort of OK as long as I had support in administration. I could shrug it off, continue to publish a mix of books, except…there was a big threatening cloud on the horizon. While I had given institute publishing an identity as Aboriginal Studies Press, a notional sort of independence, this didn't really mean beans. The academics were used to having the ear of administration members. Were used to dropping by or picking up the phone, expecting to be heard and taken notice of. Was there some hint that a manuscript might be rejected by that Horton fellow? That's what he thinks. A quick call and that decision would be reversed, even with the support that I had. Someone's manuscript was sixth in line, based on when it had been submitted after the five in front of it? No, no, can't have that, it must be out in three months' time, conference on – and up it would go in the priorities, disrupting all schedules. And then they would be disrupted again by another phone call on behalf of another manuscript, and another. Can't afford a big launch in Sydney for this book? Oh yes, you can and will, even if it means dropping someone else; who cares? And on, and on. If it was this bad under these circumstances, what would it be like when circumstances changed, which they surely would soon (principal and chair were both term-limited)?

But I had made it to 1988 and published a big institute book arising from a library project. There were demands from council that the editor and project coordinator, Penny Taylor, should not have her name on the book. I insisted that it be there – in hindsight, I should have seen this as a warning. I published many other books, enjoyed the ferment of this historic year. A year which was to see another decision made, in response to another source of influence and pressure, that was to radically affect the institute's future, my future, the future of a great many individual people, and, potentially, the future of Aboriginal people themselves. But it was a publishing decision, and given the pressures and hatreds that swirled around publishing at the institute, it was going to be fraught with problems.

10

Forms known by pure reason

'Take nothing on its looks; take everything on evidence. There's no better rule.' – Charles Dickens

Not knowing that a major life-changing decision was coming my way at work in 1988, I decided on making another at home. One of my daughters, from the age of twelve, had a pony, which was kept down the road on a farm that had a riding school and boarded horses for people. Then my mother gave her a second horse, and the logistics became more difficult. Perhaps we should look to moving to a small farm where we could keep the horses ourselves? Yes! No! Yes! Where? What about this one? Oh! Yes! Let's go!

It was perfect – forty acres, an interesting newish house, a separate two-bedroom block for the kids, stables, great views, at the end of a quiet dead-end little country road, but all on the border of the ACT, so no further to drive into Canberra to work than it had been from the outer suburb we had lived in since we first arrived (and which, in a similar way to the house in York, had seen us getting to know a group of people who had all arrived when we did, and making lifelong friends).

We sold the old house and we were off. So much land – look, one border fence is way over there, and the front fence, way down there! Can't even see a neighbour unless you have very good eyes, look, way down the bottom of the valley (cheating a bit, there was a somewhat closer neighbour's house just several hundred metres away, but on the other side of the steep hill and so quite invisible).

Happy horses, but what else? So much land, what to do with it?

Now in spite of my generations of farming ancestors among Youngs and Mauds and Carters, my farming knowledge (big brown sheep, remember?) could have been written on the margins of those little green tags you removed when opening a bag of lucerne chaff to feed the horses.

I looked around, discovered there was, because of the numbers of people moving out of Canberra on to small farms on the outskirts, a course at the local technical college for farm managers. My enrolment was one of my best decisions for several reasons. First, I learned a lot. Oh, the lecturers weren't all good, far from it, but the chap who ran the course (Dave Brown), and taught great chunks of it, was a good teacher and seemed to know everything there was to know about farming. Much of the theory stuff I could have read for myself, but the practical classes, for example on fencing (which I discovered, surprising myself, I was good at), were to prove invaluable. Secondly, the other people doing the course, mostly men, were an interesting mix from all kinds of occupations and experiences, united only in living on a small farm (or wanting to) and determined to make a good job of it. It was interesting to chat in tea breaks, or in the field, about all kinds of stuff, with people I ordinarily would never have met. The course was dumped the year after I had completed it (in three years), a great mistake.

But in the short term the big plus was that it formed a break from the increasing horrors of publishing at the institute. On tech nights (once or twice a week), I would leave work early at six p.m. and head to the technical college. Eat a packed lunch style dinner sitting in the car, and then spend three hours thinking and talking about something completely different to the day's events. It was a mental and physical break in much the same way as doing an arts degree while also doing a PhD and teaching had been all those years earlier. And, in a small way, it helped to maintain some emotional well-being in the face of those events, but only on a day-to-day basis.

Events which would have included some or all of the following: demands from an author to have a unique contract agreement different to all others; or to have a book published in a month, or with colour photos, or with a launch at the Opera House; a phone call from a council member demanding that an author's impossible demand be acquiesced to (the worst of these, but only by degree, I described in my diary as follows:

> Got a call from [councillor AB] telling me [author YZ] has cancer and I have caused it and furthermore I am preventing the treatment being effective. And the method I have used? Refusing to activate the deal she did with [a particular] bookshop [there had been endless nitpicking from the author concerned about the absolutely standard simple contract. The bookshop 'deal', a very minor proposition, caused some complication with our distributors which I needed to resolve]! Felt like asking if I had caused AIDS, El Niño and ocean pollution. It would be funny if it wasn't so sickening.

Other events might be some intractable production problem; an insoluble dispute based on personal animosity between two or more staff (at one stage, two separate tea rooms were operating on opposite sides the corridor); a computer problem; a speaker for a launch dropping out at last minute.

Such problems became more frequent and more difficult after the administration change in 1990. I don't think a fencing session distracted me from accusations of not only causing cancer but preventing its treatment while carrying out an ordinary administrative negotiation, but for many of the other things it helped keep me sane over a thre-year period. And gave me some ideas which eventually saw six pregnant Wiltshire Horn ewes arrive from Victoria on a stock truck.

'Where's your ramp, mate?'

'Thought you would have one built in to the back of the truck.'

'Nah, need a ramp.'

'Haven't got a ramp.' And so on.

But in the meantime, just as the truck had arrived, the culmination of about a year of thinking and planning (I had decided forty acres wasn't big enough for cattle, and there was absolutely no point in having a few specimens of a major breed like merinos, couldn't do much with that. No, if we were going to achieve anything with the farm, and we were, it had to be a very rare breed, and the Wiltshire Horn, I discovered, was at the time the rarest in Australia. Oh, and it had a lot of very interesting features: they shed their wool, and they don't flock like other sheep, move around as individuals or pairs – seemed a good match somehow).

I happened to look down the valley and there, unbelievably (this was winter), was a column of smoke, apparently threatening the visible neighbour's house. So, while arguing with the truck driver about the non-existence of a stock ramp (clearly a philosophical question that only René Magritte could have answered), I was also wondering what to do about the smoke, who to call.

Anyway, the impasse was broken.

'Can't waste any more time, mate, gotta get these sheep off.'

So he proceeded to grab each ewe and toss her off the end of the truck to where I was standing on the ground, ready, like a slips fielder, to catch them as they flew towards me. In spite of my fears, they coped with this better than I did (and had fewer bruises), and trotted off to where I had left little piles of lucerne in a welcoming trail. I paid the grumpy truck driver, and then raced inside to phone the neighbour.

'You have a fire.'

'No, I don't.'

'Yes, you do.'

'Just a minute.'

I heard him put the phone down and could see him, tiny figure in the distance, go out his front door, look around and go back in again.

'No, I don't.'

'Try the back door.'

I heard the phone put down, footsteps, a door opening, an exclamation, and then the phone hung up. Seconds later, I could see his truck heading up the road, the column of smoke now hanging over his house like a tornado in Texas. I headed off, too, job done of leading him to the problem, to find the fire brigade at work putting out a fire that had begun in a pile of wood and had started to spread rapidly. I stayed to help with the mopping up. Then at last went back to see my new sheep, quietly grazing, and unaware of all the fuss.

It was 1991, and I had two big projects, one academic, one farming, under way. Both tended often to involve telling people something which was a cold hard fact, only to have them reject it because they were looking in the wrong direction.

Still, things might improve at the institute. And sheep might fly.

The report at the end of my first term of first-year high school included a note from H. Hoad ('First Mistress') – 'Has not worked to capacity must try hard for scholarship.' Jacky Hos had become a friend at university because her name was the next one after mine in the Junior and Leaving exam lists, and then she turned up doing zoology ('Oh, you are Hos, JW!'), her name again next to mine in the lists (I discovered too that her father had been our gym teacher at high school). I ran into Jacky again when I came back to Perth briefly after the Melbourne year. She said that she was very disappointed I hadn't lived up to expectations (not working to capacity, in fact) and made better use of my talents. I could only agree with her of course. At the age of twenty-one, I had done surprisingly little (compared to Sagan!).

But there was a problem – what on earth was my capacity, and how was I going to know when I was working to it? I was now, I thought, settled as a scientist and a writer, so what capacity did I aim for? As I said earlier, the ethos in my undergraduate years, expounded by Bert Main, was that the research was the important thing. That you aimed to know the truth about something, and that was a good end in itself. You might publish, to let other people know about something of importance, but you published rarely, and only when you had something really important to say. Each publication should be, if possible, a perfect Platonic ideal of a scientific paper. His publication list, given his enormous knowledge and hard work, was relatively small.

And then I went to New England and came under the supervision of Hal Heatwole, whose view was that publication was the main thing, that research was only of value when it was published. He could, at times, it seemed, publish the results of a single experiment, a single observation, a single day's work in the lab or in the field. His publication list consequently already ran into the hundreds when I knew him.

Later, when I reached the institute, Peter Ucko took me back to the main philosophy – 'Make sure your first book is a good one,' he said, his first book having been a good one.

A happy medium somewhere? I guess so. I would try to publish as much as I could, but I would aim to have at least some of my papers be important ones. So, by the time I had finished my PhD and post doctorate year, I had published a dozen or so papers in lizard taxonomy but also on larger-scale issues of biogeography. Not a bad output, by most people's expectations, but I still felt I was cruising a bit, not working to capacity. Oh, I don't mean it was easy stuff, or that I didn't put everything into it, but I just felt that I was within a comfort zone. If things had worked out differently, I could have spent the next thirty-odd years producing similar kinds of papers on similar topics at a similar rate without being able to go back to Hester Hoad and saying, 'There you are, capacity achieved.'

So then I was into prehistory at the institute and I had to work even harder, see what my capacity was. I determined to reform the theory and practice of archaeozoology, turn it into palaeoecology, oh, and the history of archaeology in Australia needed looking at. And then there was the early colonisation of Australia, and fire, and megafaunal extinction, and ethnoarchaeology. I would lead people who didn't know the way. There were recent coastal sand dunes to dig, and Pleistocene swamps, and sandfly-riddled islands in Cape York, and much in between. Australian archaeologists, like anthropologists, tended to work on a single site or region, and write about single topics. The only other person who had attempted, was attempting, the range and depth of topics I was tackling was Rhys Jones, a brilliant archaeologist and thinker who I liked and admired.

All of that was satisfying and challenging, I was spending months in the field each year, analysing thousands of prehistoric bones, publishing a number of papers and monographs each year. Added to involvement in institute committees and other activities, raising children, getting on school boards, creating a garden on bare clay, building a house extension, coping with my mother (who had remarried and lived nearby), maintaining old friendships and developing new ones; moving on to a farm; breeding sheep. If this wasn't working to capacity, it must have been very close to it.

But again I felt that I was back in a comfort zone. I knew my topics, knew how to analyse a site, could see the future clearly. It must be time, for example, for that good first book, discussing Aboriginal prehistory and environmental issues like fire and extinctions – I had plenty of material. Then more of the same research and maybe a second book, and then, who knows, a third and a fourth. I had finally got to that place that great expectations had mapped out for me when I was a very young fellow indeed, being read to by my grandfather. (Not entirely: my grandfather had begged, on his deathbed, that I be taught the piano, not just, I think, in the sense of 'it would be nice if the boy had some lessons', but in the sense of 'I want my beloved grandson to be the professional pianist that I could never be because of family circumstances'. At least that is how my mother and grandmother interpreted it. Not only did they insist on honouring his dying wish, as a wish, but I think they saw it as a way that he would live on through me. Massive burden.)

Or had I?

If I pictured myself as a young teenager, daydreaming when I was supposed to be studying, imagining what I was going to be when I grew up (an impossibly long time in the future), life as an archaeologist didn't quite seem to fit the bill. Nothing out of the ordinary about it, no awfully big adventure, no glittering prize, no major contribution to Australian or indeed world society and culture. Had I reached capacity in a fairly mundane way? Would I recognise an opportunity to extend myself if it came?

And then, out of the blue, came the proposal for the *Encyclopaedia*, and it was suddenly obvious to me that this was it, this was Capacity with a capital C. And more importantly, this was a way of showing that the family had been right to journey to the Australian jungle, a way of exorcising the ghosts of nervous breakdown-inducing (in my grandmother faced with an impossible life in Margaret River in 1929) ghostly, arm-waving, dead trees. And even more importantly, this was a way of establishing Aboriginal studies as a serious discipline not a collection of disparate disciplines, an aim I had begun with editing the institute journal. And, of ultimate importance, here was a way of promoting the interests of ordinary Aboriginal people, of educating schoolchildren and the general public about the value of Aboriginal society and culture, here was a way of making a big difference. I was going to be finally testing my limits, but my cause was good, my aim extremely worthwhile. If it wasn't my first book (which I had just published – a history of Australian archaeology) which was going to be a really good one, my second book was going to be great. And my third, on prehistory and environment, would just have to wait a while (eventually a decade) until I could get this *Encyclopaedia* done.

If my life to that point had been in retrospect a preparation for the task of creating this *Encyclopaedia*, then the institute, begun nearly thirty years earlier, could be seen as having been created with the *Encyclopaedia* in mind as a major achievement. The *Encyclopaedia* would be, I was determined, a major showcase for all the collected material, and collected wisdom and knowledge, that the institute had been developing through these decades. It would be the perfect encyclopaedia with the ideal form. I chose as the logo for the *Encyclopaedia* a piece of rock art showing a group of Aboriginal people heading off to hunt – it was meant to symbolise all of the people, academic, Aboriginal, institute staff, *Encyclopaedia* workers, me, who would be undertaking this adventure together. All for one and one for all, a band of brothers and sisters. I should, in retrospect, have noticed which way the spears of the followers were pointing in that logo.

But how did it begin, this capacity-testing task? Clyde Holding was Aboriginal affairs minister in the Hawke government until 1987, when he had a falling out with Hawke after trying to introduce national land rights legislation only to have Hawke apparently block it. His wife Judy was an artist who developed a strong interest in Aboriginal art, I suppose at least in part because of Clyde's ministry, and as a consequence decided that what Australia needed was an encyclopaedia about Aborigines and that the institute was the obvious place to do it. With, I presume, Clyde's facilitation, the proposal was made to the institute in 1988, an auspicious year for such a suggestion, given that the bicentennial celebrations in general of course were heavily weighted towards the Arthur Phillip First Fleet side of history.

Senior institute staff in a meeting about the proposal suggested I was the obvious person to look at the practicalities of the project. I produced a dummy of what it could look like, wrote a number of trial entries, consulted with an experienced encyclopaedist, and started to list entries (derived from all the indexes of a series of major works in all subjects of Aboriginal studies – most of them by some of the same people who would later viciously criticise the contents). In 1989, this proposal was approved by council with me as general editor, and also approved hiring two staff, a senior editor and editor (the only financial contribution the institute was to make to the project as it turned out). The publications committee acted as a sounding board initially while I put in place a system of advisory editors. This groundwork got under way in 1990. The good ship *Encyclopaedia of Aboriginal Australia* had set sail.

But as it was raising its anchor, casting off the ropes, sounding its fog horn, there were big changes underway in the institute. The size and function of the council was radically altered to turn it into the executive body directly running the place; and, the terms of Ken Colbung and Warwick Dix coming to an end, a new chairperson and principal took their places. It was as if a migrant ship (the *Vedic*, carrying my family) had set off for Australia in early October 1929, with the world in a certain condition, and landed its passengers in November 1929 after the great Wall Street Crash, in quite different circumstances.

The question for the *Encyclopaedia* now was whether it would even be able to reach its destination as a result of these changes (and the sense that now, floating invisibly in the air, like virus particles after a sneeze, or poison gas in World War I, there were unfavourable council attitudes to Aboriginal Studies Press in general, and to myself in particular). And a question for me was what would be the state of my health by the time I reached that destination. I had to give up smoking my pipe, and I had to give up now before things got too stressful or I would never be able to when they did (and if I had known the degree of stress that was coming, unimaginable in 1990, I would have been even more convinced).

But if I was apprehensive, and I was, there was nothing for it but to roll up my sleeves and get on with getting this massive project organised. The first two appointments were made, with that of editor (Dallas de Brabander, cool, organised and unflusterable) being especially important. I was determined, given the thousands of possible sensitive topics, that we would undertake an unprecedented level of consultation, with every word being made available to every advisory editor and to others where needed, and it would be up to Dallas to coordinate and maintain this information flow, and keep track of an extensive system of indexing and cross-referencing I had planned.

I had decided that two additional integral components, to be worked on simultaneously with the book, would be a map (only the second attempt at mapping Aboriginal Australia, and the first since 1974 –Tindale's map, which had been based on work from the 1930s) and an electronic version of the book. Second, my work with the press, in itself a more than full-time job, would have to be combined with being in charge of the *Encyclopaedia*, also a more than full-time job. I was determined that no one would be able to say, honestly, that work on the *Encyclopaedia* was preventing other books being published (though of course they did, dishonestly).

The map was down to me. I started from scratch, colouring in (and using up a box of coloured pencils in the process, worn down to stubs – I knew how they felt), on a big map on the wall, one group at a time, starting at the tip of Cape York and working around in a big spiral until I did the last one in central Australia. For each group, I went to the library and came back with every available reference on that group. Then I would spend several days reading all the material and relating it to my other reading on neighbouring groups. I paid particular attention to works that had been done in cooperation with Aboriginal groups, and also to what Aboriginal organisations said about their country and what they called themselves. One difficulty was that the map tried to represent all groups at a single time, but in reality the information comes from different times and is of different quality depending on circumstances. Another difficulty is that groups of this size had different structure and meaning in different parts of Australia. But again I tried to base what got put on to the map by relating it to what Aboriginal people themselves saw as their identity – in some cases they see themselves as being part of a small group, in others part of a much wider group.

For the electronic version, I turned to Kim McKenzie. Kim, a filmmaker, had been at the institute nearly as long as I had. The film unit had been closed down (yet another change) and Kim was therefore floating as a lone person. We had talks about how he could become part of the general publishing operation, and the *Encyclopaedia*, and Kim's computer and design expertise made this happen in a concrete way. There were no computer/electronic educational resources at the time, so we were creating the whole idea from scratch, even down to the medium to be used. At one time, two very convincing salesmen for video discs came along. The quality was good, but it was clear to me that the future lay with the much smaller CD-ROM technology, and that's the way we went. The Apple system included, way ahead of its time, what we now call html but in the Apple context was just called hypertext. I was a competent Apple user, and taught Kim hypertext programming. It enabled us to create all the special effects and linkages that the electronic version would require, but I could also set up the original database of text for entries so that it was eventually automatically transferred, with added formatting, either to the CD-ROM or to the printed version. No one else in Australia, possibly the world, had ever done anything remotely like it at the time.

Finally, keeping the press running at normal speed was down to Stephanie Haygarth, who had just taken over (another change!) from Robyn Lincoln as senior editor, and who succeeded magnificently, by working incredibly hard. She also, of necessity, had a major hand in planning the production of the *Encyclopaedia*, and therefore had to work doubly hard. Stephanie and Kim were the two people on whom I depended absolutely to complete the project. They both knew everything that was going on, were both extremely smart, and I could rely on both to give me good and honest advice. It was much less lonely at the top, facing slings and arrows, with those two as my strong right and left arms. I also relied a great deal on Robyne Bancroft, Bundjalung woman, who, if she wasn't related to another Aboriginal person, seemed at least to know them. She was not only well-connected but doing a university degree, and therefore straddled the two worlds the *Encyclopaedia* was straddling. She was enormously important, particularly for the electronic version (where sound and film added another dimension of concern) in advising me on what Aboriginal people wanted from the *Encyclopaedia*, and in letting me know, forthrightly, when I got something wrong.

As the planning for procedures and functions was getting under way, I was also putting together the panel of advisory editors (whose roles included advising on such things as structure, style, essay writers, entries, writing the main essay which would overview their field, reading every word that was written and providing feedback). These were critically important to ground the work firmly in both the academic world and the Aboriginal world. They included people who were among the most senior figures in their respective disciplines; included about one - third who were either current or recent past members of the institute council; included a number of senior Aboriginal figures (notably the wonderful Charles Perkins, for whom my respect grew as I got to know him). One member of the advisory board, while knowledgeable in a particular field, was there because I wanted them on the inside of the tent pissing out, not on the outside pissing in. What I hadn't anticipated was that they were just as happy pissing inside the tent while being inside the tent. Not unique as it turned out.

Beyond those twenty were some ten times that number (ranging again from extremely senior figures down to junior but upcoming figures, again with a significant proportion of Aboriginal people ranging from young ones to elders, and including a large number of the professional institute staff) employed to write particular entries in their fields of expertise. It was an extraordinary collection of people – there were few names familiar to anyone knowledgeable in Aboriginal studies who were not included. The gatekeepers were all safely inside the gates. If you wanted credibility in both the world of Aboriginal people, and academics in Aboriginal studies, and a firm grounding in institute history, you couldn't go past a team of people like it.

In later years, people would say to me, with a sympathetic note in their voice, 'Well, it must have been hard navigating your way through all the complexities of Aboriginal politics and society.'

'No,' I would say, 'that part was easy.'

The *Encyclopaedia* was under way by 1991, and so was my sheep breeding. Those pregnant ewes, thrown off the truck, had lambed, and I had bought a ram for the following year. Sheep breeding was vital in maintaining my sanity through the grim *Encyclopaedia* years that were coming. It was hard physical work and so it kept me fit after twelve to fourteen hours sitting at a desk reading and writing. And it was a whole different world – a world of actual life and death where reality was inescapable. Such a change, mentally, from the institute world in the 1990s. After the first lot of lambs were grown up, it was time to go on the sheep show circuit. I knew almost nothing about it, except for my long-ago brief childhood experience in flower and dog showing, but it seemed like a good way to announce the arrival of a new breed and new breeders in the area. It was also, now I had finished my technical course, a way of having a short break each day from the madhouse involved in running a press and writing an encyclopaedia simultaneously, in the face of gradually strengthening resistance. And so we would head off very early on a Saturday morning with a truck full of sheep, unload at some showground, breathe in all day the heady aroma of sheep, their droppings, their hay and grain, the developing ammonia from their urine in the straw. Chat to newly made friends, eat inedible hot dogs and drink undrinkable coffee. Relaxing in a whole different world.

What an odd world it was and is, though. There are people involved in showing who not only have never heard of DNA, but haven't yet caught up with the work of Gregor Mendel in the mid-nineteenth century. They speak in terms of blood, infusing with blood (an old view also familiar in anthropology as we have seen, with its talk of full-bloods and octoroons). The ram is of primary, indeed almost sole, importance, the ewe doing little more than acting as a receptacle, an incubator, for the 'blood' of the ram, and now we are back into mediaeval times and earlier.

The whole show philosophy, indeed, dates back to Plato and his idea of perfect forms or types, each object having an ideal form, from which, in the real world, individuals diverged, but the aim was to keep trying to achieve the perfect form. A breeder, or judge, of sheep (and the same applies to other domestic breeds of animals and plants), has a perfect ideal form in mind for the particular breed concerned. In breeding, he (very rarely she) is striving to produce sheep that match that ideal as closely as possible; in the show ring, the judge is ranking the animals before him (very rarely her) according to how close they come to the ideal type. Curiously, the same process applies in a very formal way in biological taxonomy.

When I went to England in 1973, one of the things it enabled me to do was check the types (technically the holotypes) of the lizards I had worked on. When a new species of plant or animal is described, a typical single specimen is lodged at a museum. When other similar specimens are collected later, the question to be asked is, 'Are these specimens similar enough to the type to be the same species, or are they so different that they must be from another species?'

It is a concept that precedes Darwin of course and precedes our knowledge now of natural variation in a species around a mean. It also ignores our knowledge of the way genes work as discrete units – one specimen could appear to be radically different to another simply because of the presence of the dominant allele of one or a small number of genes. There are many species described on what turned out to be just minor variants.

Judging in the show ring based on divergence from the ideal type fits with the eighteenth-century view (and unlike my father's) that inheritance is through the blood. As one senior sheep person put it a few years ago (1999!) – purity is purity to type not 100% purity blood. The same chap was encouraging the infusion of breeds with each other because there couldn't have been enough variation among the animals on Noah's Ark to suit all our purposes today (I thought this was a joking remark, and said so; it turned out not to be – 'I hope my book of reference, the Bible, was also documenting the truth,' he said). As does the showing ideal that an animal is judged on its looks, not on age, weight, muscling, amount of wool produced, or indeed any objective measure at all (so, in practice, the sheep are being judged on some unknown combination of nature and nurture, whereas what they are wanted for is purely nature, which can be passed on). No, an expert sheep judge, one could call him a gatekeeper for a breed, knows instinctively which are the best sheep. Just knows, needs no other information, has a good eye for a sheep.

Naturally, though, a view of which sheep in a line up-most closely approximated the golden type for that breed was a very subjective view (at the end of judging, a judge is supposed to explain, for the edification of breeders and spectators, the reasons why this one wins first prize, this one second, by reference to objective differences to them.

One judge I heard espoused this concept by explaining, 'This one was a very good sheep, so was this one, but not quite as good, and this one wasn't quite as good as that, but still very good, and this one…'

If you had doubts about which one was closest to the ideal type, then there was a sure fire way to confirm it. The individual sheep are not made anonymous by some kind of random numbering system (as happens, for example, in wine judging or even poultry judging) but are exhibited in the ring while held by the breeder or members of his family. Stands to reason, does it not, that a leading, and long-established breeder, will have much better sheep than a novice breeder (like an archaeologist editing an encyclopaedia)? No question.

Similarly when it comes to the interbreed judging (in the so-called British Breeds section, Merinos are judged quite separately), all breeds are judged against each other to see which is the best sheep, no question but that the long wool section will be won by a Border Leicester, the short wool by a Poll Dorset. No pretence of seeing which of the specimens representing each breed was closest to the golden mean for that breed – the logic of the earlier judging. No, the big breeds were expected to win, and they did.

Look, it was fun for a while in an *Australian Idol* kind of way (and such competitions could have been modelled on sheep judging, where the hundreds of sheep that arrive on a cold morning in the sheep shed are gradually whittled down by a series of eliminations through a hierarchy, to leave just one standing at the end), but it quickly became obvious that it was a waste of time if you were just trying to breed good sheep that performed well, did the job they were bred for. So I gradually stopped, although I have occasionally judged (in the blood, I suppose), and done my best, since then. But it really isn't my kind of thing – surface impressions, subjective opinions. I think judgements should be reality-based. Hard to find those kind of judgements anywhere, though. And not, by and large, at the institute of the early 1990s.

11

Year without a Summer

'I would rather be wrong, by god, with Plato...than be correct with those men.' – Cicero

I began creating the *Encyclopaedia of Aboriginal Australia* with the feeling that all of my career to that point might have been aimed at ensuring that I was perfectly, uniquely, equipped to do the job. And that all of my ancestors, themselves lacking opportunities, held back by circumstances, knocked by outrageous fortune, had combined, rather in the way that gymnasts build a human pyramid, to act as my support and lift me up over the wall. That I had, to use Newton's thought in a different way, 'stood on the shoulders of giants'.

Just as the palaeoecologist job had combined my twin interests of science and the arts, so the *Encyclopaedia* combined my knowledge of Aboriginal studies and publishing.

A brief summary of where I was up to as I began the *Encyclopaedia*. I had four university degrees – Bachelor of Arts, Bachelor of Science with Honours, Master of Science, Doctor of Philosophy. I had been a staff member at the institute for sixteen years, and for thirteen of those years two principals had liked, trusted, relied on me, sought my advice, involved me in major decisions. I had served on a variety of committees and even council. I was forty-five years old, at the peak of my mental powers, and had under my belt professional careers in science, archaeology, publishing.

In archaeology, I had undertaken more fieldwork than most Australian archaeologists; had been involved in excavating very diverse sites over the whole length of eastern Australia; had made significant contributions (and published many papers and monographs) to prehistory theory regarding major issues such as colonisation (I wrote that woodland areas, not coastal ones, had been colonised first), use of fire (I wrote that Aboriginal use of fire had little or no ecological effect), megafauna extinction (I said climate change, not hunting, was the cause), Tasmanian prehistory; had radically altered the way archaeozoology was done in Australia. I had attended many archaeology conferences and in 1990 was keynote speaker at the Australian Archaeological Association conference, and had examined a number of PhD theses. In 1990, I published my first book on the history of Australian archaeology. By any conceivable measure, I was a major figure in Australian archaeology.

I was also a major figure in Aboriginal studies in general. Had been editor of the institute journal *Australian Aboriginal Studies* for five years; had supervised the publication of a wide range of books, some fifty by 1990; had played a key role in establishing the Aboriginal-run press Magabala Books, in Broome; had served on a number of institute advisory committees. I knew the ethical and philosophical questions, had hired one of the first Aboriginal members of staff; had returned the first skeleton to a community; had published work that had significant implications for the way Aboriginal people were viewed.

I was recognised as a significant figure in Australian publishing, attending conferences, book fairs, taking institute books to the point where they began winning awards, were selling well, being reviewed in newspapers, were leading the way for other publishers to copy us in publishing autobiographical works, community histories, children's books. I knew the nuts and bolts of publishing from manuscript to distribution, with editing and design and layout skills, printing knowledge, familiarity with the intricacies of finance and distribution and promotion. I had extensive computer skills and had introduced Apple computers to publishing in the institute before many other publishing houses had done so.

I don't list these attributes in a boastful way but for two reasons.

First to point out that I wasn't, as I started the *Encyclopaedia*, some unknown young graduate in a single discipline still wet behind the ears, nor some bureaucrat who just happened to have been in the right place at the time *Encyclopaedia* editorships were handed out. I wasn't one of the grand old figures of Aboriginal studies, but I was part of the next wave, the grand middle-aged figures, and there was no one around my age who I had any need to feel inferior to.

And second to illustrate how chance events, random decisions, lucky breaks, can put together (rather in the way that mutations and environmental accidents can lead to the evolution of a species ideally suited to a sudden major climatic change) a CV which just happens to be ideally suited at the right time to a job that arises, I knew that if someone had said to me, in 1963, 'Listen, in twenty-five years' time, the institute is going to be looking for someone to create the *Encyclopaedia of Aboriginal Australia*, this is the plan we want you to follow in order to be qualified for the position,' then it wouldn't have been much different to what I had done.

So anyone looking at the situation in 1990 would have seen that a significant figure in Aboriginal studies academia, with bonus ability in publishing and computing, with a long history as a respected institute staff member, with a track record of having saved a sinking institute publishing operation and turned it into a major player in Australian publishing, and with a sound plan for developing an encyclopaedia, was about to start work, they would have heaved a sigh of relief and thought, that's all right then, lucky we had David available. And while I felt a bit like a diver in the final of the Olympic Games, faced with a triple somersault with a handstand start and pike and tuck, I also felt like I had done all the training, had the skills, was going to give it my best shot. For my ancestors and for Aboriginal people. I felt great expectations on me.

And I, looking back in 1998 (beware, plot spoiler follows), could see that I had maintained the publishing performance of the press, while at the same time obtaining outside funding to produce the Encyclopaedia (in an astonishingly short time) at no cost to the institute, producing and selling a record (for the institute) number of copies, which returned even more money to the organisation; had won major awards for the book which had been launched by a prime minister; had received positive feedback in reviews, and from the Aboriginal community and from schools; had published both an Apple and Windows version of an electronic version on CD-ROM, again to popular accolades and awards; and had produced a map of Aboriginal Australia which sold in its tens of thousands and was seen on walls from one end of the country to the other. Looking back, then, you could see that our anonymous predictor in 1990 would have been quite right, though in fact their expectations would have been very understated against the actual achievements.

So why was it that throughout those eight years there was scarcely a day when someone wasn't screaming abuse at me in person or down a phone; or spreading rumours behind my back; or lying about what I was doing; or reversing, with bad consequences, a decision; or trying to cause trouble for me with someone outside the institute; or causing endless delays; or running me down (at the time when I had been for some years working fourteen-hour days, weekends included, day after day, the then principal told someone that I 'didn't do any work')? Why were some academics behaving towards me in ways they wouldn't have dreamt of behaving towards any other academic, and in ways they would have been outraged had they been applied to them? Why were a handful of Aboriginal people making demands about things that went against the interests, frequently expressed to me, of the great majority of other Aboriginal people?

The reasons for what happened can be easily summarised – two people (in fact, there was a third, but I didn't discover this until years later) who hated me intensely were in a position to act on that hatred; and given that hatred, other people saw the chance to refight the battle many of us had thought settled in 1974 – was the institute only to be about pure academia, or did it also have a role in informing the general public about Aboriginal society and culture, and should ordinary Aboriginal people have a voice in deciding how that informing should be done? The institute publishing operation in general was a target over these years, but the *Encyclopaedia* provided a large and convenient single target to focus all of the rage that some people connected with the institute felt because they had been on the losing side of the debates of 1974 and subsequently. And furthermore that I, perhaps because I was still there long after Peter Ucko was gone and out of reach, perhaps because I was seen as just institute staff, not a proper academic, by some university academics, was going to be a particularly welcome target. This, it should be reiterated, was friendly fire from inside the organisation, not bombs being lobbed in from radicals outside.

And as the captain of the good ship *Encyclopaedia*, I was a bit like the captain of an ocean liner cruising up a river too narrow to turn round. The work had to be completed;, no matter what damage I sustained, there was an endpoint that had to be reached. I was bound to the institute like two different metals bound together in a thermostat: whichever way one went, the other had to follow. Council was trying to bend towards the terminal of the off switch, I was determined to bend towards the completion terminal. A struggle.

How on earth do I tell such a complex story? It seems to me an important story and one where public perception at the time was quite different to the reality from the bridge. Where even the memories of some participants are wrong, or only represent part of the truth, rather in the way that, after a car crash, eyewitness accounts differ markedly. So the record needs putting straight, history too important to be left to the winners (those who caused the damage) to write.

Academics in Aboriginal studies have levels of mutual obligation, patronage, reciprocity, payback, tribalism, feuding, kinship, hatreds, that would leave members of bikie gangs, the Mafia, and, yes, even the NSW Labor Party, looking like rank amateurs organising a Sunday school picnic.

Now, the same could be said about academics in any discipline (think C.P. Snow *The Masters*, or perhaps Kingsley Amis's *Lucky Jim*, or the story of the discovery of the double helix) but there are a number of factors that make Aboriginal studies particularly virulent.

There is no question, in the minds of anthropologists, that theirs is the premier discipline, rather in the way that America sees itself as the world superpower. And, just as the US consequently sees itself as the world's policeman, anthropology sees itself as policeman for Aboriginal studies.

All Australian anthropologists are related. No, not by blood (though sometimes by marriage), but by the even more important linkages that develop in university life. All anthropologists have at some time been a student to one anthropologist, a teacher or supervisor of another. An older academic will have preceded someone in a chair, a younger one be a successor. Important linkages can be forged from the UK, with new staff members having perhaps shared a supervisor in Oxford with an existing one. In addition, there are marriages, divorces, affairs, co-authorship of books, co-organisers of conferences, people who have hosted you for a sabbatical.

Strong ties that bind? Yes, but also forces that divide. The university base provides a strong sense of territory, as does the state the anthropologist calls home. But in addition, most anthropologists develop strong ties to a particular Aboriginal community where they conduct the majority, perhaps the entirety, of their lifetime research. If the anthropologist spends some time there, the community will assign them a place in the kinship system – they will become brother, son, cousin, given a relationship to every member of the community in order to give their presence there, and their interactions with people, a firm basis in Aboriginal law.

The anthropologist will have obligations (providing transport or food, for example, to senior members of the community) and responsibilities, and will receive benefits in turn, just as other members of the community will be obligated and entitled. To have such relationships also provides status for the anthropologist back in the academic community – it means they are a real anthropologist, part of a very exclusive club. A club which has its own obligations and rewards.

A middle-ranking academic will have received benefits in the form of appointments to lectureships and subsequent promotion, thanks to his supervisor and or professor, will in turn be able to provide such things to his own students. And will help to protect the academic reputation of his benefactor, while expecting his students in turn to do the same for him. The currency is often in the form of papers, editorships of journals, presentations at conferences. Particularly in relation to the institute, anthropologists saw this as a source of academic wealth in the form of book publishing potential.

If someone had demanded and got publication of your book manuscript through the institute, then in turn you would return the compliment to them, or apply it to one of your students. Getting a book published was a major credit towards getting a job or promotion, and so being able to deliver such a prize was a powerful source of status, and the creation of future reciprocal obligation. For it to work, though, it couldn't be done in the normal way of having to run the gauntlet of readers and editors that you would have to do at, say, Penguin. That would create uncertainty, a lack of guarantee that you were indeed powerful enough to get a book published for your student. It had to be done through the institute where, for many years, books were simply published on request or demand.

And then I came along and tried to turn the publishing operation into a proper press, where publication depended not on academic mutual obligation but on actual publishability of a manuscript. Cat among pigeons. Horton not a gentleman. Even more so because I wasn't part of the club ('you won't like this chap, he's not an anthropologist'). A club whose function, as well as providing glittering prizes, was to guard the purity of anthropology. Those who had become elders, big men and big women anthropologists, were the ones who decided not only who would be admitted to the club, but what research and writing would be considered to be, accepted as, part of the canon, part of the holy writ. They were gatekeepers to wisdom.

And I wasn't part of the club. I had done archaeology, not anthropology, at university, owed no obligations to senior anthropologists, and therefore had no right to even comment on the discipline. A discipline too which, somewhat unusually by this time, in either arts or science, had absolutely no interest in educating the general public (including, in the case of anthropology, the general Aboriginal community). Other disciplines had tried to reach out, had created popular works aimed at the public, even at schools, where the latest findings in, say, physics, or archaeology, were being written in a way that was as jargon-free as possible. Anthropologists saw this as a cop-out, a terrible dilution of standards. Instead of believing that if a thing couldn't be explained simply, you didn't understand it properly, they believed that if a thing could be explained simply, it was wrong.

All of this, just as with Catholic Church doctrine, gave rise to a great many occasions of possible sin, and I, over a ten-year period, was considered to have committed every sin in the anthropological bible. I had made the publication of books by the institute not something purely in the gift of senior anthropologists, and had dared therefore to act almost like a gatekeeper, which I, not being an anthropologist, had no right to do. What was worse, perhaps, was that I was encouraging the publication of books by Aboriginal people themselves, who should have been content to be the subjects of anthropological research, and had no right to write books themselves – what was the world coming to?

And then I started the *Encyclopaedia*, and it all became a thousand times worse. I, some kind of scientist/archaeologist thingy (you won't like this chap, he's not an anthropologist), was presuming to be the general editor, when such a glittering prize belonged to someone from the anthropology club. Further, I was daring, again, to act like a gatekeeper, communicating with anthropology advisory editors and writers, editing their work, and, heavens to betsy, presuming to write some short entries on, say, kinship terms, where I took the original work by a real anthropologist and made it understandable. Why, it was criminal; the public would start thinking anyone could understand anthropology. And on top of that I was including stuff about modern Aboriginal issues, and about communities and individuals who weren't proper traditional Aborigines. I was even letting some of them write entries – this Horton fellow was evil, and his so-called *Encyclopaedia* (which, as one anthropologist said, he thought would have more high anthropology) would be the end of civilisation as we had known it since the first anthropologists began working among the natives on every southern continent in the nineteenth century.

By God, if he wanted a fight (he didn't), then he would get one, this would be war, and war to the bitter end, and if Horton thought he had some sort of control over the project as general editor, then he was very much mistaken. He was about to find out where the real power in Aboriginal studies lay. And how strong the bonds between anthropologists could be.

My friend Les Hiatt, one of Australia's great anthropologists, used to make the following observation about how Aboriginal people viewed culture. If you were to take a group of Arnhem Landers to Washington, he said, and visited the Smithsonian, they would have little interest in the exhibits relating to white culture, or that of native Americans, or that of Australian Aborigines, or that of Australia in general. What they would want to see is any artefact derived from Arnhem Land, especially one derived from their own community, especially one made by, say, the grandfather of one of the group. Aborigines had, thought Les, a very particular personalised interest in culture, not the more general one of Western society.

From the early 1970s onwards, Aboriginal people began using one of two routes towards closer involvement in, and recognition by, the wider Australian society. Some, especially the younger Aboriginal people, followed the lead of Charlie Perkins and began enrolling in university courses and obtaining degrees, often in subjects relevant to Aboriginal issues, such as anthropology, history, archaeology. The other stream of endeavour was from Aboriginal people without university education, often in fact with very little education at all, beginning to tell their personal history, or that of their community, or to put together traditional stories, perhaps for children.

Both were valid approaches. Those who went to university tended to have a broader interest in Aboriginal culture and politics, and were starting to be employed in academia and the public service, and, by the time I began work on the *Encyclopaedia* in 1990, were playing a significant role in the institute. On the other hand, I had been promoting books by Aboriginal authors, giving a voice to people like Ida West or Bill Cohen, with barely a primary school education, but whose stories were an important, and never told, part of Australian history. It would be vital to include both groups in the development of the *Encyclopaedia*.

So obviously vital that it never occurred to me that it could be an issue, especially in the form the issue was used personally and politically. My aim was to have the *Encyclopaedia* cover the whole spectrum from high anthropology right through to stories of Aboriginal people not generally known about, and so on. The academic side of things would be done to the highest possible standard – all the leading academics writing, with careful checking, referencing, indexing, and with the later addition of extensive appendices. If a university student was looking for an introduction to some aspect of linguistics or musicology, say, this would be the place to go.

On the other hand, if Les Hiatt's Arnhem Lander, say, was looking for something about his community, or its leading figures, or its material culture, or history, then he would find it too. And for that well loved publishing icon the informed general reader, and for high school and even primary school students, the language used and its style would enable even the most complex of issues and events and ideas to be easily understood.

Hard to see anyone being unhappy with that approach? Well, they were. A number of white academics were outraged that there would be entries by or about non-academic Aboriginal people, and so were a number of Aboriginal academics. The latter had become another form of gatekeeper, apparently believing that only those who had university degrees were qualified to contribute in any way. That the days of the community leader presenting their autobiography were long gone, and had no place in the new world of Aboriginal politics and culture. It was a holier than the Pope approach.

So the more I published books by ordinary Aboriginal people, and the more I included them in the fabric of the *Encyclopaedia*, the more the outrage grew among some black and white academics, outrage expressed behind closed doors in venues where it mattered. All the while, Aboriginal people in the community, like the 'Eaglehawk and Crow' protest group of 1974 (outraged that the institute was holding an all-white pure academia conference), were telling me that they wanted more, not less, of this kind of general interest material.

It was a conflict impossible to resolve. No matter how much high-quality formally academic material the *Encyclopaedia* contained, it was never enough to compensate for the relatively small amount of non-academic material. In fact, it seemed that even a single drop of non-academic blood would be enough to irrevocably pollute the *Encyclopaedia*. As a consequence, there were those who set out to damage or even completely stop the *Encyclopaedia* (and publication of non-academic books by the institute) on the grounds of quality, and others helping them who were simply determined, on personal grounds, to destroy me.

Still, even given all that, I was still part of the institute staff (and its elected membership), and that should have provided a firm base from which this vicious nonsense could be resisted. But it didn't. And I had once thought that I had been accepted into the aboriginal studies club. But during all the attacks on me, on the press, on the *Encyclopaedia*, no archaeologist, or anthropologist, or linguist, came to my defence. One anthropologist indeed came to my office one day with a letter of support to 'keep hidden in my top drawer for comfort' because they couldn't be seen to publicly support me.

In 1815, the year of Waterloo, a major volcano (Mount Tambora) erupted in Indonesia, throwing ash into the air to a great height. Its effects were felt the following year (the year without a summer) on the other side of the world, even by a farmer in Kippax, Yorkshire. So unusual were the effects of this distant event that it prompted my four generations removed great-great-grandfather Joseph Carter to begin writing in a kind of diary in 1816 – 'The corn was so damaged with the wetness of the weather as to render it almost unusable it was so sprouted.' The following year, the effects were still being felt – '1817 There was a long drought in the spring. The wet weather commenced about the 28 of May and continued three months. The corn began to sprout again which made the people despair.' Unforeseen consequences from distant, unknown (in Kippax), events.

The only physical thing I remember about my grandfather was that when he took off his hat, it left a red ring around his head, just above where the hair ended and the bald dome began. As a result, I thought (I was very young) that the hat had caused his hair to mostly disappear, perhaps as a result of abrasion cutting off circulation, though I doubt I had a clear-cut theory. Anyway, cause and effect – though I had, as can happen when young, got cause and effect precisely back to front. He was not bald because he wore a hat, he wore a hat, at least in part (the other part was convention and fashion, all men, and women, his age in those days of the 1940s and 1950s wore hats), because he was bald. But not wanting, myself, to go bald, for many years I wouldn't wear hats.

I was told later that he had become bald as a result of rheumatic fever, cause and effect again, but whether or not that had accelerated his hair loss (his increasing baldness, at the age of just twenty-one, is clearly visible in his wedding photo, some sixteen years before the fever), the actual cause of his bald head was buried in his DNA, perhaps through the Carters, his mother's family. His grandfather (another Joseph) Carter's bald head shines out from his photo.

Crown baldness from one side, pattern baldness from my father, whose thinning temples are visible quite early in photos, the only knowledge I really had of him. I was doomed by my DNA to go bald in middle age, whether I wore a hat or not. But I didn't. In photos after the age of about two, I never have a hat. Not fashionable for my generation. The earlier generations wore hats, therefore we didn't, and in birthday shot after birthday shot as I grew up, none of my friends have hats either.

Nor did we wear suncream, and so, as a result of the blazing West Australian sun, and a life lived mostly outside, my generation were creating little ticking time bombs in our cells, which would explode later and send skin cells into a frenzy of division. In my case, it took about sixty years before I became aware that spots on my now balding head were growing, itching, sore, sometimes bleeding, and began the process of removing new ones every few months. Fortunately, none so far the malignant melanoma that kills people regularly in sunny Australia, but some SCC that can also kill.

In talking to my skin specialist, she advised about hats and long sleeves and lotion and staying inside, but also pointed out that the damage was long done, the time bombs long in place with fuses ready to be lit, that I was paying the price for doing innocent things when young whose consequence was completely unknown at the time.

Things could have been much worse, I suppose, if I had, like the rest of my generation, spent long days unprotected from the sun on beaches. I didn't because of the consequences of measles when I was aged five or six. A bad case left me with a perforated eardrum and, as I've said, this in turn meant that I couldn't go swimming without earplugs held in place with a female bathing cap with flaps that covered the ears. Which meant, of course, that I couldn't go swimming. There were enough odd things about me without adding a woman"'s bathing cap to the list of things other boys could tease me for.

The other consequence of a damaged eardrum was some deafness in one ear. And in turn, thats probably led, unknowingly, to some unfortunate conversational sequences where I, trying to guess what had been said, nodded and smiled when I should have been shaking my head and frowning, or perhaps looking sympathetic when I should have looked cross, or vice versa, and unintended consequences may have often flowed from perceived insults or failures of empathy, or any of the thousands of human interactions where a foggy hearing of a word sequence may lead to disaster in the long run.

On the other hand, as my deferment for education (with my Masters) came to an end, and Vietnam loomed, my deafness was to have the consequence of making me medically unfit, the chance of miscommunication having even more dire consequences in that grim war. I was also unfit for army service as a result of a self-inflicted wound. I had begun smoking very occasionally as a teen, but had taken it up seriously (along with alcohol), as a badge of sophistication for the ultimate unsophisticate, while in Melbourne, and rapidly become addicted as that awful year unravelled my self-esteem.

Such was my genetics, as it happened, that even the desultory few teenage cigarettes had triggered chronic bronchitis, which got worse as the addiction deepened. At sea level and in humidity, my lungs were so congested that I slept badly night after night, and it was only the move to the higher altitude of Armidale that would eventually start to partially cure the problem. But in the meantime a breathing problem which was worse in humidity and at low altitudes was also not going to be a military bonus for someone with partial deafness, and the doctor signed the form to say I should stay away from Vietnam.

A good unintended consequence following a bad one? Yes indeed, but as with the damaged skin cells, I hadn't realised for a long time that my lungs were getting damaged, even when I switched to the benign (and grandfather-precedented) pipe smoking. Eventually, an odd feeling in my lip and a biopsy showed that pipe smoking could indeed kill you if you kept going after finding pre-cancerous lip cells, and I gave it up. Not soon enough, though, because, reaching sixty, and getting increasingly short of breath, the doctor told me that chronic lung disease was the inevitable result of early smoking, and even though I had stopped many years before (as I began the *Encyclopaedia*), the ticking time bombs in the lung cells, like those in the skin, would just keep exploding.

Life is full of historical and structural factors that affect the way we live our lives – wars, financial depressions, coal mines closing, unexpected severe illnesses and deaths – we can't prevent the causes, can only deal to the best of our ability with the consequences.

The things that happened to me, that were done to me, in the 1990s were partly the consequence of historical and structural factors to do with the way the institute was run, the political environment of the day, the philosophy of the discipline of anthropology and the battles for Aboriginal self-determination and expression. Being caught up in this conflict was like being caught up in a melee between two opposing classes in a rumble in high school. But I was much older and wiser now, and knew how to take these things into account when starting out to make an encyclopaedia in such a contentious area as Aboriginal studies. But all were things I understood, had trained for, could deal with. What I hadn't expected, hadn't allowed for, were vicious personal attacks resulting from hatreds which were based either on nothing I was aware of or some incident so trivial as to be forgotten, by me, a day later, but incidents which festered away in a few people like damaged cells becoming cancerous.

And just as a bitter feud with a work colleague who later becomes your stepmother is personally disastrous (to my grandmother); or a fight between a father and son over something as trivial as a radio will result in the two never speaking again and the son (my father) ending upon the other side of the world; so minor misunderstandings between me and people who would find themselves in positions of great institute power became the excuse for inflicting any kind of damage upon me that they could manage to inflict.

I hadn't imagined such a situation when I was reading, and loving, Arthur Mee's *Encyclopaedia* as a child. I suppose I pictured him contentedly working away with the support of a team whom he led, a happy project with a consequently happy outcome.

So let us turn to that outcome.

12

Arthur and me

'The greater part of a writer's time is spent in reading, in order to write: a man will turn over half a library to make one book' – Samuel Johnson

In 1933, when she was twelve years old, my mother was invited home by a friend from a wealthy family and commented years later to me, 'To show how rich they were, they had a set of Arthur Mee's *Children's Encyclopaedia*.'

Perhaps this always rankled, in the back of her mind, because about twenty years later, when a door-to-door salesman came calling with a later edition of that encyclopaedia, all ten volumes in an attractive wooden stand, she bought it for me. Or, more likely, agreed to pay it off at some few shillings a week, it being a purchase far beyond our means in the early 1950s.

She may have felt satisfaction, a kind of retrospective cocking of the snook at the Storeys, 'who had decided by then I was a rude cheeky girl and unfit to play with Marjory or eat at their place'. There we were, with a set of Arthur Mee's, as good as anyone. But she also thought, correctly, that if I was going to achieve something in life, I was going to need a kind of boost above what came from the school, and a high-class set of encyclopaedias was just the thing. It became a focus of my reading. Oh, I read plenty of other books. Each Saturday morning, my mother and I went walking a few kilometres each way to the Claremont public library, and came back with four books each, the maximum allowed. By the time I got the *Encyclopaedia* (aged perhaps seven or eight), I had reached the point where I had worked my way through everything I wanted to read in the children's section and had moved on to adult books.

However, I knew the encyclopaedia was different. It was a kind of super-book, the ultimate source of knowledge, and I avidly browsed the volumes day after day, learning all kinds of esoteric things which might have come in handy in later life. If I thought I might one day write a book, and I did by then, I never imagined writing an encyclopaedia, which was on a higher plane to my aspirations of novel writing (although when I was underway as general editor of an encyclopaedia, in that early period of optimism and pride, before the nastiness began, I once visited the Canberra Show, and going through some displays, came face to face with the modern equivalent of the door-to-door encyclopaedia salesman.

'Like to buy an *Encyclopaedia Britannica*, sir?'

'I don't buy encyclopaedias, I write them,' I said, with perhaps just a touch of hubris. But I was proud. I was going to be part of that select club with Arthur Mee and Robert McHenry, then *Britannica* editor in chief).

The *Children's Encyclopaedia* was on a higher plane not just because of the massive depth and breadth of content, but because of its form. Arthur said that he was inspired to create his encyclopaedia by his daughter asking, as children do, lots of questions which he couldn't answer. And he wanted to create a Big Book, a gift to the nation. To that end, no expense was spared in production – the paper is heavy and shiny, the covers are made to look like red leather with mock gold lettering, there are colour pictures throughout (beginning, with absolute intended symbolism, with a picture of Shakespeare).

The whole thing must have been put together (the colour pictures retain the instructions of where they are to go) and bound by hand. There is no doubt that Mee intended this to be a magnificent work to symbolise the importance of childhood. This is 'the first book that has ever tried to tell the whole sum of human knowledge so that a child may understand'. Mee thought that children were important to the nation (the British nation of course) and the empire, and the form of this work would show how important they were, how valued they were.

He also understood something else about the way the encyclopaedia should be written, a conclusion I was to reach independently (for I doubt I ever read the introduction, or absorbed it if I did) nearly forty years later. An encyclopaedia need not have a restricted niche audience – it you got the language right, it could reach everybody.

> It is a children's book that children can understand. It is written in the words the children know. The writers of this book have been simple by being natural; they have made a children's book without childishness, a book that children may read because it is simple, and that men may read because it is plain.

Arthur also realised that an encyclopaedia had another huge advantage over a single book (necessarily written for a specific audience) – there was so much content that readers could pick and choose according to their needs and knowledge, and in doing so grow with the work over a long period of time.

> Left to wander in this field, the child will find whatever it wants. For the youngest of all its nurse will find her lullaby. The child in the nursery will find its nursery rhymes and the best stories that have ever been told. The child who can be left out of doors to play will find here [as I did] the beginning of its interest in the natural world. For the boy and girl at school these pages teem with precious things; for fathers and mothers, teachers and governesses, they may well become invaluable. It is a book for grown-ups and children.

The other big thing Arthur Mee realised is that an encyclopaedia differs from a book in that you read as much or as little as you want. You read a book through from start to finish, it has a beginning, a middle, an end, and the information, the arguments, the analysis are determined for you by the author. An encyclopaedia can be dipped into anywhere, and, having dipped in, to look up a particular piece of information, you can be led on to additional information, and so on, spending as much time, and absorbing as much information, as you choose. You could start in the middle, or the end, and go in any direction, and you could be distracted by finding another interesting thing on the page of your initial topic, and be set off along a new line of inquiry, and so on. The reader creates his or her own reading experience. This was a concept that I completely failed, apparently, to get across to my critics or indeed my advisory editors, none of whom, it seemed, had been raised by Arthur Mee and his Big Book.

Hard to imagine anyone of sound mind undertaking to create one encyclopaedia, impossible to imagine anyone agreeing to do a second. So each new encyclopaedist comes to the job innocent and virginal, not knowing what the sacrificial altar, or the ducking stool, holds for them.

Also impossible to imagine, even though it is a small select band of brothers, and sisters, anyone establishing a club or an association for encyclopaedia creators. While we have things in common, the commonality is much like the survivors of an air crash – uniquely placed to understand each other's stories of survival, each of which has individual elements, but unwilling to relive the experience by discussing it with the others.

An encyclopaedia isn't a book in the sense the word is usually used, nor does it come into being in the same way. It is a pity that many Australian academics, their experience of publishing a book restricted to the publication (often by the institute, on demand) of their PhD thesis, didn't understand that. The creation of an encyclopaedia is better thought of as analogous to making a film. A film is not made in chronological sequence, but pieces shot in any order that suits and reassembled later to make a coherent whole.

In terms of structure, there were two choices. Either the *Encyclopaedia* could be organised by subject (as in the *Cambridge Encyclopaedia* series. My friend Robin Derricourt had sent me copies of some of them, *India* and the *Middle East*, to see if I wanted to model my *Encyclopaedia* on them – I didn't) or alphabetically, or somewhere in between (as Arthur Mee had done). I decided on the alphabet, because it made it very easy to find a particular topic by its position, and enhanced that capability with an extensive index and very extensive cross-referencing. The casual browser could find strange and interesting bedfellow articles thrown together by the alphabet, or follow trails of linkages. My model, in fact, was more like the *Oxford Companion* series (which I took great delight in serendipitously browsing) than a dictionary on the one hand or Arthur Mee on the other.

And so we set about the task. Some 1,800 topics were listed on a whiteboard, under the watchful eye of Dallas de Brabander, and each day Ian Willis (senior editor on the project) and I would pick a topic, any topic, head for the library, come back with an armful of books, read, digest and turn into language that anyone from a schoolchild, to Joe Public, to university students, to journalists, politicians and university professors, could read, enjoy and understand, even about topics of which they had no knowledge initially. And as we finished each one, with the addition of index, cross-reference and literature references, it was rubbed off the board. A very small dent in the enormous list at first, eventually, as three years passed, dwindling down to a precious few.

Each finished draft essay (plus those coming in from outside contributors) was put into one of the twenty-six photocopy paper boxes marked with letters of the alphabet. Each night I would take home several of the boxes and do the preliminary edit on the new essays. The major initial work needed was to cut – most writers were unable, seemingly, to hit a word limit target (250 words for ordinary entries, 500 words for the subject essays, 1,000 words for the major overarching essays). I had done my calculations – the book would be roughly this big with this number of words, this number of illustrations et cetera, and if it was this big, it would cost this much.

A two-volume set was the most compact and handy size for the average customer. So there were word limits and they needed to be met – another concept it seemed impossible to get across to many people. In the end, I would have a work of some 750,000 words and over the three years had cut the same number of words (!) from draft essays. As well as cutting, I was looking for consistency with related entries, any sensitive matters (for example, personal information in a biography), improving style, rewriting jargon and so on. This initial editing was important in setting the *Encyclopaedia* on the right path and in making it easy to read, which is very hard work.

The edits would be incorporated in a new draft attached to the original work (all drafts were retained), and when we had enough accumulated, a batch was sent out to all eighteen advisory editors (in those pre-internet days) in great heavy envelopes. They were supposed to read and give feedback, correct errors, suggest additional entries perhaps. They were being given every word written in the draft encyclopaedia so they could have major input into its development. Whatever comments they made were incorporated in yet another draft, any recent developments added, proofreading done.

And so it went on, day after day, hauling books into my room and writing, hauling boxes home at night and editing, creating the map, developing the electronic version, making endless decisions about every aspect of the *Encyclopaedia* style and contents, travelling around Australia (with Kim McKenzie and Robyne Bancroft) publicising the *Encyclopaedia* and desperately trying to raise the money needed to complete and print it (the institute having made it plain that they would fund nothing beyond the two editing positions), and in between making sure that the general press activity kept on track for a dozen books a year.

The three years passed in a blur of exhaustion. By the end of them, though, I not only had some 1,800 essays (600 a year, nearly two a day on average, every day, over half of which I had personally written), hundreds of photos, music (added to the CD-ROM version), maps, appendices, extensive index, 2,000 references – all the content of a big book – but the plans in place to produce a magnificent work that, like Arthur Mee with children, would honour the Aboriginal people of Australia (I had deliberately made the first two words of my introduction 'Aboriginal People' and the last two words of the last entry are also 'Aboriginal People' – first and last). Chapter headings used an image of Mungo, oldest archaeological site where ancient people were found in Australia. The paper quality would be high, colour was throughout (and a printer chosen who could deliver first-class work), the two volumes would come in a slipcase, the four covers would each contain an artwork by a distinguished Aboriginal artist (representing different aspects and regions of Aboriginal culture), the layout was open and clear with many illustrations, there had been enormous attention to every detail (only one typo, in a year date, occurs in the whole work). It would also be a gift to the nation, and I thought of it that way from the start.

Finally I added an epigraph which summed up my approach, and my belief, as much as any single paragraph could:

> I wish to make it perfectly clear on behalf of our people, that we wish to accept no condition of inferiority as compared with European people. Two distinct civilisations are represented by the respective races… That the European people by the arts of war destroyed our more ancient civilisation is freely admitted and by their vices and diseases our people have been decimated is also patent, but neither of these facts are evidence of superiority. Quite the contrary is the case … [We] have also noticed the strenuous efforts of the Trade Union leaders to attain the conditions which existed in our country at the time of invasion by the Europeans – [we] only worked when necessary…we called no man 'Master' and we had no 'King'. (Fred Maynard 1925)

In any other organisation, looking forward to the production of this magnificent work, I and the team would have been supported, nurtured, given every assistance. In some organisations, perhaps we would merely have been given encouragement. In a few, possibly, though this is hard to imagine, we would have been ignored, left to get on with the project until it was finished, the organisation having more important work to do. In no other organisation would senior people have set out to deliberately disrupt, delay, damage, denigrate the project and those working so hard on it, set out indeed to prevent the project ever being completed. And I couldn't understand this at the time, impossible (as for a soldier in a battle) to stand back far enough to see the course of the war. But since then, and with the benefit of twenty-five years of hindsight, I have, I think, managed to get to the fundamentals of the attack.

During my late teen years, some cousins-in-law (cousins of Trevor, my cousin by marriage) came to Perth from Sydney for a holiday. One of the things they really wanted to experience was the sun setting over the ocean, they having always, being from Sydney, only ever seen the sun rising over the ocean. I took them to the beach late one afternoon to witness such an event, only to have an additional treat for me. There was a rainstorm coming in from the sea like a great curtain. It was the first time I had ever been in a dry area while I could see rain elsewhere. Growing up in the suburb I did, in a house at the bottom of a steep hill and in a valley, I had only ever experienced rain as an on-off thing – either it was raining or it wasn't. You never saw it coming, or going for that matter.

When we came back from the year in York, where people had failed to think I was English, we landed in Perth.

'Where you from then?' asked the customs guy.

'Where do you think?' I said, thinking that at least an Australian might think I had regained the English accent I had as a child.

'Well, I thought you were an eastern stater,' he said, and I was plunged back into Perth parochialism, and into dealing with perceptions about who and what I was, and wondering if I would, as a foreigner, be let back in through the gate by the gatekeeper.

Another difference between a Perth boy and an eastern stater, we realised, was that for me the feared summer wind, roaring over a hot dry continent, growing in ferocity, was an easterly. For them, the westerly was the bad guy, the easterly a gentle cool breeze from the ocean.

Later, in Armidale, I was to discover for the first time that ground could be so cold that moisture from the air could freeze on it; water in pipes get so cold it could burst them. Later came, goodness gracious me, snow, falling like a scene from *Pickwick Papers*.

At school, I had learnt about those likely lads, intrepid sailors William Dampier and Dirk Hartog, not that James-come-lately Captain Cook, who seemed to be of some importance in New South Wales.

All part of the learning experience of growing up, of finding that things you had thought immutable, incontrovertible, part of the common mental baggage of all Australians, were all different depending on where and how you had grown up. And, as I gradually, and uncomfortably, experienced, values and attitudes you had been given by your family (or school – my school's motto was the somewhat severe admonition to 'Persevere and Advance', an approach which would be invaluable for the *Encyclopaedia*), that you had taken for granted, were no more fixed than whether you had grown up seeing the sun rise or set over an ocean.

Does knowing that make it easier to deal with the realities of everyday life? Probably not. When I was young, I used to think that everyone was equally intelligent. That if I was talking to someone and their eyes uncomprehendingly glazed over, then it must be my fault for not explaining it well enough – must try harder. And I thought that people generally had good motives (with the exception of crooks, Nazi spies, and the Sheriff of Nottingham) so that if they did the wrong thing, it was because they didn't have enough information, had been misinformed. Rather in the way that for a long time we thought that climate change deniers, if given enough information, would eventually see the error of their ways.

But I was wrong. There are many people in all organisations whose activities bear no relation to facts, aims, achievements, reality. They are motivated instead by one of the four horsemen of organisational apocalypse – Greed, Ignorance, Malice, Stupidity. Some people will act as a consequence purely of one of these horsemen, others may combine two or more. The precise combination of motives, and the number of people affected by them, will determine the nature of the organisation.

So here is Horton's Law (just like Parkinson's Law and the Peter Principle, both of which were also fully in action in the institute of the 1990s): the level of dysfunction in an organisation (D) = the proportion (P) of members acting according to GIMS x the square of their levels of power or influence (I).

High levels of D can be reduced by good leadership, democratic processes, and freely available and exchanged information. Conversely, D will be increased by secrecy, paranoia, bullying, poor leadership. It may increase so fast that it can engulf you like a sudden rainstorm whose approach has been unseen, and which blots out the rising sun.

The time of *Encyclopaedia* creation coincided, exactly, with high and rising levels of D in the institute. It wasn't merely a matter of seeing things differently, East meets West and so on, but the result of fundamental differences in values and behaviour. Writing the *Encyclopaedia* was like being part of a bimetal strip, pushed backwards and forwards as the intellectual tides changed. For the three years 1991 to 1993, I seemed to be living simultaneously in parallel universes, one of which involved extensive travelling.

I had travelled a lot in my archaeological life before 1991, both to conferences and to excavation sites. A once-in-a-lifetime opportunity was an expedition to Princess Charlotte Bay in Cape York, organised by the Marine Park Authority and using their research vessel. John Beaton would be excavating some sites, my friend Dermot Smyth would be collecting plant specimens, John Chappell was along doing geomorphology, and oddly Hal Heatwole, my PhD supervisor, and Jeanette Covacevich (curator at the Queensland Museum) were along doing reptile studies. There were also two old Aboriginal men (I was never told their names) who had been born (presumably the last generation that was) in the bay. The archaeology had only previously been looked at by Norman Tindale. So in one trip I was experiencing past and present, and anticipating the future when I would make a Horton map to replace the Tindale map.

Tropical archaeology, or biology for that matter, turned out to be not for me, thanks to sandfly allergy, although on a later trip to Broome, also sandfly-infested, I discovered a protection that could get me through the most savage of attacks. The local chemist had invented some brew (eye of bat and ear of toad, or perhaps the reverse) that made me invisible to sandflies. I was in Broome because the locally based Kimberley Aboriginal Law and Culture Centre had decided they wanted to establish a publishing house. A prophet with honour away from the institute, I was asked to go and give workshops on publishing, do some initial training, work out a framework for the operation, conduct interviews for the initial senior positions.

So having girded my loins, and everything else, against the stings and arrows of outrageous sandflies, I walked into the workshop room to begin my first session (I was going through the whole publishing process, a couple of hours per topic – writing, editing, design, typesetting, printing, promotion, sales, finances, staffing). I had never been faced with a more daunting teaching prospect in my twenty years or so (to then) university teaching experience. Sitting at the end of a long table and looking down along it, I had, on my right, a row of six or seven senior old men from the bush, each representing a different Aboriginal community in the Kimberleys. On my left were six or seven young Aboriginal women.

The young women, formally educated, were there, I think, because they could see publishing as a trendy occupation, a career, travel, life in big cities. The old men, with little or no school education but immense bush knowledge and immersed in their culture, were there because they saw publishing as a way of telling their stories to the wider community, and, in doing so, ensuring that they were preserved – oh, and make some money for their communities. I was going to have to present the information in such a way as to reach two quite different audiences. I did, then led the interviews and chose the first staff, advised on setting up the structure, and Magabala Books would be successfully launched and do good things.

My first trip to tropical Australia had been ten years earlier. The Aboriginal community on Groote Eylandt had asked the institute to find and return to them the skeleton of an Aboriginal elder who had died some years before (in the 1950s) and his skeleton had been stolen as an anthropological specimen. After some detective work, I confronted the person in Melbourne who had them, and took them back (in a box on my knee in the plane, all the way to the far north of Australia – he wasn't luggage and I wasn't letting him out of my sight) to his home. The then minister (Ian Viner, not a bad fellow from the days when big L Liberals could also be small l liberals) offered the use of his VIP jet to get me and the bones to the community.

I'm not sure what I, or Mr Viner, were expecting when we got there – some kind of impressive welcoming ceremony, I suppose, with speeches by grateful elders, and 'don't mention it' speeches from me and the minister. There was a big group waiting on the tarmac. We got out of the plane, I handed the box carefully to the leader of the group, they turned, quickly loaded themselves into a number of utes and four-wheel drive vehicles and disappeared rapidly from sight. I had learnt, I guess, that in Aboriginal society you do things because they are the right thing to do, not with any sense of reward. In this case, I think, the community had seen remains removed by a white fella (and the horror of it, in such recent times, still stuns me), and another white fella had brought them back. Fine, now the important thing to do was conduct the appropriate ceremonies, and at last give their countryman a decent and respectful burial. They didn't have time for speech nonsense. I was, as I saw them disappear, glad I had done the right thing, and pleased that there had been no speeches. But I have digressed even further.

I also had much travelling during the *Encyclopaedia* years. Shouldn't I have just had my nose to the library grindstone writing and editing as fast as I could? Yes indeed, and in a rational organisation, the work of raising money to complete the work and publish the *Encyclopaedia* would have been the business of council and management, making calls to their powerful friends. They wanted nothing to do with any such thing. If I wanted to finish the project, and they clearly didn't want it finished, then I would have to find the outside funds myself. If I didn't, that was that, the work would have been killed without them having to be seen to pull the trigger.

Indeed, my suspicions were that, in places where some of these people did have influence, it was was being used not to help me find the money but to stop my appeals being successful (and later, similarly, to block awards), or perhaps delay them so long that it would be too late to be of use. False information about the project was given to the minister's office, attitudes to me were influenced ('you won't like this chap'), other council projects were given money ahead of the *Encyclopaedia*, and so on.

To get money, I was going to have to rely, initially at least, on organisations where senior institute figures had no involvement. An approach confirmed when, in their only comment on fund raising, council abused me for having dared to tell someone that I wouldn't seek sponsorship from alcohol or tobacco companies. How dare I decide such a thing (because I had imagined an *Encyclopaedia of Aboriginal Australia* 'brought to you by Tooheys and Benson and Hedges' and the decision was a no-brainer), I had no right to make any decisions, and if council decided that sponsorship by such companies was needed, then by heavens I would seek it. One of the many episodes that seem too crazy to be true, but true they were.

There was a second reason for being on the road, and that was to raise awareness of the project and to get feedback, from both Aboriginal and academic/educational groups, as to how we were going, what was wanted. This was not a work being carried out in an ivory tower but one that needed to be firmly based in the community.

The essential part of our baggage when talking to people was the electronic version of the *Encyclopaedia*. While I had printed a mock-up of a few pages to show what the printed version would look like, it necessarily had only a few entries, and gave no sense of either the scale or structure of the enterprise. The computer version had a lot more entries (several hundred from memory) and the very big advantage that by clicking on 'links' (a foreign concept to most people then – this is all pre-internet, and the hypertext language was unique to Apple), you could bounce around the work in a way that practically and clearly showed my concept of the structure. There was an added advantage of being able to include sound and film material (the latter to a limited extent in those days, but short clips were possible) as well as the photographic images, so this was a rich interactive experience.

So the road team (myself, Robyne Bancroft, Kim McKenzie) would set up a computer at an educational or publishing or community event, put up a poster, put some mock-ups and advance order forms (part of the funding would come from advance orders) on the table, and then depending on circumstances, we would just wait for people to drop by, or I would give a talk first on what the project was about, what it would look like, and invite questions and people to come and have a look.

And this is where the feeling of parallel universes came in. Everywhere we went, everyone we met – individual Aboriginal people, teachers, community leaders, booksellers, politicians, education bureaucrats, computer people, other publishers, academics – was wildly enthusiastic about what was being done and what was coming. No one had any criticisms of my approach, or the content and style of the work I was putting together, just the opposite. People would spend long periods playing on the computer version, talking about the contents, discussing ideas.

The big question from everyone was was, 'When can we have it, when will it be available?'

One teacher said, 'Can I take this? I want it now,' meaning the short version we had on a computer disc. We were met with warmth and friendship and enthusiasm and encouragement and thanks – my well-being levels restored a little. When it came to fund raising, the educational people we approached came on board, joined the team, did everything they could to help raise the money. My vision of the happy little group working together to achieve the goal was true outside the institute.

We would return from one such trip, still basking in the warmth of our reception, encouraged to get back into harder work than ever, try to get this wonderful work out to Aboriginal communities and schools and universities as soon as I could, to be plunged immediately back into the grim institute world where half a dozen people were piling abuse on the project in general and me personally, and doing everything they could to hinder and damage the work – my well-being reservoir evaporated. Back out on another trip to friendship and support from total strangers, back in to virulent nastiness from people I knew. Over and over, as if I was two different people, with two different projects, one visible to just half a dozen people, the other obvious to the rest of the world. A prophet is not without honour, et cetera.

Eventually (through much anguish and sleepless nights), the money began to come in, and as I reached the goal of over $900,000 (mainly from four different sources, after some hiccups – but some of the last chunk was diverted for use elsewhere in the institute, in spite of my protests) it was finally clear that the *Encyclopaedia* could be completed and printed, at least in financial terms. What wasn't clear was whether the institute would let me complete it.

That battle was played out over the years from 1991. A battle recorded by me, day after anguished day, in a detailed diary, where I was trying to make sense of the senseless.

13

Penguins can't fly

'Every effect that one produces gives one an enemy. To be popular one must be a mediocrity.' – Oscar Wilde

Even after thirty years, reliving the events described here has me reliving the particular anguish and misery they caused me, notable even among all the misery that the *Encyclopaedia* project as a whole caused me. Because the event is complex and developed almost daily over a period of six months, detailing that complexity would make for a boring read, and I have summarised what happened, because the events described here are so extraordinary, so mad, so irrational, even in the context of many mad *Encyclopaedia* events, that I fear the reader may think 'this must be an early case of fake news, couldn't possibly have happened'.

And yet it did, and living through it was what it must have been like being the one mediaeval villager who hadn't eaten mouldy bread and wasn't suffering ergot poisoning and watched in amazement as those around him went off their brains.

It all began innocently. Among my management duties as director of the press, which included hiring staff, arranging work schedules, organising author and printing contracts, supervising design, setting prices, I was responsible for arranging distribution of institute books to bookshops. Once the press grew bigger, and started producing at least a few books which weren't tables of data from an ANU lecturer, it was no longer sufficient to sell books only to institute members (though that continued) but to get them into bookshops. To do that, you needed a distributor. I forget the details but before my time, there had been one or two distributors negotiated by my predecessors, and I had negotiated a new deal with Cambridge University Press, partly because their own output fitted with some of ours (and therefore their agents felt comfortable promoting it) and partly because I knew it would feed into the Anglophile/Oxbridge sentiment of our academics and make them a little happier with me.

At the time I arranged the contract with CUP, I had looked at other options, including of course, Penguin, the biggest publisher in Australia, but was told that we were too small for them and in any case they weren't taking on any new publishers for distribution. So CUP it was, and that was okay, they were efficient, they were nice people, they sold more books than we could have done without them. They would call in from time to time to talk to me and other staff, and every few months I would go to their headquarters in Melbourne and talk to their sales staff about new books in the pipeline, and get them excited about the potential of some of the interesting things we were now doing. There would be great enthusiasm from their agents at such meetings because we were often doing more interesting things than they were and they enjoyed being able to expand the range of books they carried in their cases when they visited bookshops.

It was comfortable and easy, and while I would have liked higher sales figures from them, I recognised that they had a big task in competing with the likes of Penguin for space on bookshop shelves. So, no use pipe dreaming, just get on with things.

But towards the end of 1992 a bolt from the blue – Penguin had heard about the *Encyclopaedia*, and, like everyone in Australia except institute management, recognised its importance and enormous potential. Could they have a chat with me? Er, yes, of course, always happy to talk about the *Encyclopaedia*, anywhere, any time. And then was stunned to find that they weren't just expressing polite interest in a major publishing project from another publishing company, they were expressing serious interest.

So I talked to their people in the equivalent position to me and was told that what they wanted was to publish a paperback one-volume version of the *Encyclopaedia*, wear all the costs, and pay the institute royalties on sales. This was amazing, all my previous Christmases rolled into one. I had struggled, against internal resistance, to raise enough money for the cost of publishing the hardback edition. Council was hellbent on stopping that if they could, and there was no way they would have invested in a follow-up paperback.

But if Penguin would do it, then the sky was the limit – the *Encyclopaedia* would fly into bookshops and into homes, would reach a huge audience beyond the 15,000 hardback copies I could afford to print. As well as libraries and other institutions, it would reach individual students and others, and would achieve the aims of increasing knowledge and awareness of Aboriginal society, culture, history throughout the country and influence public opinion favourably. They had done their research and could also sell it widely overseas (something my tour of university bookshops in the UK showed was not possible for us)!

But play your cards close to your chest, Horton, don't give away how enthusiastic you are. Because there was a second consideration - as well as the *Encyclopaedia*, I was still head of Aboriginal Studies Press, and I wanted to boost the books of all those authors, get their work into bookshops in big numbers with extensive promotion.

'So,' I said, to my opposite number, 'interesting offer on the *Encyclopaedia*, but of course we would also want you to take on the distribution of the rest of our output.'

Hmmm, long silence, glances exchanged between publisher and deputy publisher. 'Oh, don't know about that, your output is really too small and specialised for us, it's really the *Encyclopaedia* we're interested in.'

'Take it or leave it,' I said, 'the whole press output or nothing.'

Silence. Have I blown it, I wondered?

No. 'Okay, we'll take the lot.' They needed to look at our sales figures, but in principle we were ready for take-off. They showed me a draft contract (standard for the distribution deals they had with a number of other larger publishers than us).

'Oh, and by the way,' I said, deciding I might as well get everything I could for the institute, 'this only covers books. From time to time, we may be doing special projects.' (I was thinking of things like the map and the CD-ROMs, but other people in the institute did come up with other things from time to time, for example the 'After 200 years' photography book, or films, or music, and I wanted it all to be potentially distributed with the power of Penguin).

'Yes, okay,' they said, 'we'll write that in as potential, because not every project would be suitable for our distribution network, but we would be interested in most things.'

'Finally,' I said, 'we would want to also keep selling from the institute directly. Our members expect us to.' (I was very nervous about this because it was taking some sales away from Penguin and I knew the other publishers they distributed for wouldn't be doing such a thing). Seemed like even this was okay, they were so keen on the wonderful *Encyclopaedia*.

I felt like cheering but made myself wait until I got outside – this was incredible. The institute would become much better known by its products, and would get a much bigger income from sales. The main negotiator asked me to send him sales figures for the last few years, so they would be able to fit the finances in with theirs.

A few days later, I got the contract, which was as promised. Standard but with an agreement to consider any special projects, and they had built in a floor level of income. Based on our sales figures, he had included a base figure of $75,000 – if our sales fell below that in a year, then we would need to make up the difference (that is, pay them, say, $1,000 if our income was only $74,000; it was to ensure that they covered all their costs of warehousing our books, sending them out, managing finance, paying their agents and so on). But this was purely a formal thing to satisfy his finance people – he had seen our figures, and set a lower mark far below what we were currently earning. And what we were currently earning of course didn't include the *Encyclopaedia* nor the sales boost from Penguin distribution. A pure formality. The publishing staff celebrated with champagne, to which we invited the principal to tell him the great news. Apparently, champagne didn't agree with him and he wouldn't drink any.

I got a copy of the contract off to the Attorney-General's department – all major contracts for every department had to be checked. No time to waste, Penguin could change their minds, decide it wasn't worth their while. Got it back quickly, no problem, and at last I could take it around to the administration area to the principal, who would need to sign on behalf of the institute. On the way, I happened to bump into Russell, one of the people who, working for a big finance company, was paid by the institute to assess our budget, staffing and so on.

'Look at this,' I said, almost too excited to speak.

'Wow,' he said. 'Congratulations, this is enormous. If you'd pulled off something like this in our company, you'd be instantly made a partner.'

Russell was something of a god to the administration of the institute (unlike most of the staff), and if he could instantly see the importance of this then what could go wrong? I wasn't expecting to be promoted, not even expecting any thanks or recognition, thought the principal would be congratulated on this massive achievement and given a bonus. No matter, I had set the *Encyclopaedia* and the press on a great new path, and that would do me.

I dropped off the contract with the principal with an explanation of the importance. I just needed his signature to get the exciting development underway.

'Just sign here. Look, the Penguin people have already signed.'

'No, I can't do that. I have to take it to council.'

'Okay, yes, they should be informed of course.'

'No,' he said, 'not for information, but to get council's approval.'

'Um, no, you don't need to, this is a management decision, always has been.'

But I already knew I was wasting my breath. This was a leader who would never make a single decision without asking the real leader. Still, even council must see the value of this and, uttering glad cries, get the principal to sign after warmly congratulating him. Mustn't they?

No, even I had underestimated the depth of hatred for me. The screams began immediately, it seems.

'Who did Horton think he was, daring to negotiate publishing contracts?' [As director of publishing, and general editor of the *Encyclopaedia*, it's part of my job to negotiate author, printing, publishing contracts…]

'Look at this, what he's done, he must be insane, he wants us to pay Penguin $75,000 a year.' [Um, no, that is a very generous lower level guaranteed minimum way below what they will be earning, and, in any case, it only refers to making up a small amount to that level in unthinkably dire circumstances, and in such circumstances, there would need to be further discussions…]

'Ah, look at this, Penguin will be wanting us to do "special projects", That is crazy. *We* decide on special projects.' [Yes indeed, and so you would continue to do. Penguin is very generously offering to look at distributing them for you even though it isn't obliged to].

The screaming went on and on, with a resulting motion that I was forbidden to make any contact whatsoever with Penguin, on pain of dismissal, and if there was any negotiating to be done, the principal (whose knowledge of publishing could have been written in big letters on a very small chewing gum wrapper) would do it.

Oh, and this awful *Encyclopedia* must be looked at closely and stopped. There were two white anthropologists on the council. One of them was asked to have a good look at the anthropology entries. This anthropologist was one of the advisory editors, had been totally involved in the planning of the *Encyclopedia*, had been kept informed and asked for input all the way through to this point, and had been asked to comment on and edit every entry so far written (including all the entries the map was based on). He apparently neglected to tell the other council members those embarrassing facts and instead agreed that, yes indeed, Horton was running wild and, ludicrously, said I had been ignoring all his editing (which a thirty-second phone call to me would have confirmed was, of course, not true). But this was still not enough in this rage-filled meeting – the other anthropologist was commissioned to look at every single entry and provide a report to council on whether the project should proceed.

Now this anthropologist I considered something of a friend (as indeed I did the other one), had known him a long time (and had, a few years earlier, published, with enormous personal effort, a very difficult, long-delayed book for him). He must have known that twenty senior academics were vetting all the entries already, and that I as general editor was reading and editing them all based on that feedback, and he must have known that I had the ability to do so. Still, he was prepared to override all that and take it upon himself to be a sort of super-reviewer – an insult not only to me but to every one of the advisory editors and all the other contributors.

Would he have been willing to carry out such an insulting procedure against anyone else in Aboriginal studies? No, of course not. But, caught up in the rage, and apparently scared of saying no, he agreed. Oh, and the chairperson was concerned about some entries (written by Aboriginal people) and wanted to go through them and make changes.

So this looked like the end. At best, these two anthropologists were going to endlessly delay the work (because whatever demands they made would involve not just fixing a few typos but working out the spin-offs in relation to 'See Also' links, the index, the bibliography. Everything in the *Encyclopaedia* related to everything else, a fact that had escaped all the council critics). And, at worst, these two might give council the excuse to close down the project. Well, neither happened. Anthropologist number two came up with a few typos and a few unhelpful comments. He had expected more 'high anthropology' – well, there was a lot from all the leading anthropologists, and to have more would have made it an encyclopaedia of anthropology, would it not?;

And he was puzzled by the excessive number of Aboriginal organisations in the early pages – then, belatedly the penny dropped. 'Oh, this is because it's arranged alphabetically'…

Anthropologist number one kept making changes to one sentence in one short article dealing with the work of an anthropologist he disagreed with (who was professor of anthropology at an English university). Backwards and forwards it went – 'Change the order of these two words', 'Changed', 'Ah, no, the start should say…', 'Changed', 'Ah, no, the phrase at the end should be…', 'changed', 'Ah, no, the middle isn't quite right.' This went on for months. The rest of the *Encyclopaedia* ready, the printers waiting for it, until at the end I said, 'Enough, no more.' Neither gave the council ammunition for a shut-down. Oh, and the chairperson seemed to lose interest after the initial muscle flexing on one entry.

But the rest of it turned out to be much more damaging. I was not permitted to even tell Penguin there was a problem, and they must have thought the silence was both inexplicable and rude. In addition, when things were settled, I wanted to advise Cambridge, out of courtesy and friendship, rather than have them hear on the grapevine. In the end, they did.

'But,' I hear you ask, 'surely you would have just explained to council that they had misunderstood things and then away you would go?'

Yes indeed, in any normal organisation, but not the institute at that time. Ordinary staff members were not permitted to speak to council, the door always closed, only the principal, who in theory was on top of all activity in the institute, would represent staff concerns and interests very effectively. Except he wasn't, couldn't and didn't.

As soon as I had heard the outcome of the rage session, I wrote a note to council explaining, politely, the situation and suggesting they had misunderstood. I gave it to the principal to pass on, as demanded, only to have him tell me that he refused to pass it on because it would make them very angry! Weeks went by. I wrote another note, and insisted that it go to council. Or tried to insist. The principal said, 'Be it on your head', or words to that effect. He had told me not to, but if I insisted, I had only myself to blame. I sat back and waited, only to be told that the chairperson had refused to pass on my communications to other council members. I could knock politely, or hammer on the door of the council room all I liked, but those inside were deaf to my pleas.

Only one possible outcome. Penguin, who had been very patient, finally after six months said they couldn't wait any longer and were withdrawing their offer and were taking on another publisher instead. And that was that. Neither the *Encyclopaedia* nor the press would be flying with Penguin and a huge potential opportunity had been deliberately wrecked. Still, they had damaged me very badly, so nothing else mattered.

I have restricted myself to the bare bones of what happened over those six months or so. Almost every day, there was something new. It was an almost death by 999 cuts. Among all the obstruction and nastiness and mad decisions were rewards of promotions and bonuses and staff assistance for teacher's pets, and punishments for imaginary sins for me. To give you the flavour, it was like the Trump White House, except worse.

Some months after all this in a conversation with the principal and finance officer about an aspect of publishing management (stock levels), the finance officer asked if the matter would have to go to council.

'No,' said the principal.

'That's good,' said the FO, no good if everything [that is, management decisions] had to go to council.'

'Everything doesn't have to go to council,' said the principal.

Indeed, I later negotiated another distributor for the press!

Anyway, there we were, another couple of months wasted while an anthropologist ploughed through every entry – entries that had already been seen by every advisory editor and many of which were written by advisory editors themselves and other outside experts – and grudgingly said it was okay. So back in business now. I was typesetting, doing design and layout, finishing the last bit of writing and so on, arguing with the other anthropologist about minor changes to that one small entry desperate to get it to the printer with no further delay. Then off it went. The *Encyclopaedia* was finally at the printers at the end of 1993.

I got on with the map and the CD-ROM and meanwhile had to check page proofs, check colour of photographs, check that all the thumbnails I had drawn were in position and so on. Finally, the first two proof copies arrived and I clutched one to my chest (and gave the other to Stephanie) overcome with emotion that I had got through all the difficulty and the obstruction and it did exist, just as I had envisaged when I gave a public seminar about it to anyone interested back at the start. Now, it needed to be launched. Prime minister of course. The *Encyclopaedia* was a significant event, funded by various government agencies, and a very important symbolic event for reconciliation, a subject dear to Paul Keating's heart. And important for the institute to have produced such a significant work. So the PM it would be. We just needed to arrange a date and we could swing into action and organise a great launch for institute members and get media publicity to boost sales.

Problem. I was not permitted to approach the PM's office, nor the minister's office. That, I was told, was the principal's job. Time went by. Had he done it yet? No. More time went by. Still no action. Months were now going by and still we couldn't release the *Encyclopaedia,* piled up in store rooms. And the calls were coming thick and fast. One of the critical things in funding had been to take advance orders from people, and they had come in abundantly. Where were their *Encyclopaedias?* Calls from distributors, calls from bookshops: where were the copies they had been promised months ago, why weren't we launching? And on and on.

Finally, for whatever reason, the principal did speak to the minister and the prime minister's office. Yes, Keating would launch it but the only date he now had available was in three days' time. We frantically manned the phones, inviting institute members and others, trying to get media interest, organising a room at Parliament House and getting it set up. A huge job achieved in record time, but many people of course could not come on such short notice and were angry or disappointed. Press attendance was necessarily limited and we got very little publicity benefit from what should have been a huge free publicity boost for institute and *Encyclopaedia*.

On with the CD-ROM and map, no time to nurse wounds and bruises. I had to make up for all the time that had been wasted for me. I had finished all the research that went into the map, five years' worth. I had for the first time arranged individual groups into regions and described the regions. Had put together all the relevant anthropological, archaeological, linguistic, material culture research. And this was important. I had decided that the basis for the map had to be published work, or at least theses, and all references were in the *Encyclopaedia*. In the map, I had put together over 100 years of linguistic and anthropological work, not invented it as my critics seemed to believe. I had wherever possible followed what local Aboriginal organisations and community groups wanted done in terms of orthography and geography. Every advisory editor had also seen every entry that the map was based on.

I then had to supervise the digitising process from the base map I had drawn by hand, the smell of coloured pencils in my nostrils as each group was completed. Then supervise the printing process, deciding on colours and inventing a process of bleeding colours into each other to make it clear there were no hard boundaries. Then added a region map, and then added the index of all alternative names on the back (vitally important because for most groups there was no universally accepted name or form of name – no one else had tried to do this or seen the necessity for it; my map can be referenced whatever your preference of orthography and historical or social context – my work was descriptive, not prescriptive). Designed the cover to match the *Encyclopaedia* and CD-ROM covers, to make it obvious this was a single project. Added information about the institute, about the *Encyclopaedia*, about how the map had been created. Added a disclaimer notice, making it clear that this was not intended for land claim use and that people should contact relevant land councils for 'detailed information about the groups of people in a particular region'.

But in addition I had made the boundaries fuzzy, so no piece of land in between groups could be claimed on the basis of the map, and having thought about it very extensively, had not included on the map any known Aboriginal sites, nor any towns or mining resources et cetera, that fell geographically somewhere between groups. A moment's glance at the completed map would have shown anyone concerned that not only was the map not suitable for land claims, but would be of no use in them other than for general background information. And no one could have sued the institute on the basis of information included in the map.

After careful thought about how to identify myself as author, I decided the best course was to copy exactly the way Tindale was presented as author on his map. There, I thought, no one can say I am big-noting myself, because I am precisely copying the Tindale map format. But it clearly identifies who made this map, relates it importantly to the *Encyclopaedia* (as Tindale's map related to his book), gives Aboriginal Studies Press a plug, and promotes the institute. It also identifies the map as a kind of sequel, and an update, of Tindale's map, which was important to give people the context. And finally it showed my pride in my achievement. An achievement shared only with Norman Tindale. Then I gave the okay to run off the first few thousand copies from the printing presses.

At some point after the map was printed and ready to be released, something again erupted in council. There were apparently heated discussions and more abuse of me, and it was seriously suggested that the map should be pulped, destroyed, because otherwise the institute would be sued, taken to court. It would wreck the whole land rights process (clearly no one had looked at it, and of course no one asked me what precautions, not being an idiot, I had taken). The sky would fall in on the institute.

It's worth noting again that the map was based entirely on published material from the institute's own library. More delays while accusations raged for some days and weeks. Finally, some kind of sense prevailed. A sticker must be printed and added by hand to say 'not suitable for use in native title and other land claims'. The stickers were printed and stuck onto maps individually by hand. Apparently, no one had told council, and no one had noticed, that the map already had a detailed disclaimer – the sticker was of no value at all, except to delay things yet again, and to make the map look a bit shoddy and downgrade its importance with the suggestion that it was somehow inaccurate.

But it was done. I had two more years doing the Windows CD-ROM alone, a very difficult job. I didn't want to start from scratch using the raw materials of entries and other material because that would have meant a whole new quality control process. So I needed to be able to convert the Apple Hypercard version into a Windows program. The only way of doing so was a small program in beta version developed by a couple of guys in America. They had created a Windows version of Hypercard. But it was full of bugs and had never been used on a real product for sale. So the *Encyclopaedia* became a sort of test project in which I would run it, find glitches, advise them in America, they would put in a fix, try again, find new glitches and so on. All done through posting discs backwards and forwards in the absence of fully functioning internet. A particular problem was the sound and video files and these I had to re-digitise manually over and over again.

Another problem was that it had to be able to run on Windows 3.1, Windows 95, and the new Windows 98. So I had to constantly test it using all three very different systems, and have all three versions fitting on the disc. I don't think there were any Windows interactive media discs available at that time, and no one had attempted to produce an Apple and a Windows version of any project, let alone one as big as the *Encyclopaedia*. It was really ground-breaking stuff. I spent two years from 1996 to 1998 in a room by myself doing it. I had asked for and been refused any kind of help to do this part of the project (even though there had been *Encyclopaedia* money remaining which had been spent on institute furniture). I was just doing it alone, and I was very inexperienced with Windows. For that whole period when I worked alone, there were demands from the outside world for their orders to be filled, and all that time I was being constantly abused by council for not getting it finished.

When it was finally complete, my job as director of publishing was written out from under me and I was forced from the institute. I had asked for promotion in the last twelve months, a request rejected instantly in spite of achievements and refusal to allow me to receive prize money. A promotion in that last year would have helped with superannuation.

But they were not finished with me yet. A couple of years after I had left, I got a phone call from a friend who still worked at the institute. Did I know the map was being reprinted and my name had been removed from it? No, I didn't. So I rang the deputy principal to find out what was going on. My name had been removed from the 'cover' of the map (that is, the part you see when it is folded on the shelf of a shop) and the only indication of an 'author' was Australian Institute of Aboriginal and Torres Strait Islander Studies in big letters. And on the inside, my name as author had gone.

So I was no longer publicly recognised as the author/creator of the map. I said to the deputy principal (who would only have given the instruction on orders from the principal, who in turn would have been acting on council instructions) that I claimed the right to be recognised as the author of the map, it was my intellectual property, and I wanted my name put back immediately.

The deputy principal (who two years earlier, on the day I had left the institute, in a rare moment of being nice to me, said, 'They put you through hell, but they can't take your achievement away from you,' and was now actively taking one of my achievements away from me) said I had no rights at all, that I had been an employee of the institute and this was an institute map.

I said in that case I would need to get legal advice.

He roared down the phone, 'Try that and we will hit you with the full weight of the Attorney-General's department. Think you can afford to go against them?'

I hung up.

Some time later, I discovered that a sticker with my name in small letters had been added to the cover of the map. But my name as author was kept off the front of the map, the only place it would be seen on the tens of thousands of copies of the map on walls all over Australia.

One of my achievements had indeed been taken away from me in a way no other academic would have been treated. Some years later, it became even worse, with the title, in large letters, changed to *The AIATSIS Map of Indigenous Australia*, my name below, part of the caption in small letters. Intellectual property theft complete. A complaint led to the response that they could do what they liked with my map, none of my business. If 'what your work does is tell people you've been alive', as Lucian Freud observes, the institute has hidden my existence from the world, like the identity of Henrietta Lacks was hidden.

In early 1998, it was twenty-three and a half years since I had proudly and nervously marched into Peter Ucko's office wearing best jacket and tie, and we told each other we were both younger than the other had thought. Ten years since Judy Holding had convinced Clyde that an *Encyclopaedia of Aboriginal Australia* to educate and inform the general public was something he should try to make happen. Eight years since I had interviewed candidates for a senior editor and editor for the *Encyclopaedia* and began sending out letters commissioning essays, and seven and a half years since I had written the first entry.

Four years since the *Encyclopaedia* was launched by a prime minister and began to receive worldwide acclaim and began winning prizes for excellence. Three years since the groundbreaking electronic version for Apple computers was released, again to acclaim and awards. Two years since the amazing map was released, already on its way to becoming by far the best-selling institute production of all time. And finally, after two more years of hard, grinding and solitary work, I had succeeded, uniquely at that time, in producing a Windows version of exactly the same *Encyclopaedia* for IBM machines.

In the years between the book *Encyclopedia* being launched and the completion of the Windows version, the *Encyclopedia* was very well received by the Aboriginal community outside the institute. For example, a phone call to me in 1994 from an Aboriginal community in the Kimberleys told me they needed a new copy because the schoolkids had worn it out. In 1997, Sam Watson from Queensland was telling people how great and useful the *Encyclopedia* was and how they had worn it out using it for teaching Murri kids.

It also won many formal awards – the Australian Award for Excellence in Educational Publishing; a WA Premier's Literary Award (beaten by Dorothy Hewett for the main award; I congratulated her enthusiastically, and I am almost sure my disappointment didn't show); Australian Interactive Multimedia Association Award for best Multimedia Title; Centre for Australian Cultural Studies Award for 'an Outstanding Contribution to Australian Culture' 1994; NSW Premier's Literary Award 1995 Book of the Year 1994; NSW Premier's Literary Award 1995 Special Award; Print Industry Gold Medal for excellence in printing; Doctorate of Letters, University of New England. It extraordinarily did not receive the Human Rights Commission award, nor the institute's own Stanner Award for publishing!

Stephen Wild (who I had known since childhood and who had arrived at the institute, as ethnomusicologist, just after I did) was sent to tell me that the greatest ever institute publishing project would not be given the institute's own publishing award. I imagine he was told something like 'Think of any excuse you like, but make sure he doesn't get it.' So Stephen came up with 'It can't win because it's multi-authored.'

So after five years of being abused and damaged as the sole editor of the *Encyclopaedia*, having created, designed, edited, and personally written over half of the words, I wasn't to be recognised for having helped break the 'Great Silence' because there were other contributors, a fact that had been ignored for the previous five years. Stephen, I suspect, was embarrassed.

My guess is that something similar happened with the Human Rights Commission. The winner of the award was an author who had been one of my advisory editors who was working on a book manuscript at the same time and incorporated what he was writing into the *Encyclopaedia*, where it comprised a small part. So a publication that was a tiny part of the *Encyclopaedia* was judged to be a much better contribution to human rights than the whole *Encyclopaedia*. I congratulated Colin Tatz, it wasn't his fault, and headed back to Canberra in disgust.

Anyway I saw the Windows CD-ROM through production and it went on sale and I sailed out of the institute, the push to get me out, somehow, anyhow, having finally succeeded a few months earlier. The final event was drinks in the courtyard of the place I had been part of for so long. There were hugs from some staff, tears from others. Undoubtedly, still other people, not present, were having a laugh and congratulating themselves on mission accomplished. I had asked for, and was given, a Galileo thermometer as a farewell gift from the staff club (none from the institute itself). The thermometer operated on a similar principle to the thermostat I had marvelled at in those long ago school days in physics class. I also had a feeling of kinship with Galileo, dealing with people who wouldn't listen ('and yet it moves'). At the bitter end, I could say of the *Encyclopaedia*, 'and yet it exists'.

I had got out of the institute. It was over. I had left a solid achievement behind me in the four pillars of the *Encyclopaedia*. Now I was away from the nightmare of the last seven years or so, I needed to try to get back into equilibrium, rejoin the real world where I was a chap who was liked and respected. I tried not to think about the institute at all, didn't need to, didn't want to. It caused misery and sleepless nights when I did as a result of a chance news item, or hearing from a friend still there. Instead, I had plunged into a variety of projects. I was trying to get my new book accepted by a publisher. At last I had been able to summarise, expand on, all of my original work on Aborigines and the environment, work delayed (and as a result beaten to press by Tim Flannery's book) while I finished the *Encyclopaedia*.

My agent found me a publisher, and I began working with an editor (Venetia Somerset) to massage the manuscript. Odd to be on the other side of the fence, as it were, but I was also continuing to edit as a freelance for a publisher, taking a number of books from draft manuscript to final product, trying to supplement a drastically reduced income.

I was also taking advantage of a bigger farm to develop and expand the sheep flock at last, with time to spend on it. Both children were overseas, one worryingly so (because she was working in Russia). The dog had been mated and was having puppies, who proved difficult. And I was learning to relax, spend some time with friends, where seldom were heard any discouraging words. My emotional well-being was being topped up again.

But the main effort in 1998–9 was getting my new book finished. Working with a major commercial press was an experience that I wished (but don't think about the institute, don't think about the institute) I could have shared with some of the authors (and their supporters) I had come into contact with over the previous thirteen years. Once you had signed the contract, the business of 'your book' was in the hands of the publisher. They had the final word on title, cover design, internal design, size, number of words (in my case, for example, four chapters dropped entirely to reach a size goal), chapter headings and epigrams, extent and style of editing, publication date, print run, promotion, price, sales, royalties. I could make suggestions, for example provide several alternatives to my original and much preferred title which had been rejected out of hand, but that's all they were. 'You want to publish a book with us? These are our rules.' And fair enough too (although I did, of course, like many authors before and since, grizzle impotently in my study).

Anyway, it was nearly finished, Venetia came to stay for a couple of days while we worked through her final editing queries, and then it was with the publisher. It took a couple of years from the time I had finished the manuscript and sent it off to the publisher to the time it appeared. Again, a time frame it would have been good to share with some of the authors I had dealt with. But it would make no difference. Every author since there were such things has wanted their immortal words available to the public within hours, at most, of typing the words 'The End' on the last page of a rough draft manuscript. Sometimes before they reach the last page.

Out it came, there it was, in bookshops, but with absolutely no promotion by the publisher. I was on my way again. A few good reviews and a not so good one (in *The Australian*, who would have guessed). A great interview with Phillip Adams on *Late Night Live*. There I was in the Canberra studio of the ABC, a place of echoing dark corridors, late-night dead, just me and the sound technician, and a big pair of earphones. And then there was Phillip, on line, informed as usual, ready to ask questions that needed instant answers, no ums and ahs and maybes and on-the-other-hands.

I swallowed nervously, concentrating, not too close to the microphone; don't cough whatever you do. But it went well (I thought), Phillip ended by saying I was one side of one of the great scientific rivalries and debates of Australia, would I be happy to come back and debate Tim Flannery? Any time, I said, any time. But it never happened. Just as when I ran for federal parliament a few years later, against an entrenched local member, Alby Schultz, with a majority of a gazillion per cent who I challenged to a debate – why would he? And why would Flannery when my own publisher was not pushing the work as a major contribution to important debates?

Wedgwood Benn said, 'We do not choose our convictions, but they choose us and force us to fight for them to the death.'

In 1974, the cause that chose me, by chance and a bit of luck, was the study of Aboriginal culture, society and history, and its promotion to the wider Australian community. First, it was my involvement in getting the institute interested in contemporary Aboriginal interests and politics. Then it was my work which argued against a kind of new conservatism of thought about Aboriginal prehistory and the role of Aborigines in conserving the environment. Then, again by chance, I helped many Aboriginal people find a published voice, as I played a role in extending institute publishing to not only include academic works but those of communities, and elderly individuals, and authors wanting to tell children about Aboriginal culture. And finally came the *Encyclopaedia* and the map. The latter, even without looking at any of the detail, was a symbolic and actual statement about total prior Aboriginal ownership, and its great variety, of the continent. No wonder that ATSIC made use of it in fighting a conservative government's action against native title, but aside from such concrete uses, just seeing it, in its deliberate beauty, will have had a subliminal effect on many thousands of people. Indeed, it was used in a number of artworks, most notably by Imants Tillers in his magnificent *Terra incognita* in 2005.

And then the *Encyclopedia*. As I said in my speech at the launch in Parliament House, Grandfather's pocket watch in my pocket, Paul Keating sitting nearby, I hadn't been taught anything about Aboriginal people at school in the 1950s, and my children had been taught nothing about them in the 1970s. I had been driven (much like Arthur Mee) to create the *Encyclopedia* by a desire that this and future generations would learn about Aborigines in schools.

About the time I was finishing the Horton map, the government of Australia had changed from that of Paul Keating's Labor Party, to John Howard's Liberals. Just as with institute principals, change the prime minister and you change the country. Keating had given the Redfern speech, recognising Indigenous history, Howard gave a speech decrying the 'black armband view of history' (by which he meant the real history of Indigenous Australia). It would have been harder for Howard to push that line if the *Encyclopaedia* had been not just in 15,000 libraries but in tens of thousands of homes as a result of Penguin distribution.

For a quarter of a century, I had used all my talents and energies in promoting Aboriginal interests, had hammered on doors to get the attention of the wider public. Now I had been told that I was no longer wanted, get lost, vamoose, close the door behind you as you leave. And don't come back. So, causes choosing me again, I moved on to looking not at how perceptions of the environment affected Aboriginal interests in society, but how perceptions of past Aboriginal interaction with the environment affected conservation. In short, a mistaken view of the role of Aborigines in causing extinctions in the distant past, and a mistaken view of the extent to which they had used fire to modify the environment, both ideas deriving from some other work of my co-mapmaker Norman Tindale, but recently popularised and extensively quoted in environmental debates, were issues that I needed to devote my attention to over the next decade. Sound the fire alarm, here comes Horton.

14

Following your career with interest

'For substantially all ideas are second-hand, consciously and unconsciously drawn from a million outside sources, and daily used by the garnerer with a pride and satisfaction born of the superstition that he originated them; whereas there is not a rag of originality about them anywhere except the little discoloration they get from his mental and moral calibre and his temperament, and which is revealed in characteristics of phrasing.' – Mark Twain

I have spoken earlier about some of my excellent teachers. Harry Creeper stood out in primary school, Stan Richards (of four great teachers) in high school. Harry stands out because he clearly saw potential in me, thought I was a good chap, did some nurturing, gave me some confidence, gave me a foundation or tradition from which to grow. I think the reason Stan stands out was that he not only taught our class as if we were adults, but he taught us to aim at being creative, original. As a result, I can surprisingly remember some lessons, some work that we did. I also, out to impress, wrote some things without being asked, poetry, short stories, prove that I was a budding writer. He was good about that, treated the work seriously as if by an adult, whereas other teachers might have been dismissive. I was straining at the leash, looking for a voice, trying not to be affected by all the books by great writers that I was devouring. Trying to imagine what my style, my subject matter could be.

One poem I wrote called 'Nothing new' railed against the writers who had come before me and had left nothing new to do, no possible approach that hadn't been tried, no avenue to be truly creative. After complaining about tradition and wanting it over with – let us new men get on with things – the narrator suddenly realises something. If no one is interested in tradition, no one will remember his work when the time comes. So perhaps tradition better stay, eh? I only realised later, perhaps I saw something similar, that many other writers had the same thought, and that what I saw as an original bucking against the bounds of 'tradition' was itself a tradition. Indeed, this very paragraph, being, I think, original in complaining about the lack of originality in my younger self's complaint about the lack of possibility of being original, is not original either, and so on recursively. Mark Twain beat me to it.

Having encouraged us towards being original, Stan then took us the other way in a few lessons. We had to try to write, I remember as if it was yesterday, a couple of short stories, one in the style of Charles Dickens (hooray, a doddle), one, for something completely different, as Ernest Hemingway (we were doing *Old Man and the Sea*, which I hated, but I liked some of his other work). I reckon I made a fair fist of them, though I bet they would be embarrassing to read now. But they were very good lessons. Don't just read this stuff and take it for granted, but work out how they did it, what were the skills, the techniques. Once you know how other people have done things, then you can go on to discard traditions and do your own thing, but you have to know what you are rebelling against to rebel.

Throughout my life since then, I think, I have always aimed for originality, tried to do things a little differently, explore new ideas, try new techniques. The *Encyclopaedia*, for example, while firmly anchored in the tradition of other encyclopaedias and companions, still contains many original touches, new structures, new styles. Maybe, in turn, others will copy me, then branch out in their own directions. And so it goes.

I guess humans have used fire metaphors ever since they have used fire, and metaphors. So, as a widely read and well-respected writer, it's time I invented my own. Show my mettle which has been forged in the fiery furnace of *Encyclopaedia* creation…you get the idea.

I got interested in the role of fire in the environment in the mid-

1970s. There was a popular and prevailing hypothesis (the result of articles by zoologist Norman Tindale and archaeologists Rhys Jones and Sylvia Hallam) that Aborigines had used fire extensively in the past (and into the present in northern Australia) and that this use (a major motivation being the desire to increase the area of suitable habitat for animal species being hunted) had caused major changes and shifts in Australian vegetation patterns. All sounded pretty reasonable to me, and I set out, as a zoologist turned archaeologist, to see if I could put my zoological knowledge to use to discover if, in addition to altering vegetation, this Aboriginal use of fire had affected animal species.

To save you jumping to the end for the answer, let me say briefly here that the more I studied the hypothesis, the more I realised that it was unsoundly based, and contrary to the real world as observed.

But first my fire metaphor. There is a very old one, perhaps the oldest of them all, that relates to gossip around the campfire, and rumour and reputation: 'No smoke without fire'. That is a beauty, isn't it? It now forms the basis of the whole celebrity industry and its parasitic gossip magazines and online sites. It has also come in useful in the not dissimilar business of modern politics. Oh, and in war propaganda.

Nothing could be easier as a technique, and it is extensively used by Donald Trump ('just asking'). Tossing a verbal petrol bomb is an effective way to get fire, and smoke, going, but it's a bit risky. Someone will have seen you doing it, you might be confronted, challenged, called to account, forced to recant (doesn't matter, still no smoke without fire). Much safer is the way that some arsonists start fires – throw a lighted cigarette butt into the bush (two or three to be certain in case one or two don't catch), and then be on your way. The butt can smoulder for a while, set fire to a twig here, a leaf there, a tuft of grass going this way. Invisible to the watchers – no smoke, so no fire. And then, given favourable circumstances – a wind springing up, a pile of dry rubbish, a hillside of dry grass – the fire can suddenly erupt, seemingly out of nowhere, and burn down a forest, or a neighbour's house. And even when it has been put out, at great cost and effort, there remain, all over the forest, small hot spots, smouldering logs, or termite nests, or tree stumps, or a hollow branch, that can, when the firemen have gone home, weary but satisfied, if the wind gets up, start a whole new firestorm.

Now the rumour may not go anywhere for a while, just be passed one to another as idle chat, signifying not much. The person is of course innocent of anything and may be perceived generally as a good chap. But given favourable circumstances – a row perhaps between the target and someone significant; or some mistake that is the subject of criticism; or external pressure on an organisation which looks like resulting in some people losing jobs – the piece of malicious gossip (for example, some staff were once told that the reason they had poor funding for library activities was because the *Encyclopaedia* was taking all the budget money) can take off and be repeated as fact.

It can become confirming evidence (especially if it falls onto fertile ground where the target is perceived as having some undesirable qualities, stubborn perhaps, distant, arrogant, too serious, works too hard) that the person is no good ('you won't like this chap'), shouldn't be promoted, shouldn't be praised, should be sacked. And the person can try to put out the rumour fire as carefully as possible, but bits will still smoulder away to emerge next time he, or she, applies for a job, starts a project, seeks a pay rise. And they will be left wondering where on earth the new round of criticism came from.

I mean, you would have to be utterly ruthless and amoral to behave like that, but if you have those qualities, then it is a sure fire way to block or dispose of an office rival, or punish a perceived enemy, without risk of exposure. Once the perception has been created that they are a bad person, your work is done, rather in the way that a sneeze can leave invisible virus particles lingering in the air.

But I digress, carried away with the joy of a new metaphor. The hypothesis that Aborigines had massively altered the Australian environment by the use of fire fell onto the fertile ground of public perception and common sense.

On to a long-standing Australian philosophy that the bush was there to be dominated by man. Those greenies had kept on saying that Aborigines had lived in harmony with the land for 50,000 years and we should try to emulate them – less of this chopping and clearing and burning; in fact, try to preserve some of the wilderness, some of the natural world, bit of a downer to development really. And then along came Jones (and one or two others) and said it was all okay, Aborigines had been burning the bush forever and there was no wilderness, nothing natural, they had altered it all anyway, so go for it, chaps. Oh, and since they burnt so much and had stopped recently, we had better get burning again, quick smart, to restore the bush to what it had been 200 years ago. And tree clearing? Don't worry about that, since Aborigines stopped burning, there are all these trees growing, more than ever before in fact, so clear away, fellers, clear away to your heart's content. Popular theory or what!

And then I came along, spoilsport, and said that all this was not fact but hypothesis, and that the hypothesis was based on very shaky ground indeed. In fact, wasn't true. So could you guys, please, stop clearing trees again, and if you keep burning those forests, you are going to cause untold ecological damage. Popular do you think? No, and not just among the usual suspects. Even the conservationists had become convinced, had perceived, that 'fire-stick farming' was a good, indeed indisputable, theory. Had invested philosophical capital into it, weren't about to change just because Horton said it was all wrong. Couldn't be all wrong, they had believed in it. And the people presenting the theory were good chaps, geniuses, everybody said that. Oh, plenty of ecologists got in touch, said, 'Thank goodness you said that. Always thought this fire-stick farming idea was rubbish.' But they said it quietly, not wanting to be perceived as greenies, when real men still knew that the bush needed a damn good thrashing, just like those blackfellas had given it.

Hard to make people change perceptions when their sense of self requires those perceptions to be true. All you can do is stubbornly keep chipping away, persevering, trying to get perceptions matching reality again, leading people back to the real world. It's an important cause.

Doesn't make you popular, though, sailing into the wind, swimming against the tide. Using metaphors. One newspaper columnist wanted people like me (perhaps it was just me) strung up from lamp posts (probably not a metaphor…). Nothing new there then.

When the *Encyclopaedia* had been out there for a while, it was accumulating awards (at least from places where there was no institute influence) but garnering no academic interest at all, because no academic had bothered to read it, see what it was about. Nor recognised what the map was based on, aiming at, instead just sneered at it. Nor had any idea what interactive media were and how advanced the *Encyclopaedia* was in this new field. Anyone else who had achieved even one of those things would have been praised by all others in the field, been promoted to the media, been invited, perhaps, to apply for chairs.

Instead, there was silence. It was as if it had never happened. So I decided to submit it for a Doctor of Letters degree at my University of New England (had to be where I had done the BA). Sent off the three copies. Waited. And waited.

I finally got a reply saying the *Encyclopaedia* 'wasn't enough' (!) and I would have to submit additional material, other publications. Oh, and it had been sent out to three very senior Australian academics as referees; here were their reports which would explain everything. Read the first two. Brilliant, the work was excellent, important, deserving of a D.Litt., no question, of course, congratulations. So, um, what was the problem?

I turned to the third report, which 'didn't think my work was great'. Said I didn't have much to do with the *Encyclopaedia* and the CD-ROM was done by technicians. Yes, it had won awards but that was because it had 'Aboriginal' in the title. Okay for Aborigines and children but not an academic work. When I challenged the writer (more in sorrow than in anger) on those statements, instead of apologising, outrage was expressed that UNE had let me see the referees' reports. And more than just the unfounded criticisms, the writer demanded that I be made to submit all my pre-*Encyclopaedia* work in addition. There was no getting around this bastard. I bundled together my most significant research papers and sent them off. Very quickly came the reply (I imagined the university had been pretty embarrassed) that, yes indeed, now I would be awarded the D.Litt.

So I headed to Armidale to receive the Doctor of Letters. Borrowed a resplendent gown (thought briefly about buying it, wearing it often in public), visited my old department of zoology, where I was greeted in the tea room as if I had just been away for a day or so and a conversation could now continue, and then headed out on to the lawns behind the wonderful old administration building Booloominbah. I would be called up first, ahead of PhDs and then the Bachelors.

I walked up to Chancellor Pat O'Shane, doffing my cap, she handed me the degree and said, warmly, 'We have been following your career with interest. Well done.' Oh, this was more like it. Pat O'Shane knew who I was, what I had done, so that was something. But as I walked away from her, scarlet robes billowing, the first of the PhDs had reached her, and I heard her say, warmly, 'We have been following your career with interest. Well done.'

So that was that, had got my D.Litt. in spite of the obstruction. But this person had done more than obstruct me getting recognition for the *Encyclopaedia*. They were on the publications committee through all the critical *Encyclopaedia* planning years. In committee and letter (there shouldn't be Aboriginal authors otherwise it wouldn't be scholarly, but that if I had to use some then they should be undergraduates, not 'radical elders'), this person demanded that Aboriginal authors not be in the *Encyclopaedia* because it would lower academic standing. I would love to have told people this, but didn't. Obviously they were saying how poor the *Encyclopaedia* was right through to the D.Litt. By 1993, people were told behind closed doors that the *Encyclopaedia* should never have gone ahead and had wrecked our production of other books (completely untrue as I had made sure would be the case). Again, I reiterate, this person was consulted throughout the planning process – saw the strategy, the advisory panels, the author lists, the topics, the style and so on. They argued the case against Aboriginal authors (I don't remember any other specific criticisms, but the committee decisions were all consensus) and was defeated. From then on, all those committee members were kept fully informed of progress until the committee composition changed.

Partly this incident got to me because it was so typical of the denigration and insults and misrepresentation and lies that I had experienced for the previous five hard years. But I had thought it over with. The *Encyclopaedia* had been published, in spite of the best efforts of a small group, and it had been praised, contradicting the criticisms of that group, so that, I had thought, was the end of it. Instead, I had discovered that the ratbaggery was continuing, would never end.

But there was a far worse aspect. I had considered the person concerned a friend for some twenty years. And a supporter and adviser who had been heavily involved in the committee which supervised publishing in general, and the *Encyclopaedia* in particular. As a consequence, they had been given all of the information right from the very start when I began putting together the structure and philosophy. Had been aware of everything I was doing and had been asked to comment and advise. And yet, at the end, pretended that there had never been an opportunity for input every step of the way.

But wait, there's more. After this nasty episode, I began putting clues together, got information from people, that showed me that this person, this friend and adviser, had been bad-mouthing me for the whole time of my work in publishing and the *Encyclopaedia*, behind closed doors, whispering into receptive ears.

And, finally, this was a person, friend, adviser, so familiar with my work, who I had asked to be a referee for jobs I had applied for over the years, and who had happily agreed. I knew now why I never even got an interview for anything I applied for in spite of my obvious achievements and abilities. After the *Encyclopaedia*, and after another institute staff member with far less achievement than I had been elected to the Academy of Humanities, I asked this person, a senior figure in the Academy. whether they would put me up for membership.

Oh yes, they said in a letter, happy to. After the next round of membership when I was again conspicuous by my absence among new members, I asked a friend who worked there if he could tell me why I had failed to be elected after being nominated by such a senior figure. He looked puzzled and told me that I had never been nominated. I had asked someone to ring a doorbell for me, thinking it was ringing away down the academic corridors. I should have hammered on the door myself.

All my life, I had accepted people at face value, thought they were okay until there was reason not to. And all my life I had tried to conduct my professional life openly and honestly, and assumed others were doing the same. Now, after fifty years, in 1995, I had discovered that these approaches had failed me. And discovered that the apparently inexplicable events surrounding the *Encyclopaedia* were not simply the result of the two people who hated me working behind closed doors, but of someone I had liked and trusted doing the same thing. Arsonists setting a whole lot of small hidden fires which would eventually combine into an inferno.

After my new book came out in 2000, it led to me writing bits and pieces in the *Canberra Times* and one or two magazines. It also led me to meet some conservationists, who had seen and liked my book, most notably my friend Ric Nattrass from Queensland (who would suddenly and shockingly die, very young, of a heart attack just a few years later). Meanwhile, I was becoming more and more concerned about global warming, the use of 'prescribed burning' in Australian forests, and about the tree-clearing river-drying climate-change-denying antics of John Howard and his government.

I had to do more than write letters to newspapers, or even occasional columns, and I had to do more than shout at television programmes where some minister would announce that the environment would get in the way of development over his dead body.

So I broke the habit of a lifetime and joined a political party. Yes, the Greens, of course. It was only a quixotic gesture, charging the windmills in a very conservative country electorate with a firmly entrenched conservative federal local member, but what the heck, what's that saying about good men doing nothing? It was 2003, and I joined in the lead-up to the state election. My good friend Bob Muntz was our local candidate (up against an equally entrenched female state member), and I happily trudged up and down the steep hills of my nearest town, shoving flyers into letter boxes for him and trying to avoid the attentions of furious dogs, conservative and angrily anti-Green every man-Jack-Russell of them.

Other members were trudging too. I always laugh when I hear some radio or newspaper shock jock denouncing the radical young greenies, painting them as crazed teenage Marxist revolutionaries determined to bring an end to the world as conservatives love it. In fact, I wasn't the oldest of the members in this country electorate, there were parents, grandparents (like me), even, I think, a great grandmother. Occasionally, some youngish folk in their thirties or forties would turn up, but mostly it was us oldies holding the fort, ready to storm the barricades. Ready anyway to come out on late nights and sit in freezing cold rooms, smelling of a bar heater and instant coffee and the dust of an old building, for monthly meetings. Ready to trudge around long country streets letter-boxing. Ready to stand in windy school gateways handing out, with frozen fingers, how to vote cards at election time. Passionate about their concern for the future and what kind of a world would be handed down to children, grandchildren, great-grandchildren. A lot of very nice people in the Greens.

The following year, I decided to take the plunge. I was nearly sixty and I hadn't yet run for federal parliament; my internal political clock was ticking. Besides, I thought I could do a reasonable job as a candidate. Had ideas, had experience in speaking to audiences and the media, reckoned I could hold my own in debates or on street corners. Give it a go. So I put my hand up, got preselected, and the campaign kicked off. Dreaming of a political career? No, not for a Green in this electorate.

But it was interesting and tiring and stretching. I was speaking to groups I would normally never have come into contact with – Rotary people, for example, a retirees group, and well-informed compères from odd little community radio stations. I drove many kilometres to set up stalls on street corners and banter with passers-by. I had dinner in Parliament House with Bob Brown and other Green parliamentarians. I wrote columns for local newspapers, and started a political blog.

When the campaign first began, I was at a function where Alby Schultz, local member and my opponent, was launching something or other. Never hurts to be polite, I thought. Democracy means hating the policy not the person, and so I walked over and put out my hand, said who I was.

'I know who you are,' he said, ignoring my outstretched hand and turning away.

Finally, I had the great feeling of going into the polling station at the local school and being given a voting paper with my name on it. Yes, I did vote for myself. A great experience, all things considered. And good, too, to watch the results come in and see that over five thousand people had decided I wasn't a crazed young (if only) Marxist revolutionary and had voted for me. I had increased the Green vote over the previous election. Okay, honour saved.

I was going to run again in 2007, had learnt a bit, woiuld make an even better job of it next time, but in the end I didn't, left it to someone else. Went back to handing out how to vote cards and then dropped out of party membership entirely. Not because of any policy disagreements, or of changing my mind about trying to do something about the world my grandchildren were going to find themselves in, but because I really, when it came down to it, wasn't happy in a political party. I was a political junky from way back – right back to 1961 when I had told my grandmother to vote for the appalling Menzies and had been trying to make up for it ever since. I had ideas about how to campaign, present issues, what were good strategies, didn't agree with some of the practical issues with the Greens campaign people, didn't like the rigid policy structure. In a party, you have to go along with what everyone else is doing. So I left.

But in any case, I had decided that I could be more effective writing newspaper columns, blogging about issues, than I could be as a party member. So that's what I began doing. Winning hearts and minds? Probably not, but it helped me settle my own ideas in my head, and if doing that helped me to lead other people to see things in a new way, then that was good enough for me.

15

In the blood

'The purpose of literature is to turn blood into ink.' – T.S. Eliot

Did 2001 mark the start of a new decade, century, millennium? Or was it the year 2000? Did the publication of my new book mark the end of my previous careers, or the start of a new one? I think, looking back that it was the former. In *Pure State of Nature*, I was putting together a set of my related research activities, updating them, adding explanations, creating a coherent account out of what, as I was doing the work, seemed to be not very closely related strands of thought. I was checking the accounts, adding up the figures, balancing the intellectual budget, closing a set of books (as I am doing in this memoir, twenty years on).

So the new decade, new millennium, first year of the rest of my life was 2001, not 2000. It was one of those decades where you suddenly feel yourself as not just an individual but as part of the sweep of history. One of those momentous events you read about in history books, and wonder how your ancestors felt at the time, is suddenly happening in your time. One of those many decades you find in your own family history where you can see generations turning over; paths not taken, or taken; births and deaths and marriages and employment and movement and other events that stitch one generation of a family into the long thread of that family's story.

It was a decade in which my mother's death cut my direct link to earlier generations, while the arrival of grandchildren gave me a link to future generations. The decade wasn't very old when the event came that apparently changed everything forever, as American hyperbole would have it. An event I was aware of in a place and state of mind that could have hardly been more distant, but which we were linked to by various friends in far-off places (as, I suppose, most people around the world were). This is how I recorded 9/11 in my diary (9/12 in Australia):

> My mother calls at 5.30 a.m. to announce the terrorist attacks on America. We watch the effect of the insanity of religion and barbarism. We watch transfixed in horror, then I go out to the sheep. 824 has that look in her eye and a little later goes off and has a ewe lamb quickly and effectively. I contrast the peaceful idyllic scene of a mother sheep caring gently for a new born baby with the madness of destruction and hatred inflicted on New York. It rains all day keeping the [other] lambs inside the shed…. Various ewes lose track of various lambs during day and I round them up. We watch tv all day. xxx anxious about yyy until she hears that he is ok, not having an office in the Trade Centre any more. Then we anxiously realise aaa worked there earlier in the year. Try to phone [aaa's parents] without success, Day ends with bbb, back in Djakarta, saying that this obscenity will be the finishing touches of John Howard [who was in New York by chance] getting back into power. Finally do my rounds [at night]. Chase eyeshine of fox via northern ridge all way back into zzz's place. All nightmares about my lovely lambs return. Hope alpacas stay alert.

My mother died, ultimately, to save the life of a moth. I wouldn't mind that for my own epitaph. She was walking from her kitchen to front room to answer the door bell, unsteady on her feet in her eighties. She went to take a step, and looked down to see a moth on the carpet where her foot was about to land, life and death a matter of perhaps an inch. She changed the angle of her step, to avoid treading on it, and in doing so lost her balance and fell, damaging her back and being taken to hospital. The damage she had done was sufficient to stop her walking, and it was quickly clear she couldn't go back to living in her own home and needed nursing home care. Sorting that all out took me three difficult weeks, and a fair bit of angst for both of us. Six months later, she contracted pneumonia and was dead in twenty-four hours, long before I could get back to the other side of the continent. Still, she had told much of her own story in her own way, and I think, most of her old friends and family having died, that she was ready to go.

Anyway, as we talked about family history, the only non-fraught topic we had, really, in those three frantic weeks, the smell of hospital in my nose, when I tried to sort out her big, and final, change of circumstances, she said that she hoped I wasn't going to go on wasting my life as a farmer. I was going to say she didn't mean it like that, but she did. I think it was partly her memories of the family's unsuccessful and sad experience in farming in 1929, but mainly her view that what she saw my destiny as being was the life of the intellect, the life, specifically, of the writer. 'Why aren't you writing?' she kept asking, plaintively, from her hospital bed.

But the question needs expanding a little. She knew of course that I had written, published, the *Encyclopaedia* and other books. Had copies of them on her shelf, showed them off, proudly, to visitors. But what she meant was why hadn't all that been a springboard to being a professional full-time writer who appeared on breakfast shows and in newspapers (and there was really no way to explain to her why the *Encyclopaedia* hadn't led anywhere unless I wanted to unleash a new Lizzie Borden onto the world). I think she thought I was wasting, had wasted, the opportunities, and had just sunk back into the bucolic sloth of farming life. She herself felt that she had waited too long to write her own autobiography. The part she had done, 100 pages handwritten in an exercise book, was anxiously handed over to me to take care of and do something with. I tried to say that I was indeed still writing.

The previous year I had run for federal parliament. ('Are you going to win?' she wanted to know, expecting the answer would be yes. I tried to explain the reality of running for the Greens in a country electorate.) That had led me to writing a regular column for a local newspaper and starting a blog. I had kept both going, even after my unfathomable failure to unseat the big-margined Liberal member in the election. And in

2005, I had also begun writing, the only Australian contributor, for the American *Huffington Post*, then just started as the first of the new breed of websites combining news and opinion in a big way.

Our relationship honed over sixty years being what it was, I alternated between trying to explain what a blog was (she didn't know and it wouldn't have mattered – more books were what she wanted) and telling her that, yes indeed she was right, quite right, I was going to waste the rest of my life being a farmer. But the other thing she didn't understand, although she might have from the evidence of the way she wrote about her experiences in Margaret River seventy-five years earlier, is that the 'farm', this piece of land – with its sweeping views of low blue hills (like those of my childhood), and Cunningham's skinks (bringing back memories of those long ago days working on the species in New England), of butcherbirds calling in the still autumn mornings (bringing back memories of doing archaeology on the Liverpool Plains), and spiders and deafening crinia frog calls (reminding me of zoology in Perth); with its sheep (which I now know are not small white cows) and horses and alpacas – was a constant source of inspiration to me and my writing. Directly and indirectly. That, good times and bad (and there are plenty of both on the land), I felt at peace in this place, and, at peace, felt creative again (by 1998, the battering I had received had left me not wanting to think, write, create, be involved, ever again. If that was what a small number of people could do to you when you did, then I would never try to achieve anything again.

But coming to this magic place had refreshed my vision, got me started on new aims, and I wrote, early in my new book,

> As I write this, I look from my window to the east. Above the fog, I watch the sun rise over a pair of high, rounded hills. The first rays shine through distant branches, an irregular fringe of angular forms and dark green foliage. Anyone sitting on this hill waiting for the sunrise to bring warmth to the morning would have seen the same view at any time in the last 50,000 years.

My aim, I said, was to 'observe locally and think globally'.

We had discovered the place by accident (and the timing, which in 1997 I had thought wasn't good, turned out to be exactly right – after the ordeal I had been through from 1991 to 1998, I was in need of serenity) just as I was about to leave the institute, retire, or perhaps, like a cause attaching itself to you, it had found us, but it was now an integral part of who I was, in my blood. Part of my emotional well-being.

I could no longer separate being a farmer from being a writer, if someone had asked, as I had been asked about various dichotomies in the past (science or arts, Australia or England, archaeologist or scientist, researcher or publisher) which one I was, I would say both.

And another dichotomy had been resolved, though I didn't try to explain this one. If my book *Pure State of Nature* (no, it wasn't my preferred title, it was the publisher's choice, and gave quite the wrong impression) in a way marked the end of my old research life, summed it up, put it to bed, it also marked a beginning of a different kind. My research career in the institute had been entirely focused on an Aboriginal-eye view of the world. It wasn't so much a question of whether I was in Aboriginal studies or ecology, the latter took second place to the former. In 1998, as I was leaving the institute behind and putting my new book together, I began to be aware that global warming, until then something only specialists knew much about, was a clear and present danger to us all.

I mentioned it in the book, pointing out that the extinctions of giant animals in Australia's past, the result of climate change (not human hunting), gave us a taste of things to come. In fact, it was clear to me that both of my particular ecological interests, extinctions and fire, were not only of relevance to Australian prehistory, to Aboriginal history, but to the future of the country and indeed the world. So my blogging (I later added writing a blog monthly for a major Australian blog site on the ABC) and column writing, as the decade progressed, became more and more focused on trying to lead the public to understand the dangers we faced. I was hammering on the door marked 'Public Intellectual'.

If many Aboriginal issues remain to be solved – in fact, pretty much the same issues that needed to be solved in the decades I was putting every effort into helping solve them – then it is also true that unless we stop climate change, and the parallel damage that is being caused by the use of fire, tree clearing, overfishing and hunting, the pollution of rivers and oceans, then none of us have a future. So I kept niggling away, doing what I could.

What else did I do in this concentrated decade? I took on the editing and production of our local community newspaper, using skills I first learned when tackling the institute journal backlog in 1985. A challenge each month to get the material, meet the (self-imposed) deadline, find advertising to support the self-funded production, but compared to the publishing activity in my distant past it was a doddle, easy peasy, walk in the park. Anyway, it was a contribution I could make to the community, and I think community is increasingly important, will be more so as we all face the difficult times ahead. Also reached, I guess, the peak of my sheep-breeding program with a three year stint as president of the breed association, after years of being secretary, and years of being involved with genetic issues on an industry-wide basis (drawing on my old zoology training). Thankfully, my emotional well-being had been topped up in these years, because it was about to be drained.

Ten years after I left the institute, I had a heart attack. I didn't know I had, though. A year or two earlier, I had been involved in a horrible event over the road when a man dropped dead of a heart attack a long way from medical help. But nothing as dramatic as that with me, or I wouldn't be here to tell the tale. None of that movie stuff of clutching the chest, sweating, pains down the left arm, collapsing in a heap. No, just a kind of burning sensation, weak enough to make me think of indigestion, strong enough to make me have to sit down until it had passed. If you get anything like that, go to hospital. If they tell you it's indigestion, it's less embarrassing than being dead (I suppose).

I did, eventually, the burning becoming more frequent and insistent, and there I was, having test after test that showed nothing. I had pretty much been told to go home, nothing wrong with you, hypochondriac, was getting my clothes back on, somewhat embarrassed, when, rather in the way that in American movies an innocent man is about to be hanged when a sheriff rushes in clutching the last-minute reprieve from the governor, except in reverse, the one last test was positive and I was taking my clothes back off again. Operation a few days later.

I was being operated on, magically watching my blood vessels on a TV screen, my mind wonderfully concentrated, a small object being poked along them, and then a rush of dye being released. And going nowhere as it hit an obstruction. Soon opened, by the magic of stent insertion up a long thin tube from the groin. A day flat on my back, talking to a chap who I was sharing a room with, whose earlier experience with dye being sprayed had revealed the need not for a stent but an open heart operation and quadruple bypass. I felt a bit of an imposter as I escaped hospital food the following day, but not in a bad way. The only after-effects of the operation were frequent nightmares – often the aftermath of traumatic events, I find.

Finally, this was the decade when I got seriously into family history. One surprising fact I immediately discovered was that my name should be Orton, not Horton. In 1870, Thomas Orton walks into Edensor church in the English potteries region (the family were pottery factory workers and miners) to get married as an Orton and walks out as a Horton, the vicar, having assumed a dropped aitch, has helpfully added it to the marriage certificate. Like Snout, my ancestors were playing with identity (his father remained an Orton), and I kept on doing that as I went along.

I felt like I had walked from the eighteenth century coal mines of the English Midlands and the eighteenth-century farms of Yorkshire all the way to the twenty-first century farm in Australia. Walked along with a few people to begin with but gathering more and more numbers as I travelled through the decades, until there were hundreds of relatives all around me in a virtual cloud, cheering me on.

There have been, along my personal road, a number of blockages, obstructions, dead ends, false starts, new beginnings. Most of them, I guess, fixed with a mental stent, some needing major bypass work. There have always been a cloud of family, friends, supporters, to help me over the hurdles, across the swollen rivers, through the closed doors. And a few other people, emphatically not friends, wanting to drown me.

They say that the best revenge against people who have done you wrong is living well. Not true at all. People who say that have never really experienced the efforts of bad people. Marcus Aurelius has it right as he so often does: 'The best revenge is to be unlike him who performed the injury.' Still, I was basically living well in the new millennium, but it wouldn't last long.

So I'd had a heart attack. Okay. Still alive apparently. You know how you wonder, in idle moments when you are young (in your fifties), which human ending has your name on it? Are you going to be run over by a bus, eaten by shark, get incurable diseases from a dishcloth, fall off a cliff, get cancer, die of a heart attack? I had had the heart attack bullet. And survived. I was bulletproof. Come on, Mr Reaper Man, is that all you've got? Anyway, that was it, my brush-with-death story. Get on with life.

But a couple of years later, I visited my GP routinely for a new prescription for an anti-cholesterol drug. I was an old-hand heart attack survivor now, take two pills each day and Bob's your uncle (as indeed he was, which made that saying a family joke that never grew stale when I was young). Call in, see my nice doctor, have a chat, through the worst news you could get as a sixty-something fellow, bit of an old hand at this surviving medical emergency business. Something of a medical veteran, got the prescription ribbons to prove it, got the scar.

Anyway, while I was there, I casually mentioned that a few days earlier, while showering, I had noticed a lump on my leg. Nothing much, old scar tissue from collision with sheep, or perhaps a cyst. Nothing to worry about, eh, Suzie? Within a minute or two of her checking it, she was on phone to get me an ultrasound scan and a blood test, refusing, somewhat ominously, to take part in my light-hearted banter about collisions with sheep.

A week later, having had the blood test, I walked into the medical imaging rooms, feeling a little as if I was walking along edge of cliff. But hey, what could go wrong, had my intimation of mortality, heart was where it was at. This was a nothing, the unimportant lump of an ageing hypochondriac. But it was a morning that would turn out to be a microcosm of the next six months of my life.

First came the ultrasound. Not unpleasant, rather like a massage in fact. Sort of interesting, looking at screen, oh, they're blood vessels, eh, and those are lymph nodes, a muscle, yes fine, bored now. Then a wait. Doctor on duty came in took a look at the scans. We chatted about them – blood vessels, lymph nodes et cetera.

'They are fine, aren't they?' I said.

'Are you a doctor?' he asked, having no doubt used the question to shut up nosy patients many times.

'Yes,' I said.

'Anyway, yes, they were fine. Fine, er, wait, bit of enlargement there. No, look normal to me.'

'So,' I asked, 'I don't need a needle biopsy, do I?' (a grim but remote possibility my GP had mentioned.)

'No, no, don't think so. Looks OK.'

'Thank goodness,' I said, my hypochondria confirmed, preparing to swing legs off side of surgical bed.

But he was still glancing at the scans. Still, it seemed, thinking. 'No, you better have the needle biopsy to be on safe side,' he said, and my heart sank. Back he came with a long needle, rather in the way they do in cartoons. I hadn't realised he would need to do it using the blurry ultrasound to get his bearings, and that that meant he would need to take a number of shots, in both groins, before getting the places he wanted to sample just right. To say the process left you dreaming of a wisdom tooth extraction for light relief would be to underestimate the unpleasantness.

I staggered out, some time later, feeling like the victim of an attack by a homicidal maniac with a stiletto. Wrote in my diary that night, 'Scary ultrasound, even more scary, and painful, aspiration of four lymph nodes. Am I in big trouble? Feeling like it.'

Two days later, I had the results, my GP, unprecedentedly, phoning, so I knew immediately it was bad news. Wrote in my diary, 'I am given death sentence – lymphoma.' I had fallen off the edge of the cliff and was on my way down. A couple of days later, on a Sunday, I wrote, 'My last day of normal life.'

I was plunging down into a medical world much scarier than cardiology. Finding, as I kept falling, that I had lost control of my life. Instead of making my own decisions as to what, where, how, when, why, I would do things, they were made for me. I rushed from one set of medical rooms to another. My GP gave me a very sombre prognosis. I go for another blood test, then a CT scan. Then meet a surgeon who is (the speed and urgency of all this was frightening) rushing me into a full lymph node surgical biopsy three days later.

Next day, yet another blood test, ECG, X-ray. I get the CT scan but note in my diary, 'Avoid opening test results. Don't want to know until after I get through [surgery] tomorrow.'

Tomorrow was a long hard day, surgery being delayed to late in the afternoon, so I had nearly twenty-four hours without food or drink. Home that night with lump missing.

On the next Sunday, trying not to think about results, I wrote, 'Last day before fate is decided.'

The next day the fall down the cliff continued. Like William Dunbar,

> I that in heill wes and gladnes,
> Am trublit now with gret seiknes,
> And feblit with infermitie;
> Timor mortis conturbat me.

More blood tests and X-ray (I had fallen heavily and thought I had broken my wrist; it seemed a minor thing). GP tells me CT shows cancer is all through lymph system from groin to neck but not other organs. This seems curiously not quite bad enough for my fears.

The next day, life matches fears. As I record,

> Trying to get myself together mentally. Phone call comes from hospital. I am wanted in urgently, right now, for testing and treatment. We hurriedly get ready and rush in by about 5 p.m. Checked in. An incredibly noisy night in four-person ward. The chap in next bed, with stomach cancer, has developed lung infection. They fight all night to save him, and do, while he vomits constantly, coughs, hiccups, burps, groans; machines beep, voices question, shoes flap noisily on floor. If I wasn't in a bad enough state before, I was by end of night.

The next morning, I am scheduled to at last see the oncology specialist, find out details of my fate. Again my diary tells it best.

> Have a gated volume study of heart. Tin injected, then radioactive stuff. Heart is going well it seems. Then specialist finally comes with a gaggle of residents, interns, nurses. Gloomy faces as he examines me [and tells his students I have large cell lymphoma, very fast growing, fatal et cetera]. Then he asks if they have the surgical biopsy report yet. Yes, we do. 'Follicular lymphoma'. Faces light up. Specialist loses interest. I'm just a boring easily curable common case now it seems. Fine by me. Feel relieved but confused. Seems the needle biopsy was indeed inaccurate for some reason. No sleep again all night.

The irony here was that my GP, in a rare attempt to cheer me up, had said that the needle biopsy could be inaccurate. Neither she nor I had believed her. Yet the bedside manner attempt at soothing had indeed been true. I had gone from having a lethally fast cancer, hence the rush to get me into hospital and start treatment, to having a slow treatable one. I had to stay in hospital two more days to have the unpleasant bone marrow biopsy and very unpleasant PET scan tests (which together would eventually show the cancer was worse than had been thought – into spleen and bone marrow) then home to await instructions on treatment, now seemingly nowhere near as urgent as it had been, but still reasonably urgent.

Two weeks later, I am back at hospital to see the specialist with all test results, although I see his registrar first.

Talk at length to registrar Sam who doesn't think I need treatment, just monitoring, as he explains at length. Then he calls in his boss, who, noting that the bone marrow is 30% involved and it is in my spleen, and I am over sixty, wants immediate treatment. All still part of rollercoaster this month. Then told have to have chemo. Then put into clinical trial testing new antibody (otherwise can't get antibody until after chemo has failed!). Roller coaster continues. All sounds awful with many needles and many side effects (when I tongue in cheek complain about hair loss they laughed). Might start on my birthday or day after. Happy birthday!

A week later, I have to see my heart specialist for an echo cardiogram, more or less okay with some valve leakage, but all paled into insignificance. Heart problems were so yesterday's news. The medical circus rolled on. Just after that, I went in for my cancer treatment orientation, where a nurse scared me witless with all the terrible side effects I could get, most of them starting off subtly and if not recognised able to kill you quickly. 'Cure sounds worse than disease and up to six months of it,' I note. She showed me around the treatment ward, where terribly sick-looking people are sitting on dentist-type chairs hooked up to bags of fluid with machines going beep. It was like a science fiction film and scared me even more.

A few days later, I am one of the people in the science fiction movie, although I look ridiculously healthy. Apart from the fact that the first round of treatment took some seven hours (because they go slow in case of side effects, and partly because I had a learner nurse), my life from then on followed a constant pattern. Hooked up via cannula in hand for three or four hours. Home, several days of taking steroid and anti-nausea tablets, the former making me very tired and headachy. A blood test a week later. Another blood test and visit to specialist a week after that. A few days feeling okay. Blood test. Back on to treatment chair. Over and over again.

I was lucky. There were no real side effects during the chemo itself, in spite of my fears after the first treatment; after-effects made life difficult but were put-up-able with; and the steroid effects were bearable though debilitating. My blood tests with one aberrant exception (which nearly frighteningly put a stop to the whole process after the first treatment) were normal throughout. Making it worthwhile was that within a day or two of first treatment, the glands in my neck were shrinking. The doctor later confirmed others were shrinking too. Another CT scan halfway through treatments confirmed they were all reduced in size.

And so it went on. I was trying to just concentrate on the finishing line. Of detaching myself sufficiently to take needle after needle, cannula after cannula, tablet after tablet, hardly flinching. And I had begun as a lifelong needle-phobe.

I got to the end of the eighteen weeks (six-treatment cycles) and it was clear all the glands were smaller. As was the spleen. I saw the specialist, who agreed I had gone well, but wanted two additional sessions just with the antibody treatment. Said to be more effective. Grin and bear it. At the end of that (during which a new irritating side effect had developed, I had to have another of the dreaded bone marrow biopsy and PET scan tests. Managed to grin and bear those, seeing the finishing tape of the marathon in clear sight.

Then I saw the specialist, to be plunged into depths again. While both tests showed a huge improvement, they also showed there was still some residual lymphoma. Instead of being home free, I could have a break of a couple of months and then go into a three-monthly antibody-only treatment for two more long years. Wasn't there an Olympic race once where someone stopped running, thinking they had finished, only to be told there was a mistake and there was still another lap to go? That was me. So there I was. Back to the ward and the same pleasant nurses, same ill patients, same chairs, same beeping, same bags. Betwixt and between. Not ill, not well. Not happy, not sad. Not starting, not finishing. At the end of the beginning, but not necessarily at the beginning of the end.

My feelings about cancer by the end of 2011 and into 2012 were that I had persevered and advanced. That I had done everything that was asked of me, followed the rule book, been brave, and that, rather like spending years working hard to prepare for a big exam or conference, in the end my efforts would be rewarded. I should have known better.

Some time into 2012 and my body was going haywire. In quick succession, I was in hospital for a week with pneumonia, then suffered originally undiagnosed (because of atypical symptoms) shingles which ulcerated my eyeballs as well as many other unpleasant things and nearly blinded me. So the oncologist decided to take me off the continuing treatments because they were having bad effects on my immune system.

The idea of taking me off treatment to see if it was the cause of the shingles and pneumonia was a good idea given the constant civil war between disease and chemotherapy in the battlefield of my body. But it turned out to be wrong. To positively eliminate the apparently unlikely comeback of lymphoma as the problem I was sent off for yet another of the dreaded PET scans.

This time, to add to the unpleasantness, my body broke the computers that run the scan, twice, and I was left lying there on the steel rails waiting while the technician rebooted all sixteen of them. Bit of an omen really (as was the sympathetic treatment of me, when she had seen the preliminary scan results, by the normally very unpleasant nurse who sets you up for the scan), had I believed in omens, as it turned out when I visited my now grim-faced oncologist to get the diagnosis.

The cancer was indeed back with a capital C, stronger than before, as if the poisons that had been thrown at it, like a monster in a fairy story, had merely made it bigger. Oh shit. The promise of five years', hell, ten years' remission if I behaved and had a whole lot of extra single chemo treatments, proved as unreliable as those end of the world prophecies we hear. Five years? Hadn't had five months remission, it being pretty clear the cancer had come roaring back more or less the day after my last multi-chemo treatment. Which meant, dire omen/prophecy that I was in Big Trouble with a capital T.

Because the background remained the earlier heart problem. My original chemo treatment left out one ingredient (that is, in the rather nasty acronyms, COP+R instead of CHOP+R) which could affect my heart. My oncologist decided she (I had by a lucky accident acquired a wonderful new oncologist Ann McDonald) wanted to have one more crack at my lymphoma with mainstream treatment before facing the catch-22s, and move to CHOP from COP. But before I could have that, my heart status needed checking with yet another scan (the radiation from two years of scanning becoming of some concern, at least to me) to see if it could withstand treatment with CHOP. All clear, and away we went.

Into a new oncology treatment room in a different hospital, with new, wonderful nurses. First cycle very very slow to make sure I didn't react badly to either the ingredient (the 'R') that had affected me last time, or the new ingredient. Six hours in one of those chairs was no fun. Nor the feeling of déjà vu from 2011, starting out on a series of nasty chemo treatments that stretched endlessly into the future, and, what was worse, carried none of the (in reality false) optimism this time that I was going to come out the other end more or less cured.

But no choice, really, so on I went. The side effects afterwards were worse this time, then made worse still when my neutrophil levels dropped (a common occurrence, leading to major immune system fears of infection, but it hadn't happened to me in the first treatment) and I had to have a bone marrow booster shot to follow up the chemo. Which had its own nasty side effects. You never feel well when you are going through chemo, as if you constantly have a set of minor, but debilitating, diseases. Lost all my hair this time, put on even more weight. On through four cycles over twelve weeks. Then a pause, followed by yet another PET scan (!) to see if the new treatment regime was effective.

Yes, yes, it was! The PET scan showed no activity distinguishable from background. Did I want to stop or have two more cycles to make sure? No-brainer really. Two more cycles then back to my oncologist, where a physical exam confirmed no glands enlarged now. She had, she thought (though with fingers literally crossed; her toes, I suspect, touching wood) given me a real remission this time. Don't call me, I'll call you, come and see me in three months, after your body, free of being injected with chemicals, has a chance to recover. It was all like the telegram from the governor arriving just as you are climbing the stairs to the gallows. I walked out into the sunshine feeling…? Feeling numb if truth be told.

There were two reasons for not being 'over the moon'. One was that after two years of treatment and illness, I just felt battered, mentally and physically. No more felt like doing a Toyota jump in the air than if I had just completed an Olympic marathon. Besides which, I wasn't being given a cure. Just like there is no such thing as a recovered alcoholic or an ex-smoker, there is no such thing as a cured lymphoma patient. What you are is in remission, a remission that may last only months, as with me initially, or indefinitely, but you can never think of yourself as totally cured.

The second reason I looked out into a sunlit day somewhat blankly was the wider context. While I was going through this cycle of treatment, I heard that another dear friend Kim McKenzie had lung cancer. The kind of news that hits you with a hammer blow. Another one has joined the club that you didn't want to join because it would have you as a member.

My old friend died, horribly, during one of the many treatments by which they try to keep inoperable lung cancer from flooding the lungs. I had seen him one last time at his home in the country, where he didn't have enough lung capacity to go for much of a walk. He was pleased for me that I was in remission, genuinely I am sure, but he knew he didn't have long. Ask not for whom the bell tolls.

Then in 2015 my great oncologist retired. Doom and gloom but she had carefully arranged for one of her students to take over, and that proved to be the also wonderful Emma. On our first meeting, with what seemed to me somewhat excessive honesty, she said, 'I can't cure you, you know.'

Yes, I did know that, intellectually, but, you know… She was proved right by the very next blood test and then scan. The lymphoma cells, after hibernating, like an Egernia lizard in winter, for a couple of years ('dormancy'), had lived to fight another day. They had, once again, come roaring back (my lymphoma was unusual; everyone's lymphoma is unique because all are based on your own DNA, blood as genetics after all, my father quite wrong about its importance – in that it looked like a slow form but behaved like a fast form – 'I do not know whether to call him a slow lymphoma patient or a fast lymphoma patient.' Chemotherapy needed to begin immediately, catch it before it once again spread all through my body.

But the best laid plans of oncologists gang aft agley. My buggered body once again succumbed to pneumonia and I was back in hospital. Emma was having her baby, so I was in the care of another of Ann's students, the wonderful Maya. Pumped full of antibiotics, pumped full of fluids, the pneumonia wouldn't shift. A terrifying procedure where a very large needle was inserted into my chest cavity to draw off the some fluid to see if there was a secondary infection. Kidney function and heart performance being anxiously watched. It was touch and go to meet a deadline for getting chemotherapy underway again. I finally made it with minutes to spare, discharged from one ward, walking across the road to chemotherapy treatment rooms.

After the twin failures of COP and CHOP, this time Emma was trying something completely different, something my chemotherapy nurses hadn't heard of and were unfamiliar with. Something called Bendomustine, which was derived from the same chemical as the mustard gas of World War I which had killed and maimed so many poor buggers in the trenches, and which in 1943 had killed hundreds of sailors and civilians in Bari in Italy, when an American ship loaded with the stuff had been bombed. An American, Dr Alexander, studied the situation, and in spite of great military secrecy, discovered that the mustard gas had, in saltwater/oil solution, caused not only terrible burns but shrank lymph nodes and wiped out white blood cells. He immediately realised the implications for cancer treatment, and it was thanks to the explosion and him that seventy years later, I was going to live. Consequences, eh?

Anyway, one man's poison and all that. What choice was there? I was still determined to place my complete trust in my oncologist and nurse, so away we went, back in the old three-weekly routine for about six months. Another advantage of my liquid mustard gas was that it was said to have fewer side effects than the other treatments.

But suddenly, on about the third cycle, the chemical began to hurt going in, burning my veins. Kate, in charge of the chemotherapy ward where I now had treatment, put the next cannula into the inside of the elbow instead of the hand. That worked, and she used that method for the next few cycles. But the aftermath was scar tissue in the veins of the elbow, normally reserved for taking blood samples. As a result, I would now find it difficult to provide the three-monthly blood samples. And in general, the after-effects were very sore arms, the irritation to the veins persisting, with nerve damage leading eventually to loss of sensation in the hands and feet.

Still, it was done, finished. Blood test and scans showed good results. The mustard gas had mowed down the enemy soldiers very effectively it seemed. And just in time for my seventy-first birthday in April 2016. Odd that the best birthday present was the end of the third lot of chemotherapy in five years, over half those five years spent in a chemotherapy chair with a cannula stuck in my hand.

And curiously, my experiences with cancer have shown me how wonderful it is to have a team of people supporting you, treating you, helping you all they can, willing you to get better. What a contrast to my institute years where a team of people were doing their best to damage me, destroy me, obstruct me, willing me to fail. But in a wider sense the medical roller coaster of hope and despair, joy and sadness, sickness and health, was much like the *Encyclopaedia* years and indeed much like my whole intellectual career.

Over six years' remission so far as I write this, which means I don't know whether I have cancer or don't. Am I a normal person who used to have cancer, or a cancer patient who is now cured? When Emma passed me on to Maya at the end of 2020, did she say, 'You'll like this chap, he's a former cancer patient'?

16

The roads more taken

'Brief is man's life and small the nook of the earth where he lives; brief, too, is the longest posthumous fame, buoyed only by a succession of poor human beings who will very soon die and who know little of themselves, much less of someone who died long ago.' – Marcus Aurelius

Watching Donald Trump in action has brought back memories of my experiences in the institute. There was a real world, a real series of events, and then there was an imaginary world which was the one people were being told about. Because information flow was so controlled from above, it was possible to sell fake news. Even now, a quarter of a century later, people who were there, reading this account, will be astonished, find it impossible to reconcile with the imaginary world they were sold, will be convinced I am inventing a story, or am misremembering, will be told perhaps, by others, that that is the case. At present, the chunk of imaginary history, written from the fake news of the institution, sits there corrupting the real history (I was told by someone at the institute a year or so ago, when I asked her if she knew about the history of the *Encyclopaedia*, and why I was so bitter and angry about it twenty-five years later, that all she had heard was that there were 'funding problems'). Reality has always been important to me.

Looking back at the *Encyclopaedia*, a quarter-century on, gives me much needed perspective on the way it affected, not my life at the time – that was bitterly evident as it was happening – but my lifetime of academic work. Context is also provided these days by new internet sites on which I can compare my achievements with those of my contemporaries in terms of numbers of publications and numbers of citations.

The *Encyclopaedia* took some nine years of my peak intellectual life. My output in it was equivalent to, say, 500 research papers, or perhaps ten books. Yet because of the attacks on it during production, that output was ignored academically, in spite of the fact that it had been deliberately written to be used (among other purposes) as an undergraduate reference source, and a reference source for professionals, because it incorporated all the most recent research to 1994.

Yet it has not been used like that because of the damage inflicted on it, the misrepresentation of what it was about, what it consisted of, and the refusal of leading academics, consequently, to even look at it seriously and perhaps find their perceptions challenged. No one reviewed it in research journals, no one used it as a reference in their own publications. In one notable case, a work published by one of the advisory editors just after the *Encyclopaedia* didn't refer to his own work in the *Encyclopaedia*. This was a general pattern. People who had supposedly written major essays summarising the state of their discipline in 1993, and supervised all the essays related to that core essay, never referred to them academically. And because they didn't, others didn't and a massive review of Aboriginal studies never became part of academic discourse in Australia.

I wasn't Aboriginal, so there was nothing unusual about my editorship and I gained no media or public interest. On the other hand, it was a work all about the whole range of Aboriginal culture and society, and was written in a style to appeal to the general public, not a purely academic work, so it gained no praise from the university world. Once again, I was caught betwixt and between, hoist on the barbed wire separating C.P. Snow's 'two cultures', choking in mustard gas.

The map *Aboriginal Australia* suffered a similar fate. Having taken six years of my life, it is rarely if ever referred to academically, though it appears on walls over Australia. The map was conceived and constructed as an update of Norman Tindale's map, with decades of additional work in linguistics, anthropology, archaeology, added in to work Tindale had done in the 1930s and 1950s. Tindale's map has been referred to, cited, tens of thousands of times since it appeared in final form in 1974. So why hasn't the Horton map? Because it was attacked relentlessly by institute council members throughout its production and in its published form down to demands that it be pulped after publication.

To give some idea of the nonsense involved, here is one snippet I managed to hear about. One senior member of institute administration, in a meeting after there had been a session of *Encyclopaedia*, map and Horton bashing, turned to another senior member who had been silent to that point of the discussion and asked, 'What about you? Are you happy with the map for your area?'

'No, no.' He wasn't happy either.

Had I been there, I would have said, 'So you mean you are not happy with the work of xxx [who had written, in the nineteenth century, the only account of the particular language and group]?' The map, of course, didn't present my view of the group concerned, but simply reported on the classic work which had been in existence for a hundred years or so. The person commenting had no knowledge of his own on work in the area, nor did he seem to have strong links with Aboriginal people in the area. In other words, his opinion on this one spot on the Horton map was both worthless and irrelevant, and yet the others present took it as yet another indication of the 'problems' with the map.

I wasn't present at that meeting or at any other meeting of the institute administration. When the governance of the institute had been changed, the new council had decided that institute staff would have no direct access to the council, all communications in either direction would be conducted by the principal. So, over all the years I was creating map and *Encyclopaedia*, this small group of people in council held endless discussions about the project, made dozens of decisions, without ever *once* consulting with me, asking me for explanations, discussing the effect of decisions, nothing. It was as if I was trying to communicate with a room full of deaf people who refused to lip read, and I didn't know sign language.

The map escaped being pulped by a miracle. However, council insisted that a 'warning' notice be added, in spite of the fact that the map already had (they seemed unaware of this, and nobody informed them) a lengthy disclaimer notice. The council notice was that the map was 'not suitable for use in native title claims', which was the purported concern they had used to finally smash it with. In fact, it was clearly not a map that would or could be used in individual native title claims – a moment's thought would have made that obvious had anyone tried. It could have been used to provide general context to such claims (and in fact was by ATSIC later, making a complete mockery of the council reaction), in conjunction with the *Encyclopaedia*, which provided the references which would have themselves been used.

Native title claims rely on primary sources. The map wasn't a primary source and therefore concerns about its misuse in claims were (perhaps deliberately) wrong. On the other hand, it was a lead-in to primary sources, unlike Tindale's map, and was much more up-to-date, and therefore would in fact have been useful in relation to claims.

But the effect of the council notice (and my disclaimer, forced on me to try to counter the attacks that had come from them) was to suggest to anyone looking at it that it was not a serious or accurate map. The Tindale map had no such notice. In addition, once my name was totally removed from some editions of the map, and even when reinstated, was invisible when the map was mounted on a wall; it appeared to be anonymous, just a general institute production, not the result of six years' hard research by a single named author. So it wasn't referred to academically, in spite of selling many thousands of copies, and there were people, including some involved in the writing of the *Encyclopaedia*, who continued to refer in their own publications to the Tindale map, in spite of its known errors and omissions which had been corrected in the Horton map.

So nine years of incredibly hard and stressful work for…nothing. I didn't benefit financially from the project – I was not permitted to have the copyright on *Encyclopaedia*, map, or CD-ROMs, nor was I permitted to keep any of the money from the prizes they had won. I was, I was told, employed by the institute, so the institute, which had done its best to stop the project, owned it all. Useless to argue that I hadn't been employed to to do the project, that it had been done in addition to the work I was employed to do, which had continued. (The principal actually reduced my institute salary when I was about halfway through the *Encyclopaedia*.)

Nor did I benefit academically. The project had been hammered while it proceeded, and no promotion of it was permitted afterwards, so I remained invisible. Another chunk of my life had just vanished like rain on a desert. So when I wrote my new book and had it published (delayed by ten years because of the *Encyclopaedia* and therefore seven years behind Tim Flannery's book, which had by then firmly established itself as the last word), I wasn't known. The publishers didn't push it, didn't promote it, and I didn't have a name which would lead to publicity generating itself. So it too was born to waste its fragrance.

Chemotherapy damaged me more than the lymphoma. It produces immediate side effects and long-lasting, sometimes permanent, after-effects. My score included osteoporosis, neuropathy, colitis, pneumonia, shingles, cataracts, blocked eustachian tubes causing increased deafness, numerous skin cancers, lactose intolerance, loss of senses of taste and smell, chemo brain, weight gain, scarred veins, muscle pains, gout, and one or two others. I miss the sense of smell, feel isolated from the world around me.

My treatment by the institute similarly left after-effects on my work and career.

I guess more generally life itself leaves after-effects everything that happens to you, everything that is done to you by people, everything you do in life has consequences, and by the time you get to your seventies, those after-effects have accumulated and added to the chemotherapy ones.

The cells in your body turn over every seven years or so. At the age of seventy, you are, like Dr Who, ten regenerations removed from your original self. You are also seventy years of angst removed from the young boy playing happily, learning with awe what a big world was out there, full of endless possibilities, and trying to plan, and dreaming of, how to make a contribution to that world. Seventy years of gradually absorbing wisdom and knowledge from the world around me, using it to try and make a difference.

To stay in remission (not cured!) from lymphoma, you have to placate the crab god with a three-monthly ritual in which you make a blood sacrifice. Some poor bugger has to read the auguries in my blood, just as I had once done just over fifty years earlier. The auguries are handed to the high oncologist to read the future, the past being indicated by a pattern of dark and light numbers on a sacred piece of vellum (sorry, computer screen, carried away there).

Hopefully, the number of dark (outside the normal range) numbers gradually decreases, with each one heading towards the light of normality. With that settled, the oncologist then conducts a question and response catechism, reminiscent of the one from the Rechabites I knew as a child. Any night sweats? No night sweats. Any lumps? No lumps. Any illnesses? No illnesses. And so on. Finally you are stretched out on the altar where the high oncologist examines you for bodily imperfections, see if you meet Plato's standard of perfection.

And then you are all clear, home free, in the land of the living, once again. Until the next three-monthly exam. In the waiting room, all around you as you wait, anxiously, for the reading of the auguries, are other people going through similar cycles. Anonymous, all of us, brought together only by chance mutations, reduced to the sole status, the sole uniform, of 'cancer patient'. In a previous life, they were doctors, engineers, farmers, teachers, politicians, artists, writers, truck drivers, footballers, students, archaeologists. Distinguished careers, awards, professorships, all invisible. Just like I had been made academically invisible by the actions of a few people in the institute.

I developed anxiety. I began treatment with chemicals, unsuccessfully, but in 2017 the amazing Anna started to help me sail my leaking boat into harbour, or at least into sight of the lighthouse. I began blogging (mainly poetry) anonymously, commenting on some political threads anonymously, doing some online university courses. All got me functioning mentally again.

In 2018, the wonderful GP Natasha took over my general medical care, coordinating all the specialists who were taking arms against my sea of medical troubles. And, like the beat of a slow muffled drum, comes the three-monthly check-up. Am I still in the business of living? Every clear day doesn't mean you can see forever, but you can see for three months. So on I go, three months at a time. But when you think about it, that's really all any of us do. And now, with coronavirus, that time interval has shrunk to days.

I have told my own story almost purely as that of my education and working career. But I could have written my farming life, my life with family and friends, my life in the medical system, my life with animals, my social life, my cultural life, my life in publishing, my fieldwork life, and so on. Not all of those headings would make a book as big as this one, but all of them are only hinted at in this volume (which, big as it is, averages about three words per day of my life).

But still, this part of my life of the mind, my career, has been a major one, and my aim in compiling it, as much as I had a conscious aim, has been to take stock, to balance the book of my life. Have I worked to capacity, finally satisfying the predictions of Harry and answering the criticisms of Howieson, Hoad and Hos (note all the 'aitches' like the one added to my surname in the 1870s)? And am I happy with the way my career went (a question Rob Paterson recently asked), or should I have done things differently?

I could have done more, squeezed out some other publications, tackled my third book earlier, gone to more conferences. But not much more, especially when the *Encyclopaedia* drained away the ten years of my prime. I could have sucked up to those above me in the hierarchy, and avoided disagreeing with leading archaeologists. But could I have lived with myself? No, of course not. Should I have resolved the conflict between arts and science in my mind rather than doing both? Yes, but I'd have been bored.

Were there things I should have done differently, and would they have made a difference, provided alternative train rides through the world? Yes, of course, although surprisingly few. I should never have watched TV in 1961, should, with more effort, and based on my results earlier in the year, have had four distinctions in the Leaving, and arrived at university with more of a head of steam.

I should never have done physics and maths in first year, chemistry in second year, or physiology in third year, and instead should have popped in some first and second year courses in botany, geology, history. I would then have done much better in third year and arrived in honours year as a stand-out from topping third year, perhaps changing the perceptions which led to my second-class honours.

In addition, not doing physiology would have prevented me being offered the job in Melbourne, instead arriving in Armidale a year earlier, making a huge difference to my state of mind and resulting in me completing the PhD a year earlier. That might have resulted in me finding a job somewhere, or I might have stayed in Armidale an extra two years and then still come across the institute job.

In York, I could have thought quickly and told Mark Williamson that, yes indeed, I would love to do a joint paper with him, and was looking forward to learning from him. And gone on to a career in York.

In archaeology, my fate was sealed by the manner of my appointment and the context of the institute. But I could, I suppose, have been more flattering to the big guns, attended more seminars where I asked admiring questions, performed at more conferences (instead of staying on the fringes, not wanting to impose on people if they didn't come to me). In publishing, I was always standing back at book launches, having done the work to set them up, so that the author would have the spotlight. Another note for young self: be visible.

I should have also tried to acquire mentors, but there were few on offer. Abigail 'May' Alcott struggled to fulfil her artistic ambitions. Unlike her sister, May had help along the way. 'She is a fortunate girl, and always finds some one to help her as she wants to be helped,' wrote Louisa in her journal in 1864. 'Wish I could do the same, but suppose as I never do that it is best for me to work and wait and do all for myself.' As did I.

From 1990 on, things are pretty much fixed. You might think that I could have said no to the *Encyclopaedia*, and I probably could. But the outcome would have been much the same. I already had the experience of the then principal supposedly being the editor of the institute journal, which resulted in absolutely nothing being done for two years until I took it over. The *Encyclopaedia* would have been the same. The institute could have named a figurehead, but the extent of their involvement would have been that their name went on the cover, while I did exactly the same amount of researching, writing, editing, designing, programming, fund raising. So I had to put my hand up and from then on, given the people involved, the ten years that followed were inevitable. What I hadn't imagined, though, is that I would do all the work and they would then take my name off the map, but, hey, some things are just too way out to imagine.

After that, the publishing treatment of my next book was inevitable; there was nothing I could do to get the publishers to promote it properly. And after that my blogging succeeded on *Huffington Post* and the ABC, but both organisations gradually changed and were no longer available for my writing. *HuffPost* started rejecting any of my articles that criticised religion or right-wing politics, so I just stopped, no point in protest. The ABC, or rather its opinion site *The Drum*, also started rejecting some of my articles, but then I did protest (more in sorrow than anger; I was a few months into my first year of chemotherapy) to Jonathan Green, who had become site editor.

3 June 2011 7.47a.m.

Jonathan
    I don't know if either of the pieces I sent and re-sent yesterday

are being seriously considered but I wish to withdraw both of them from consideration.

A little while after writing to you two new pieces appeared on *The Drum*, by Lapkin and Phelps, which have caused me to reconsider my position.

For many months now I have been concerned about the great volume of IPA propaganda (there is, actually, no other word for it) appearing on *The Drum*. Absolutely unlimited instant access it seemed while at the same time I (and I assume others) was having every second piece or so knocked back, and the accepted ones delayed for weeks. I kept persisting. Partly because I knew that every one of my posts that has appeared in the last three years or so has attracted hundreds of comments, many of them extremely flattering, and it was clear I had a receptive audience. But also partly because I thought, modestly, that I was helping provide a tiny bit of contrast to the IPA stuff, and that if writers like me dropped out they would hold the field unchallenged. Silly I know, but that was my state of mind.

That was until the Lapkin and Phelps pieces appeared. These two are so outrageous, so vicious, so nasty, towards Greens and Scientists, that even the most virulent shock jock or Australian columnist would feel a little embarrassed by them. Yet here they are, on the ABC, given the ABC seal of approval by being accepted for publication, presented matter-of-factly as if they are part of civilised discourse along with all the rest.

After a sleepless night thinking about this I can do nothing else but refrain from publishing on *The Drum* in future. I regret this, I have enjoyed my time on the blog, have been challenged to come up with new ideas and analyses, have had excellent feedback, have been very appreciative of my dealings with Catherine and Aimee. But I will not any longer appear on *The Drum* and therefore help give credibility, by what ever small amount my presence might contribute, to the hateful outpourings of Phelps and Lapkin. I doubt in fact that I will even bother visiting in future.

I realise this is a futile gesture, and that my presence or absence is of little concern to you. But I have my values and beliefs, and this is a line I won't cross.

Jonathan replied that he was sorry to see me go, would welcome back any time, but the site had to be 'broad church'. And that was that, I could no longer say, proudly, I was writing for the ABC.

A merchant in Baghdad sends his servant to the marketplace for provisions. Soon afterwards, the servant comes home white and trembling and tells him that in the marketplace, he was jostled by a woman, whom he recognised as Death, who made a threatening gesture. Borrowing the merchant's horse, he flees at great speed to Samarra, a distance of about seventy-five miles (125 kilometres), where he believes Death will not find him. The merchant then goes to the marketplace and finds Death, and asks why she made the threatening gesture to his servant. She replies, 'That was not a threatening gesture, it was only a start of surprise. I was astonished to see him in Baghdad, for I have an appointment with him tonight in Samarra.'

With a few caveats then, my life ran on rails with no sidings or rail junctions where a direction could be changed – I had to be a writer, no choice; writing was like breathing. Much the same with the cancer really – at some point in my life, I breathed in or handled something that damaged a cell, and from then on the next six years or so were inevitable. On the other hand, had I not smoked for the first half of my life would my cardiac artery have blocked? Conversely, had I not forced myself to stop smoking in 1990, would the heart attack have been fatal? Cause and effect. My close friend Kim McKenzie (whose death contributed greatly to my bad cancer years) with inoperable lung cancer, near the end said to me that a year earlier he had fought a grass fire over the road and wondered if breathing in the smoke had caused the cancer! He had been a heavy smoker of cigarettes for over forty years at that point.

The Jesuits say, 'Give me a child until the age of seven and we will have them for life' (that is, in the church). Much truth in that but more generally it means that the values you absorb from parents, grandparents, other relatives, friends, literature, good or bad, will stay with you for life.

Similarly, my quest to find the schoolmates of my last two years of high school (that time when everything seemed possible), and the life stories revealed as a consequence, suggests that I say, 'Tell me what the teenager was like at seventeen, what teachers they have had, and I will make some predictions about their life for the next sixty years.' A number of us have taken side roads, diversions, only to find ourselves, almost inexorably, drawn back to a particular career. In relation to teachers and the group I was closest to, it is interesting that so many of us have been drawn into careers in the biological sciences of some kind, as a result of Mary Critch's influence (and to a lesser extent Alan Strahan's). And in having all those careers, we have all necessarily had the ability to write (thanks, Stan Richards) and perform in public (thanks, Charlotte Bruce).

So this has been an effort to keep on nodding terms with the person I used to be (still am, I think, mostly). And an accounting of the heroes and villains that have peppered my life. And an attempt to see if I agree with Stephen Graves, who told me is happy with his career, content with what he has done (and who is right to be). So, what was I trying to do, and do I rest content?

I was fascinated by maps from an early age (which also explained my interest in stamps). I would pore over maps tracing imaginary voyages I might take, countries I might visit. I loved old maps showing how the world once was, new maps showing how it was now, maps with topography, maps with events marked in position, maps with roads and railways, maps with vegetation. It was a response to growing up in Perth with its one-dimensional (to me) geography, its lack of visitors from outside, the zero chance (I thought), of ever travelling even to other parts of Australia, let alone overseas. It was also a response to being marinated in a family history that was in England, not Australia, and of wallowing in books and toys that reinforced that identity.

My choice of biogeography was a further reflection of my obsession. Receiving specimens from all over the world and plotting their origins on maps was really a more sophisticated extension of my childhood interest. As was my later interest in the organisation of Aboriginal Australia and the origins of its people.

But I could not have dreamed of being one of the fabulous mapmakers who I had marvelled at as I grew up. And then I was, a dream come true, and I had created a thing of beauty, and a great contribution to the world of map making. It was a Horton map, and then it wasn't. Now an anonymous map that just flashed into existence, uncradled.

I began my career with work on taxonomy and biogeography. Not earth-shattering, but I took on two lizard genera that hadn't been reviewed in eighty years, and did the best I could with museum specimens and no possibilities of the internal anatomical or DNA work that is now so common. Taxonomy and biogeography are still important in a world hell-bent on destroying as much of the fauna and flora we evolved with as it can before the destruction backfires and destroys us too. We need to know what is where if we are to have any chance of keeping track and trying to stem the flow of extinction.

Similarly, my work on megafauna extinction is important in showing us what can happen in a world getting hotter. And it is important to know that the loss of all these species is due to climate change not to human predation (that is to 'nature' not 'nurture'), if we are to show people what horrors we are in for in a warming Australia. In addition, I have tried to show people that Aborigines didn't use fire in a large-scale way sufficient to cause habitat change. This grossly mistaken idea (called 'fire-stick farming' by Rhys Jones) is adding to the damage caused by climate change, farming and development, as people burn the remaining forests and woodlands. But I have been disappointed to find that people quote my work, apparently without reading it, and either (a) refer to it as one of a list of researchers who support the idea that Aboriginal use of fire was important, or (b) recognise that I oppose the idea but simply dismiss me as being wrong without discussion. Ah, if only I had written the book earlier. Ah, if only the *Encyclopaedia* had been permitted to give me a public profile.

If there has been an overriding philosophy to my work, it has been to show and celebrate the extraordinary people and culture that occupied this continent for perhaps as much as 50,000 years before 1788, but to have that celebration firmly based in reality, not a mythologising of an imaginary golden age of noble savages with superhuman powers and knowledge. This isn't a philosophy that leads to popularity either. In particular, I believe that the null hypothesis in studies of Australian ecology is that any change (for example, extinction, fire) is the result of natural processes not human intervention.

And finally I have learned, believe, that nothing you do in the environment is cost-free (just as there is no chemotherapy without side effects); everything you do in the environment has a consequence. That is another philosophy (in relation for example to 'hazard reduction') that has not made me popular with people who believe the world around us is infinitely malleable. I've always had a view of history as being a real series of events with a real series of cause and effect with a real collection of people who said and did actual things, and it was my job to try to set the record straight, change from mythology to history.

Ultimately, my work has been unique because I never did resolve the dichotomy between science and the arts, and therefore approached all the questions about prehistory and the environment simultaneously from two points of view, rather in the way glasses with a red lens and a blue lens give a three-dimensional scene, something no one else was doing or has done. And I approached such questions with an intellect which was the result of nature and nurture.

Throughout my life, I have always tried to follow Dante's advice ('Think of your breed: for brutish ignorance your mettle was not made; you were made men, to follow after knowledge and excellence'), hammering on the door of professionalism, not content to be an amateur dabbler. I was determined to be the best in my university education. After coming third in third year and honours, I picked myself up, started all over again (as I would do so many times in my life and, as F. Scott Fitzgerald said, 'strength shows not only in the ability to persist, but the ability to start over'), still determined to do do my best. In my research on reptiles, I set out to do the best that could be done with limited resources. When I moved into archaeology, I was determined to be the best, solve the big questions. I was determined the *Encyclopaedia* would be the best thing of its kind ever done (including the map and electronic versions). I wanted my book to reset the debate on environmental prehistory. I also set out to bring a scientific approach to sheep breeding and be the best sheep breeder of the best sheep ever. Finally, I have tried to make this memoir the best ever written, or at least one of the best, and the easiest to read (easy reading is damn hard writing, as Hawthorne said).

So, all worthwhile, and I'm glad I did it, made a contribution, am content, within myself, that I did my best, persevered and advanced. But I'm no saint, and it would have been nice to have a little more public recognition. A few days after I began at the institute, Peter Ucko's secretary asked me what I wanted to achieve at the institute. Still having little idea of how to go about archaeozoology, and less idea of what the institute was about, I couldn't say anything concrete, so I said, 'I want to achieve recognition for who I am and what I achieve.' I failed in that ambition, and it would have been nice, at some time in the following forty-five years to be, if not showered with honours, then to have at least one of a chair (but a chair in zoology or archaeology, that is the question), fellowship of an academy (and Science or Humanities, how could I decide?), an honorary degree or two, perhaps, like Henrietta Lacks, a posthumous statue, something to underline my identity. But if I was, in my mind, hammering on the doors of recognition, then clearly no one was listening.

Neither fame nor posthumous fame going to happen now. Marcus Aurelius has the thought,

> Give yourself a gift: the present moment. People out for posthumous fame forget that the Generations To Come will be the same annoying people they know now. And just as mortal. What does it matter to you if they say x about you, or think y?

17

Consequences

'And in general it was a great pleasure all the time I staid here to see how I am respected and honoured by all people; and I find that I begin to know now how to receive so much reverence, which at the beginning I could not tell how to do.' – Samuel Pepys

My years in remission from 2016 were a time for recovering my emotional well-being. Just as well. The summer of 2019–2020 in southern Australia was a sharp taste and smell of the coming catastrophe of climate change. On this farm, dams that had held water comfortably for the previous twenty years began to dry more and more; some dried out completely. As I watched kangaroos and sheep trying to get water from these last few drops, I was reminded of my hypothesis about Lancefield, 25,000 years earlier. It was a last waterhole, I wrote, a place where megafauna congregated at the only water for miles around, then died as they ate out the small amounts of vegetation available.

In nearby mountains, tinder-dry vegetation ignited as a result of lightning or human stupidity, and fires began to burn all around this dry hill. Early in 2020, while those savage fires were burning in the Australian bush (sending clouds of smoke over this hill all summer; I smelled smoke every day, breathed in tiny smoke particles which months later would wreck my poor old lungs even more than they were by my cigarette smoking of sixty years earlier), a tiny virus, in the ultimate case of blowback to humans from cruelty to animals, jumped from animal to human in China. From that tiny inconsequential event, like the flapping of a moth's wings in Mandurah causing my mother's death, or the flapping of a butterfly's wings in Brazil causing a tornado in Texas, came chaos all over the world. Consequences.

The world had to shut down, humans had to isolate from each other. I had been isolated from the academic world, and from old school and university friends and more recent academic friends, so it has been no great shift for me. But sitting here, watching the world go by the window of my iPad, a couple of my past interests kept intruding on my consciousness, hammering on my mental door, firmly closed for some years.

The first of them brought back to the front of my mind my map. One of my many sins when I was creating it was that it was said I had totally misunderstood the nature of Aboriginal society (not of course being an anthropologist) and drawn a map in which there were 'tribes'.

Quite wrong, I was told, Australia wasn't North America. Pointless for me to protest that I knew all the debate about 'tribal organisation', that the map was in part an update of Tindale who had used 'tribes', that it would have been absolutely impossible to construct such a map at the 'clan' level, that I had deliberately produced a map with no hard lines around each group but had their colours fading into each other representing the porous contact areas between such groups (I doubt the critics had even noticed), and finally that this level of organisation was one of the major ones with which Aboriginal people today self-identified, and indeed one that anthropologists themselves tend to use for their own places of study!

No use, I was an idiot (not an anthropologist, although we are into tautology here), and this terrible map should be destroyed, this tribal thing was all wrong. James Knight's PhD criticised the map's structure.

Imagine my surprise then, when, having partially emerged from my isolation, I discovered that everyone in Australia was now referring to Aboriginal people as 'First Nations' people, based, I guess, on the North American terminology. And every time an Indigenous person is now mentioned in the news, they come with an identifier ('Barty's win is a significant one for First Nations people. A proud Ngarigo woman...) based on my map. I suppose this was some kind of vindication twenty-six years on, but I doubt there will be a flood of apologies from the institute through my email server. In late 2021, after NAIDOC Week used the map to encourage people to know who their local Aboriginal groups are, WA's Perth Airport 'has become the first major airport in the nation to acknowledge the Traditional Custodians of destinations across Australia. Boarding gates will now show both the commonly used name of the destination, along with the name of the Traditional Custodians of that place' (impossible to imagine when I first flew out of that airport in 1966), based on my map without referring to me by name. All these welcome developments (plus several artworks) stimulated by, depending on, the existence of the Horton map. Just as well it wasn't pulped twenty-five years ago.

The second development which had my old fingers itching for the keyboard was in relation to fire. Once upon a time, the desire foresters had to burn forests regularly was called 'control burning' until it became horribly obvious that little control was involved. So then it was changed to 'prescribed burning'. When ecologists and conservationists tried to point out that this regular burning was causing a lot of ecological damage, the answer was 'Aborigines used to do it so it is okay. Oh, and by the way, Australian plants are not just adapted to fire but need fire.' When studies showed that these things were not true (I wrote that 'to say Australian plants are adapted to fire is like saying that grass is adapted to a lawnmower' – some of them are, in fact, adapted to recovery after disasters like storm, flood, animal attack, drought, and, yes, fire), there needed to be another change of name, and suddenly, out of nowhere, 'cultural burning' appeared and was rapidly adopted by the media. Good stuff, culture, who could object to it? A new trendy name for 'fire-stick farming'.

You can only carry on with this 'cultural burning' approach by simply ignoring the lack of evidence for the practice and its effect, and proceeding on the basis that 'we know it to be true', rather in the way creationists work. And by suggesting there are more and bigger bushfires now simply because indigenous fire use stopped, while ignoring all the other changes (global warming, forestry, agriculture, weeds, hoofed animals, sources of fire) that have actually caused the increase. But it seems to be impossible to argue with this belief. My words fall on deaf ears. And I am too old, too unknown, to try to re-fight the battles I first began to fight forty years ago.

The consequences of my history since 1990 are that the Australian bush will continue to be burned, often, leaving me, isolated on my hill, a frustrated observer. And more generally, this 'cultural burning' meme is part of a growing anti-science movement (think creationism, the anti-vax movement, the climate change denial warriors), in this case rejecting 200 years of Australian archaeology and anthropology and ecology and related disciplines to invent a golden age of Aboriginal culture, society and economy that never was. Reduced to responding on comment threads, I am told that I know nothing about it and nor do any of the archaeologists who have studied these issues over the last two centuries.

So no more guiding the lost, no more catching in the rye, not a prophet with honour in my own country. Just fearful of the coronavirus cloud hanging over me, hanging over us all. In summer I wait, anxiously, for a fire to start to the west, and for an ember attack to set fire to garden and house, destroying years of work, of achievement. Small sparks from far away, kilometres away, can, falling from the sky, unseen at first, spell doom to your life. Small doses of some unseen chemical can years later trigger abnormal cell division and send you into a desperate battle with cancer. Some casual words, a look perhaps, an impatient grunt, a minor administrative matter, can leave resentment festering unseen in a brain which will later be turned into a major campaign to destroy your life's work. And now, small sparks of virus travel through the air, unseen, and can set a fire in your body, destroying years of medical care for other, lesser, ailments. Just as well I have my home, and a reserve of emotional well-being, to see me through.

Especially when another kind of consequence struck at the end of the awful year of 2020. I woke up one morning unable to speak or write. The result of a blood clot moving through blood vessels and blocking an artery in my brain in Broca's centre. Groundhog Day as a catheter was once again sent through my arteries (to the brain this time), and thankfully found that the chemical I had been immediately given on arrival at hospital had dissolved the clot that had caused the stroke. Faces were appearing before me, a great crowd of people, all wanting to know the answers to vitally important questions like what year it was and why did Tasmanian Aborigines not eat fish (I tried to say that it was an adaptation to cold and dangerous southern oceans). For a moment, it seemed that my life of communicating with people, leading them, had come to a sudden end. Not just because people were deaf to what I was saying, like before, and not because chemotherapy, while saving my life, had basically removed all my senses, but because now I couldn't even speak. And then gradually, over some days, speech returned, though the deaf audience remained. There seemed no end to the bullets with my name on, but all of them defeated by my reserves of emotional well-being.

And while they were scanning (hammering) my brain for blood clots, they had come across the previously unknown aneurysm, another named bullet. A tiny thing, just two millimetres in size, but a potential explosion in my brain. Could have been there all my life they said, unknown and unsuspected, like a buried, unexploded, bomb, on an old battlefield. So much lurking unseen within our lives. So many causes, so many potential effects.

In April 2022, I reached six years in remission from lymphoma, but had barely finished a small celebration when that hubris was rewarded with Covid, so long carefully resisted (and triple vaccinated against), so many virus particles floating invisibly in the air and one finally reaching my sinuses. Neither antibodies from vaccines, nor reserves of well-being, prevent determined malign forces damaging you, but they did enable me to survive. Again. Then a potentially lethal skin cancer emerged as a ticking time bomb and resisted initial attempts to remove it – a surgeon finally succeeded with a massive excavation and my skull held together by stitches.

Finally, in November 2022, came an ultimate test of my survival capacity, my aorta valve began failing (Arnagretta, my cardiologist, refusing, somewhat ominously, to take part in my light-hearted banter about how fit I was) and I was back to trying to mentally prepare (little reserve of well-being after loss of my beautiful dog) for a heart operation in 2023. But hey, what could go wrong? Had my intimation of mortality, cancer was where it was at. Or was it?

One damn huge boulder after another, as Sisyphus said – *Encyclopedia*, map, heart attack, cancer, stroke, cancer again – and now I was back to the one labelled heart attack. Oh well, off we go, up the hill. Well, up to Sydney, in fact. Valentine's Day!

Arrived at hospital in Sydney to find my map prominent in the reception area. Sorry, meant to say, found the 'AIATSIS map of Indigenous Australia' in the reception area. Its author, arriving for a heart operation, just one of the many anonymous people passing the map.

In the usual roller coaster way, first I was in for open-heart surgery and weeks in hospital and months of recovery, then back to minimal use of a balloon in a vein and two days in hospital and a week or two recovery. But in hospital I lay there as the dye, once again squirting into my coronary arteries, revealed blockages to the increasingly grim-faced balloon man (wonderful David). And revealed that two valves needed replacing rather than one being fixed. Open-heart surgery back on the table.

Next day, I lay on the trolley chatting, in a whistling past the graveyard way, to the nice anaesthetist, and a moment later I had an eight-hour operation (magic surgeon Alasdair) and four hours recovery in my past and an intensive care unit in my immediate future. Next twenty-four hours all was well, and then suddenly Sunday morning was coming down with my fibrillating heart beat racing through the roof, and blood pressure dropping through the floor.

My near-death experience didn't involve long corridors, bright lights and angel choirs (atheist, remember) but as if I was seeing a group of scientists, bathed in dimmed lights, muttering quietly, in a nuclear power station who were watching the core begin to melt down and trying to come up with ideas to cool it down. Hours later, they succeeded. They were all part of a team dedicated to supporting me through this project of the heart.

It 'had been a damn nice thing' (just like the *Encyclopedia*), as Wellington said of Waterloo, 'the nearest run thing you ever saw in your life', and, just like Wellington, I had survived. Then another two weeks in hospital (they didn't call me 'Pop') and finally home. To go back to rebuilding my stores of physical and emotional well-being, getting ready for the next boulder crashing back down the hill. Although David said the next boulder would not be heart attack or stroke, because my heart was now in good shape as a result of the fine-tuning. "So I have the heart of a nineteen-year-old?' I asked, remembering those long-ago days. But, alas, probably not, except metaphorically. Still, dying of something else was as good a bargain as I was going to get.

What's future is epilogue

'You are not finished,' I [Arthur Hastings] exclaimed warmly. Poirot patted my knee. 'There speaks the good friend – the faithful dog. And you have reason, too. The grey cells, they still function – the order, the method – it is still there. But when I have retired, my friend, I have retired! It is finished! I am not a stage favourite who gives the world a dozen farewells. In all generosity I say: let the young men have a chance. They may possibly do something creditable. I doubt it, but they may.' – Agatha Christie

No, no, Hercule, I won't have that – the 'young men' (and women) have been doing very creditable things. I just wish that my anonymity was not so complete that when they discover, say, the history of Australian archaeology, or realise that climate change caused megafaunal extinction, or that plants are not adapted to fire, they would recognise that this old fellow had known the direction home. 'Cans't boy read?' 'Yes, and write,' they would say.

'Pain or damage don't end the world. Or despair or fuckin' beatings. The world ends when you're dead. Until then, you got more punishment in store. Stand it like a man, and give some back.' – Al Swearengen, Deadwood

'Give some back' I guess is what this memoir is an attempt to do. But, with all due respect, Al, it's a wasted effort. The young folk rush past me in the rye, not even aware of my presence. Perhaps I can become the world's best philatelist, which is what I am doing instead of responding as well-meaning people demand more and more fire be used in an environment under stress from climate change and development. Anyway it's hard work staying alive, which much of my energy will be increasingly directed to in the future. It's always later than you think. My school friends are eighty! On the other hand,

> 'If you've still got your marbles and you're not incontinent, you're fucking lucky. So think of it like that.' – Miriam Margolyes

Having mentioned Chekhov on the first page, I must quote him on the last:

> 'One hundred years from now, the people who come after us, for whom our lives are showing the way – will they think of us kindly? Will they remember us with a kind word?'

www.ingramcontent.com/pod-product-compliance
Lightning Source LLC
Chambersburg PA
CBHW021056080526
44587CB00010B/272